To S.

"NEVER FORGET
TO WAKE UP
AND DREAM !"

Best

Paul
x

WHEN I WOKE UP

ONE MAN'S UNBREAKABLE SPIRIT TO SURVIVE

A TRUE STORY BY PAUL EVANS
WITH CAROLYN COE

WWW.WHENIWOKEUP.COM

This book is memoir. It reflects the author's present recollections of experiences over time. Some names and characteristics have been changed, some events have been compressed, and some dialogue has been recreated.

ISBN: 978-1-0761355-9-9

National Media Council approval number: MC-01-01-7500208

FOR MY BOYS COLE AND ETHAN,

I have travelled along many wrong paths in my life, but I have focused relentlessly on the right journey. Boys, hold my hand tightly and I will show you the way. No matter how great the distance between us, you will both always be the first thing I think about the moment I wake up and the last before I fall asleep.

I love you both with all that I am, and all that I will ever be.

Love, Dad.

A note from the coauthor

When I Woke Up is based on multiple interviews, numerous sources and the recount of Paul Evans himself. In some places, we have changed details of settings, timelines and descriptions to protect identities. Characterizations and descriptions have been altered to protect privacy, and in some instances, we have recreated dialogue based on the recollections of interviewees, especially in scenes that took place more than a decade ago. But all the events we describe are true, and most can be verified.

—**Carolyn Coe**

PROLOGUE

Every autobiography has to start with the customary dedication to friends and family, and I feel that the people who have joined me on my journey so far have blessed my life. Some have joined me for short parts, others have joined me for longer, and some have been standing by my side the whole time. I want to thank all of you, no matter what part you played in helping me become the man I am today. There is no doubt in my mind that my heart would never be as full as it is now without you. I have decided not to mention anyone by name, simply because there are too many of you. But you all know who you are; I consider all of you to be angels on earth, and I thank you from the bottom of my soul.

I dedicate this book to the people I am yet to meet and to those who have shown interest in my story. To those who consider themselves (as I did) underdogs, self-doubters, isolated and the overwhelmed, and to those who think that being different is a bad thing, I hope my story encourages you to refuse to let others define you or label you and to find your own way. I have grown to acknowledge that every person has a unique talent. The secret is discovering what your talent is and maximizing it without the ceiling of limitation or the cloud of judgment.

Because I have been given the gift of a second chance at life, I have valuable lessons that I'd like to share, lessons about the true meaning of life and happiness that I learned only by being given the chance to wake up and live again. However, please be warned, this is not a self-help book. Don't get me wrong: I wrote this book with the pure intention of helping as many people as I can, to tell a story that will hopefully reignite your inner strength and determination to overcome the obstacles and difficulties you may face in your own life. However, I'm not going to dish out advice. I can only tell you my story from a very privileged position and let you take away from it what you will.

Let's face it, we are all just trying to get through this thing we call life, and to me, life is a collection of moments in time, not all good, and not all bad—and that's OK. Time, and how you choose to fill it, is what matters. Your choices will ultimately determine the quality of your life, and I spent a large part of my time wasting those moments on things that didn't matter, until it was almost too late. Let me ask you now, what aspects of your life would you change today if you knew how much time you had left? That's an incredibly powerful perspective for anyone to consider.

I hope my story makes you smile, I hope it makes you giggle, and I hope it entertains you chapter by chapter. Above all, may it serve as a reminder that you can never fail to achieve your goals, unless you quit. As long as you have air in your lungs, you have the ability to keep going.

Good luck along the journey, and I look forward to hearing your success stories.

All my love,

Paul

**Life is a series of wake-up calls;
never forget to wake up and dream.**

—Paul Evans

CHAPTER 1

NIL BY MOUTH

El Gouna Hospital, Egypt,
Friday, July 25, 2003, 6 a.m.

I woke up with the most severe thirst. The back of my throat rasped with every attempt I made to produce some saliva. The more I tried, the drier my mouth became. My cracked, dry lips stung as my tongue licked them and seemed to just split them even more. I strained my voice to try to get someone's attention, "Water." But no one stirred; my hungover friends at the end of my bed were passed out, and my pathetic whispers weren't going to wake them.

I rang the bell for the nurse. A dumpy woman, as wide as she was tall and with thick, black eyebrows and multiple chins, stuck her head around the door. "Nil by mouth. You can't have any water," she replied abruptly in a thick Arab accent.

"No, you don't understand," I pleaded, sounding like a whining child. "It feels like I've gone forty days in the desert. Nurse, please...."

She just shook her chins and waved her chubby finger at me. "Nil by mouth. No water for you, sir."

Bitch, I thought.

As soon as I saw her round shadow disappear from view, I wrestled myself free from the tightly tucked blanket that was pinning me to my bed.

Sitting upright, I pulled the cannula from the back of my hand and left it in a tangle behind me as I pushed myself up and onto my unstable legs.

With my hospital gown barely covering my modesty, I shuffled, unnoticed, across the corridor into the nearby bathroom. Locking the door behind me, I leaned over the sink, angled my jaw under the tap, turned it on and drank like a man possessed. I gulped and slurped frantically. I couldn't drink fast enough.

Then things got worse.

As anyone who has visited Egypt knows, drinking water from the tap carries a hefty health risk. Naturally, swallowing pints of the forbidden drink led to my contracting a nasty case of E. coli. Almost immediately after I returned to the bed, my stomach twisted into painful knots and cramps and, just minutes later, my wobbly legs were shuffling me as quickly as possible back to the toilet, where I endured the most horrific and undignified bout of explosive diarrhea and violent sickness.

It didn't take long for the nurse to realize what I was up to. To prevent me from drinking more, she shut off the water supply to the taps. Sadly, she didn't shut off my thirst.

To this day, I remember the desperation and horror I felt when I returned to the tap, turned it on, and nothing came out. It makes me cringe to think back to what I did when I realized there was no other way to slake the thirst that was driving me to the very fringes of insanity. It's difficult to admit what I did while in such a state of febrile dehydration, but at the time I was out of my mind. If toilet water was my only option, then so be it.

Without pausing for thought, I picked up the little plastic cup that sat at the side of the sink, turned around and dropped to my knees. I scooped the cup into the toilet bowl, raised it to my lips and drank the water as if I were downing a shot of tequila. One after another, I knocked back cups of toilet water until I was exhausted.

A toilet. In a hospital. In Egypt. It's impossible to know how many asses had sat on that toilet. God knows, I'd been on it most of the day. Think of the amount of disease, of diarrhea, of shit, of piss, of blood, of pus that had oozed into that filthy toilet bowl. But I didn't care. I didn't give any consideration to what it tasted like nor to its gut-wrenching smell. It was water, and I didn't give a fuck where it came from.

Of all the low points in my life—and believe me, there have been many—that has to be the lowest. Today, in my kitchen I keep a supply of the best-that-money-can-buy chilled, glass-bottled mineral water sourced from European volcanic streams. However, at that moment, nothing tasted as good as the water from the bottom of that Egyptian toilet bowl.

How was I to know my body was shutting down and that I was only days away from death?

At last, the nurse showed her kinder side and allowed me to have some ice. But let's not get excited. It wasn't as if she served the smooth, shiny ice that softly melts in a glass of Cognac. No, what she gave me was rough blocks of sticky ice, which, I suspect, she had chipped from the sides of a freezer in the hospital kitchen. It was the type of ice that could burn skin. It was so cold that I had to pry it off my fingers. It stuck to my lips, making them bleed, and blistered the insides of my cheeks. But it was water. So I lay there and sucked the glorious, burning ice cubes until I passed out.

I had no idea that the next time I woke up could have been my last day alive.

Wake-Up Call 1

THE AWKWARD YEARS

CHAPTER 2

THE BOY WITH THE TYPEWRITER

Winsford,
England, 1986

I t's common for people to fear the unknown, but for me it was the opposite: I feared the known. From the moment I opened my eyes every morning, the fear was there. The thing is, I absolutely hated school. Knowing that each day was going to be the same as all the others and that there was nothing I could do about it filled me with dread.

Consequently, I always took as long as possible to get ready in the morning. I'd lie in bed, staring up at the Liverpool FC posters that covered the walls of my bedroom and imagine myself kicking a winning goal into the back of the net at Anfield and then sliding on my knees across the pitch with my fingers raised to the sky in triumph. My dreams of being a footballer usually lasted all day long.

Back in the real world, I'd lock myself in the bathroom and stand under the shower, hoping that the water would wash my worries away, until eventually my sister, Keely, would thump her fists on the door and scream at me to hurry up. Ignoring her, and as the water ran over my face, I'd close my eyes and try to imagine what it would be like to be Ian Rush rather than Paul Evans. To me, Ian Rush was the best footballer in the world, a legend of a man. I sometimes wondered if he ever felt like I did? Not likely. I needed to be like him. I wanted so badly to feel like he felt, not like I did.

At the breakfast table, I'd wind up my sister while she ate by commenting on her talents for scoffing buttery toast: "And here comes Keely Evans. Is she going to score another piece of toast? Can she do it? Oh, my goodness, yes, she can. Keely Evans has scored again!"

Then, before I could tease her further, Mum would usher me out the door with a packed lunch, some bus money and some words of encouragement in my ear. She knew she was sending me off to the place I hated most in the world and always tried her best to cheer me up. "Don't let them get to you, Champ," she'd say with a smile and hug me. "Now get a shift on or you'll miss the bus!" She'd wave goodbye to me as I dragged my heels to the bus stop, flicking through my Top Trumps football cards and kicking stones along the curb, trying to keep my nerves at bay.

As I said, I hated school. The first problem with Middlewich County Comprehensive School was that it was a 15-minute drive from my hometown of Winsford. I know that doesn't sound like a big deal, but to a 12-year-old boy, it was everything. Exactly halfway along the four-mile stretch of the A54, between the two small Cheshire towns, I imagined an invisible crossing in the road that signified the end of friendly territory. My daily bus journey to school was like crossing enemy lines, and the difference between the two places was palpable.

Allow me to explain the difference further. Middlewich is a Manchester United fans' town, and I was a Liverpool FC fan. To appreciate why this was a problem for me, you have to understand the passionate, deep-rooted rivalry between these two famous UK football clubs. Their supporters are widely considered to be the most fanatical in all of footballing history.

It was late 1986, and I remember the period well for two reasons: Alex Ferguson had just been appointed manager of Manchester United, and the local council issued me with a typewriter. Because of those two events, I became a prime target for the school bullies.

Every day at Middlewich School was almost unbearable. Not only was I from a rival town and therefore a fan of the "wrong" football team, but to make matters worse, I also had chronic dyslexia, which at the time was not regarded with the same understanding as it is today. Back then, dyslexia was just a posh word for stupid.

When I tried to write in my schoolbooks, I couldn't control the scribbles on the page. Nor could I control the order of the letters; they would spill out randomly in a jumbled mess. It didn't matter if I wrote slowly or if I focused all of my attention on one line at a time, my brain just went into a spin when I tried to spell or write sentences.

Because of my bad spelling and erratic handwriting, I became the first kid in school to be given a typewriter. I was forced to carry the bloody thing under my arm to every class. Rather than making things better, this made everything worse, because I stuck out even more. I was a constant source of ridicule. In fact, because of the typewriter, I drew so much attention to myself that I may as well have walked around Middlewich with a "Kick Here" neon sign above my head.

Because of my dyslexia I was placed in the bottom of my class for almost every subject and was noted as being difficult to teach and an irritant to my teachers. Meanwhile, I just sat there day after day, wishing I was invisible. During class, my attention span rarely lasted more than a few seconds. Instead of listening, I would stare in bewilderment at the space between my typewriter and my belly button and be swept away by my own thoughts. I would drift a million miles away from the classroom, and as the teacher's dull voice hypnotized me with boredom, I would dream I was on the football pitch.

My teachers often lost patience with me. I didn't have a problem with them, and I wasn't really a bad kid; it was just that they didn't know how to deal with me. I was a cheeky lad with the gift of gab and bags of energy, but through the sheer frustration of being constantly misunderstood, I eventually gave up trying to learn anything at all. I did all I could to avoid being asked to read out loud or write on the blackboard in front of the class. For me, being put on the spot in front of a class full of students was a fate worse than death. Yet, my teachers never picked up on it. If a teacher singled me out, I would throw tantrums and shout obscenities and usually end up in detention for making a scene.

I guess that's why my end-of-year report cards contained comments such as "Paul is arrogant and difficult to teach," "A slow learner, silly and rude," and "He has very limited potential here."

One teacher even went as far as to write, "Paul is a disruptive influence and has far too much to say for himself!"

Another suggested, "Paul needs to change his attitude if he is ever to fit in to normal school life."

But that was exactly the point: I wasn't normal, and that wasn't a problem for me. It's not as if I ever read my report cards anyway.

The real problem that I faced daily was considerably more horrific than knowing what my teachers thought of me. Perhaps they weren't aware that every time they put me under the spotlight to test me, they were making matters even worse. Maybe they were oblivious to the fact that for every stutter, stammer or spelling mistake I made, the greater the probability that a gang of bullies would be waiting for me in the playground at lunchtime to remind me of how stupid I was.

The bullies at Middlewich operated with a particularly nasty hierarchy. Each year, the senior students picked a junior pupil to beat the shit out of whenever and wherever they wanted for the rest of the year. In my first year at Middlewich, Bogarelli, the biggest and nastiest of all the boys in school, picked the boy with the typewriter.

Bogarelli became my nemesis when I became his punching bag. He was 16 years old, with fists that never tired of contacting my face, and it was a special extra pleasure for him to plant his heavy Doc Marten boots into my ribcage. Every day, he and his gang of acne-ridden fuck-wits would wait for me to walk through the school gates with my typewriter under my arm. Perhaps they'd be there when I got off the bus in the morning, or maybe they'd be lurking around the corner at lunchtime, or perhaps they'd pounce on me as I made my way back to the bus after the last bell. It was never a matter of if they'd be waiting for me, but when.

Some days I'd get off lightly with a bit of name calling. Sometimes they'd smack my typewriter out of my hands, sending me to the ground after it. They would kick my school bag around like a football and stamp on my Liverpool strip when it fell out of the side pocket. They'd take it easy on me only if an even more pathetic bastard like Fat Kenny, the kid in the year above me with the thick-soled orthopedic boot, had the misfortune of being let out of class minutes before me. But for the most part, there was no escaping it. I was a marked target, and I knew the attack could happen at any time.

By the end of my first year at Middlewich I had taken more beatings from Bogarelli than I can remember. My name had been on his list all year, and as the end of term approached, the tension grew among the students: Who was going to get the biggest kicking of their lives? Every day, he tormented me that today it could be me, until the day came and the wait was over.

I was standing in a circle of boys in the playground at break time, when I heard him shout my name. I froze and slowly turned around as the other kids stepped away cautiously. In a split second I weighed my options. I could try and fight him; that option was quickly crossed off the list. I could try and make a run for it, or I could hide somewhere. But I didn't do any of those things. Instead, I stood, petrified, rooted to the spot. I was too scared to do anything.

I knew I couldn't take him on. He was double my size and most certainly capable of breaking every bone in my skinny body. The only thing I thought to do was drop to the floor and roll up in a ball, clasp my knees to my chest, and take what was coming to me. So that's what I did.

He set upon me, thump after thump, blow after blow. His swift foot founding a fresh rib with each kick of his heavy boot. His fists pounded the sides of my skull, while my arms feebly tried to shield my face. He pushed my head sideways into the damp, gritty tarmac. There was nothing I could do. I squeezed my eyes shut and inhaled the scent of damp, earthy stones mixed with the sweetness of the blood pouring from my nose, until it was finally over.

However, it wasn't Bogarelli's boot the hurt the most. It wasn't even when he held my knees apart and booted me in the bollocks. The real enduring agony was the sheer and flagrant humiliation of the whole experience. Instead of standing up for myself, I had cowered to the bully. I had allowed the whole school to stand by and be entertained while he kicked the shit out of my spirit.

This would be the last time I'd ever let that happen to me.

CHAPTER 3

CROCODILE. COUNTRY. LIBRARY.

At school, the happiest time of the day was when the bell rang for sports time. Sports were the only release I had in that hellhole. I discovered, to my joy, that sports were the one thing that I could do better than everyone else. Unlike in other subjects at school, in sports I was never judged or singled out as the underachiever. On the contrary, sports gave me significance; they challenged me, energized me and enabled me to stand out from the crowd for all the right reasons. The only subject at high school I was ever applauded for was sports.

The boy on the football pitch, on the track or in the swimming pool was completely capable—invincible even—whereas the boy in the classroom, with his sad typewriter, was at the lowest end of the spectrum, or so I told myself. That belief in my sporting ability was the one thing that helped me survive.

By the end of spring term of 1987, I had found myself in detention more times than I care to remember. My disruptive behavior in class had become the stuff of legend, but there was one authority figure who really had it in for me: Mr. Little, the deputy headmaster.

On my way to school each day, I was always quick to check if Mr. Little's dark blue BMW was in the staff parking lot. It was a distinctive car, and not for the right reasons—much like Mr. Little's personality.

He had fitted it with cheap alloy wheel rims and a huge, tacky clip-on spoiler. He had faked its upgrade from the standard 318*i* model to the top-of-the-range M325 *IS* model using stick-on badges that he must have bought from a local market stall. He also had attached an exhaust pipe that he must have thought made his BMW sound like a rally car. But in truth, it sounded more like an elephant's fart.

Our teacher-pupil relationship instantly plummeted during one of countless detention sessions. I lost my cool after listening to his relentless predictions of my doomed future, and so I retaliated in the only way I knew would hurt him: I insulted his car.

"Think what you like," I said with a shrug. "I'm looking out this window at your scrap-heap reject! Whatever you say, one day I'll have the kind of supercar that the closest you can hope to get to will be by looking through the showroom window. Insult me all you want, but you're not exactly what I'd call a success yourself."

He didn't like me much after that. From that day forward, his loathing for me was such that if I saw his car in the Deputy Headmaster parking space, I knew there was a high chance that my day would take a turn for the worse.

One fateful morning I happened to arrive at school at precisely the same time that he screeched into his parking spot. Immediately, I regretted my timing. The start to this day couldn't have been any worse. I felt sick to my stomach as we walked toward each other, knowing that I couldn't avoid our inevitable meeting. We were at eye level and side by side when he pushed one half of the door open and made an archway with his arm for me to duck under. We were the same height, so it was a particularly awkward gesture, as he had to stretch as high as he could on his tiptoes while I, of course, had to bow to him to pass under his arm.

"Morning, Mr. Little," I huffed as I reluctantly slid under his elbow.

"Spelling test this morning, Evans," he sneered in that condescending tone used by self-important, patronizing teachers the world over.

"Yes, sir," I replied as I broke into a run to put as much distance between us as quickly as possible before we reached his classroom at the end of the corridor.

After our brief meeting I had no doubt that he was in the mood to pick on me. Reaching the classroom, I scanned the room and chose a desk that I hoped would shelter me from his predatory eyes. I sat down and prayed that he would turn his attention on some other poor sod. I waited with a mounting sense of dread for the class to start.

The bell rang for first period. Mr. Little entered the room silently while the students chattered among themselves. He stood stern-faced in front of the class, casually bouncing a piece of chalk in the palm of his thin and bony hand while he waited for us to acknowledge his arrival. He had an air of menace about him, as if he enjoyed his position of authority a bit too much. His thick, dark hair was shaved down one side and parted sharply in a line above his ear. The rest was styled into a comb-over that often fell forward, giving him the sinister look of a German army general. His tone was unfailingly patronizing whenever he opened his mouth, but on this occasion, before he uttered a word, the room fell silent, as if he had used the severe stare of his cold eyes to turn us all into stone.

"Morning, class. Now that you've all settled down, how about a little spelling test to wake you all up?"

His lip curled into a smug smile as he placed a box of index cards onto his desk like it was a trophy. As he opened the box, I shrank down into my chair and looked away. My stomach twisted, and I began biting my nails. Like so many times before, he spotted me instantly.

"Up you come, Evans."

It was the moment I dreaded more than anything. I dragged the legs of my chair noisily across the floor, got up, and shuffled with hunched shoulders to the front of the class. No one said a word as I stood in the spotlight. He knew it, I knew it and everyone in the class knew it: This was his chance to humiliate me once again, and he appeared to relish every minute of it. His nimble fingers pulled a card from the deck. He glanced at it, and with a look of smug satisfaction, slowly he pronounced the word *crocodile*.

It was like I'd been punched in the face. How the hell should I know how to spell that? I searched the room for a friendly face, but there was not even one to be found. Instead, a sea of hungry eyes watched my personal horror unfold. It was clear my classmates were enjoying the morning's entertainment.

Mr. Little passed me the chalk and waited impatiently for me to begin. As the letters of the alphabet buzzed around randomly in my head, I knew I had to make an attempt at spelling the word. My hand shook as I put chalk to blackboard and slowly began to write out the letters.

C-R-O-K-A

"Try again," Mr. Little said with sigh.

K-R

"And again."

K

"No, Evans. You were right the first time!" Mr. Little said, frowning with impatience. "*Crocodile* starts with the letter C. Let's try again."

He replaced the card in the box and selected another. As I stood and listened to the sniggers and whispers from the rest of the class, my heart rate rose. I bit my shaking fingernails and waited nervously for the next word.

"*Country,*" Mr. Little said, grinning.

I hung my head and considered the possible answers. My mind raced. I tried to decide if he was bluffing. Was he giving me another word that began with C, or should I attempt to begin with K instead? Either way, I knew I had a 50 percent chance of getting it right, so I took a deep breath and placed the chalk to the board.

K-U-N

"No, Evans, I've given you another C word!" he huffed loudly and rolled his eyes skyward.

"I'll give you another fucking C word, you fucking prick," I whispered under my breath, as my rage surfaced and I rubbed the chalky duster across the board to begin again.

C -U-N

Mr. Little stared at me with a look of disgust. His face flushed red as a vein pulsed in his neck. "Right, Evans, you obviously think this is funny! Well, Mr. Funny Boy, it's time to stop acting like the class idiot or you'll be finding yourself in detention again."

He turned to the class and opened his arms. "Who can spell country for Evans?" The class spelled out each letter in unison while I bit my lip, humiliated and desperate, swallowing the words of anger that would surely land me in even more serious trouble if they came out.

Mr. Little snatched the chalk from my hand and wildly wrote the word across the blackboard, punching an exclamation mark at the end with such vigor that he broke the stick in half. Relieved to be off the hook finally, I looked down at my trembling hands and started to walk back to my seat. But Mr. Little had other ideas.

"Evans! Don't think you're done yet. This spelling test isn't finished until you've given us a whole word!" he boomed.

The attention of every pupil in the class was now firmly fixed upon me. Silence filled the room as Mr. Little flipped though the box of cards. He paused. I held my breath. The class gasped as he read, "Library."

I lost the plot.

"Go fuck yourself!" I yelled.

The class erupted like a rabble of monkeys, jeering, laughing and whooping, "Thickoid! Spastic! Duhhhh!"

I grabbed my bag and ran for the door.

"Evans!" I heard Mr. Little scream. "Report to the headmaster's office right now!"

"Fuck you!" I yelled over my shoulder as I slammed the classroom door behind me.

I ran full tilt down the corridor, out of the school gate, and around the corner as fast as my legs could carry me. With the school building out of sight, I slumped down onto the pavement, folded my arms around my knees, buried my face into my shirt sleeves, and howled my heart out.

When I stopped crying I was unsure what I should do next. The voices in my head were buzzing with all the ominous outcomes that I was convinced were coming my way. Going back to school would mean detention again for sure, maybe worse. How would I explain that to Mum and Dad? But if I didn't go back to class, the school would contact them anyway. Either way, I concluded, my parents were going to kill me. They were already disappointed that their son was so stupid, and now this. They were going to wish they'd never even had me! I was never going to be good at anything, and they would never be proud of me. Those teachers were right, my inner voice confirmed, I was a complete and utter failure.

I took the bus home, and for the whole journey my head was filled with thoughts of shame. So many times before when I had been in trouble at school, Mum and Dad supported and forgave me, but this time I was sure I was going to discover the end of their patience. Why didn't I ever learn? Why couldn't I change? What was wrong with me? Why was I so useless?

At the time, my dad was away in Glasgow on a business trip and not due back until the next day. I convinced myself that when returned he was going wash his hands of me for sure. By the time the bus arrived at my stop, my inner demons had convinced me that I was such a disgrace to my parents that they would never want to see me again.

There was only one way out: end it all.

No one was home. I let myself in, dropped my schoolbag at the door, and made my way into the kitchen. It felt like being in a house after the tenants had moved out: empty and completely still. Normally there would be the sound of us all talking and laughing, the television would be on, and there would be delicious smells wafting from the kitchen. That day there was nothing.

Two teacups sat on the kitchen counter next to the kettle in the corner, waiting for Mum and Dad. Their first ritual once they came home after work was to have a brew together and share their stories of the day with one another. I looked at the cups and wondered if they'd be making their tea today unaware that I was lying dead upstairs.

Reaching up to the cupboard above the kettle, I grabbed all the glass pill bottles from the shelf. Using my school jumper as a hammock, I carried the bottles to the dining room and lined them up on the table. Opening Dad's drinks cabinet, I selected a bottle of whisky. I unscrewed the cap and took a deep whiff; the sharp smell felt like it was burning my nostrils. That's strong enough to do the job, I thought.

I sat at the table with tears streaming uncontrollably down my face. The bottles of pills and the whisky stood like statues in front of me. Before I began, I paused. My mind was filled with guilt and desperation at the thought of what I was about to do. I pictured my parents' sadness and felt their grief. Images of them discovering my lifeless body flashed in front of my eyes. Through the blur of my tears, I penned my parting words:

Dear Mum and Dad,

I know that you are going to be heartbroken, but this is the only way out I can see.

I don't want to let you down for all of my life, this will be the last time.

You will be better off without me.

I am sorry.
Love, Paul.

I left the note on the table. I never saw it again; I don't know if my parents ever found it. They have never mentioned it, and I have never asked them about it. To be honest, I have never thought about it until today; it's not the kind of note you treasure. It pains me so much now to think that those could have been my last words to my parents.

Then I began. A fistful of pills followed by a mouthful of whisky. I scoffed and swallowed then swigged and gagged. The alcohol stung my lips and chin. The bitterness of the pills numbed my mouth, but I didn't stop. Another handful of pills followed by another mouthful of whisky. I coughed and spat on myself until I'd taken the lot. I had to get it over with as quickly as I could. The quicker I could swallow, the quicker I could go to sleep, and the quicker this whole shitty life could be over.

Job done. I stood up and looked around the empty room. I looked at photos on the mantelpiece and at Mum's chair where she would sit and knit in the evenings. I imagined Dad sitting in his chair and me sitting on the floor with my back propped up against his footstool as we watched the footy together. I saw my sister lying on the couch with a blanket around her, having her "picky tea" (bite-sized cheese, pâté and crackers) while watching her favorite TV show, *Antiques Roadshow*. I said goodbye to my family one last time and went upstairs. I lay down on my bed, and as the room started to spin, I passed out.

I woke up about an hour later, drowsy and confused. I could hear the phone ringing downstairs. As the ringing stopped, I came to my senses with a jolt. What the hell had I done? I got to my feet, but the effect of the pills and whisky was well under way. I staggered clumsily into my bedside table as

I reached for the door handle. Trying to steady myself, I bounced from wall to wall along the landing. I teetered dangerously on the top step and tried in vain for a few seconds to regain my balance until, as if in slow motion, I lost my footing. My ankles gave way and I flopped forward, knocking a set of family pictures from the wall as I fell head over heels like a dead weight to the bottom of the stairs.

I knew I needed to get to the phone. I limped to the corner of the living room and picked up the handset. I assumed the call that had woken me was the school trying to reach my parents. I thought there might be a way that I could fix this without my parents finding out what I had done. The only person who I felt might be able to help without alerting them was Mrs. Charity, my form tutor. She had a very appropriate name, as she was the one lady I believed I could trust to understand and deal with the carnage that I had caused. I called her there and then.

"Mrs. Charity, I've done something stupid!" I cried.

"Yes, Paul, I just been trying to call you. I've just heard about the incident with Mr. Little," she said hurriedly.

"No, that wasn't the *schtupid* thing, Mrs. Charity," I slurred, as the potent cocktail slowed my speech.

"I've done something stupid just now, Mrs. Charity. I've taken all Mum's pills and drunk Dad's whisky!" I hiccupped. "But shhhhh, Mrs. Charity. I don't want you to tell them."

"Oh God, Paul, you silly…." She stopped herself from saying any more. I could sense that she was already on the move. "OK, stay where you are. I'm coming to get you," she said hurriedly.

I must have passed out again, because the next thing I remember is little Mrs. Charity, five times my age and half my size, bursting into the living room and somehow finding the superhuman strength to drag my drunken body out of the house and into her silver Mini Metro. I slumped into the passenger seat. She belted me up, wound all the windows down, and yelled at me to stay awake as she sped along the country lanes to Leighton Hospital.

Fifteen minutes later we hurtled into the Leighton Hospital emergency ward. I was lapsing in and out of consciousness as the hospital orderlies heaved me from the car and into a wheelchair. While holding my head upright, shining a light into my eyes, and shouting questions at me to keep me awake, the hospital staff whisked me past the busy patient waiting room and into a treatment room, where they pulled the curtains around me.

I began to feel nauseous. I sat on the edge of the bed and tried to stabilize myself while the nurses tugged off my shoes and pulled at my trouser legs.

"I'm gonna be sick."

"No, Paul, don't be sick! You must keep it down!" The nurses ordered me. "We're going to get it all out in a minute."

"I don't want to die," I pleaded.

They pulled at the sleeves of my school jumper. "You're not going to die, Paul. Let's just get that jumper and tie off, shall we?"

I did exactly as they said. They weren't messing around. Within seconds I was stripped down to my underpants and dressed in a hospital robe, my arms and legs flopping around like dead weights. The nurses' voices echoed as they braced me for what was about to come.

"Paul! Can you hear me? Because you have taken pills and we don't know what they are, we are going to give you a stomach pump. OK?"

I couldn't exactly refuse. I was as limp as a rag doll, lying on my side with no control of my body. One nurse held my mouth open while another pushed a long, clear pipe down my throat. It felt as wide as a drainpipe as it passed my back teeth. I tried to bite down on the tube to stop them from pushing it any farther, but they were too fast and too strong, so I gave up resisting; the last thing I needed was a mouthful of broken teeth.

The nurses funneled a solution into my belly as though they were feeding a battery hen. Then they pulled the tube out so quickly that I lurched sideways and threw up into a metal bucket that had been placed beside the bed. The putrid smell of my stomach contents filled the air as my puke splattered across the steel. Once my projectile vomit stopped, the nurses forced the pipe back down my gullet, repeating the sequence continuously until the liquid in the bucket ran clear.

My throat felt ripped to ribbons, but finally it was over. I was wrapped in warm blankets and, in a daze, wheeled onto a ward where Mrs. Charity was waiting. The doctors informed me that they'd got all the bad stuff out of my stomach and that all I needed was some rest. Mrs. Charity tucked the blankets up under my chin and with a gentle voice asked me a question. "Paul, shall we make a deal? Shall we say that from now on you'll promise you'll always let me know that when things get on top of you? If you feel that you have no one to talk to, remember that I'm here and I'll always listen to you. Can you agree to that?'

"Yes, Mrs. Charity, I promise," I coughed.

She sat with me until my eyes grew heavy and I fell into a deep sleep. I was so glad for her to be there.

The next time I opened my eyes, Mum was sitting next to me holding my hand. Relief and a sense of calm flooded over me as I gazed at her kind blue eyes. Her tear-stained face smiled back at me. I tried to speak, but no words came out. She kissed me on my forehead, and a curl of her blonde hair tickled my cheek as she whispered, "Don't worry, son. Just sleep, my darling."

At 3 a.m. a firmer grip took my hand. I opened my eyes to see Dad. But he's not due back until tomorrow? He must have driven through the night! The look on his face told me all I needed to know. He wasn't angry. He wasn't disappointed. My dread of him being ashamed of me evaporated.

"I'm so sorry you felt like that, son. Let me tell you, you have nothing to be ashamed of. Nothing is ever that bad. I promise, there's nothing you can't tell me or your mum. We will always be here for you and will be proud of you no matter where you are or what you do. No stupid tests or teacher report cards will ever make us think that you aren't destined for great things. Now come here!" He scooped me up and gave me a huge bear hug. "You're my boy, and I love you more than anything in the world."

The love I felt was so genuine and powerful. Surely, if my parents loved me this much, then maybe I was wrong after all. Maybe I wasn't useless. Maybe things would be OK. Maybe I wouldn't disappoint them for the rest of my life. As I lay in my hospital bed, I considered, for the first time, that maybe I had something special going for me. I was loved—and that was a good place to start.

That day was a directional change for me. I learned the true meaning and value of the deep relationship and the unconditional love of my parents. And from the depths of my despair, I learned to acknowledge my own value.

As for the staff at Leighton Hospital, that was the first time, but not the last time, that I would thank them for saving my life.

CHAPTER 4

THE POWER OF 143

During the summer holiday that followed the pill-and-whisky incident, I spent nearly all my time with Dad. The more time we spent playing sports and being together, the more I noticed a rise in my confidence. In the first of many boy-becomes-man lessons, Dad took me on my first-ever visit to Anfield to watch Liverpool play West Bromich Albion. With 40,000 fans shouting, cheering and singing the club's songs together, the atmosphere inside the stadium was like nothing I had ever experienced. Dad bought me a Liverpool strip as a souvenir. I didn't take it off for weeks afterward.

In addition to a love of football, Dad and I shared a love of water sports. We joined the Wirral and Sandyway Waterskiing Club and spent every weekend of the summer holidays from sunrise until sunset at the lake practicing. It was our time to bond.

During one of our many frank chats in the car on the way home from a day on the lake, I told Dad that I thought there was something different about my brain compared with the other kids in school. I explained that being dyslexic was like having a mental disease. Naturally, he was alarmed that I had said such a thing about myself. But instead of responding sympathetically, he said that I should take an IQ test. His suggestion took me completely by surprise. At first, I thought he was joking. After all, he of all people knew that I'd never passed a single academic test in my life. Despite my hesitation, I thought, What the heck, it can't hurt. And so the next day, Dad arranged for me to take the test.

When at last the letter from Mensa dropped through the letterbox, I sat nervously with my parents at the kitchen table to open it. I held the envelope in my hand and closed my eyes in prayer before I unsealed it and removed the contents. The results melted my face from a look of fear to utter disbelief. My score, to my shock and amazement, was 143! I couldn't believe it. I was in the *genius* category! The report explained that as few as 1 in 1,000 students are of similar intelligence. My jaw dropped. I was completely lost for words as my parents jumped up and hugged me, giddy with excitement.

Until that point I had genuinely believed that I was stupid. I had believed that my school teachers were right to nark me, but that was all about to change. With my IQ score I at last had the proof I needed to show them that I didn't belong at the bottom of the class! When Mum and Dad showed my results with pride to the school headmaster at the start of the next school term, I was moved up from the bottom set of all my subjects. Of course, it took a while for the change to sink in, and it certainly wasn't as if my dyslexia vanished overnight. However, with 143 fixed in my mind, I finally had a tangible reason to believe in myself.

I settled back into school much better, and Dad began traveling a lot more for work. At that time, he owned a successful sales-and-marketing company, and it must be said, although school was less painful, I probably got a better education from listening to him and watching him work than I did from all my school days put together.

I loved it when he worked from home. I would sit on the floor with my ear to his office door and listen to him. I could hear the warmth and confidence in his voice always making his clients chuckle. They never seemed to notice that they were falling for his smooth sales techniques hook, line and sinker. I would applaud when he used the "rabbit punch," which Dad defined as "an irresistible offer that comes out of the blue and hits the client between the eyes, leaving them so stunned that they simply can't decline." A salesman's proverbial kill.

Dad's work took him all over the UK and Europe and sometimes even farther afield. He once whisked me away with him for four days on a business trip to Singapore. Back then, that was like traveling to the moon. It was so far away and took so long to get there, that I slept through most of the visit due to jet lag.

My favorite of all Dad's work trips was to Club LaSanta on the island of Lanzarote. He would go there every three months or so to deliver three weeks of training to their sales force. Being sports crazy, I always begged him to take me. It's easy to understand why I became so obsessed with the place. It was a vast, new, state-of-the-art sports resort boasting football pitches that stretched as far as the eyes could see. Multiple running tracks, an enormous athletics stadium, numerous Olympic-sized pools, tennis courts and watersports—you name the sport, and LaSanta had it covered. As a facility, it was the best of the best, and at the time, it was the stomping ground for the world's best athletes.

On my visits there, while Dad was working, I enrolled myself in as many sports groups as I could. I was on cloud nine! I felt free to be myself and was literally on a level playing field with everyone else. Because I was free from the pressures of school, teachers, bullies and trying to prove myself, La Santa became my favorite place on earth. The coaches were genuinely interested in my abilities. They wanted to know how quick I was off the blocks, how elegantly I could dive into the swimming pool, or how precisely I could dribble a football. They didn't give a shit about my spelling.

To my delight, when I was there, the beloved British athletic superstars Linford Christie, Daley Thompson, Colin Jackson and Tessa Sanderson were there too, as part of their Olympics pre-season training. Every day, Linford practiced at the track with his coach, and I sprinted back and forth along the sidelines, mirroring his every move. Other kids would come and go, joining in with me from time to time, but as long as Linford was there, I never left the track, hoping that one day he would notice me.

Finally, at the end of one of his training sessions, the moment I had been waiting for came. He called me over and beaming his world-famous friendly grin, he placed his huge hand on my shoulder and said, "OK, kid, let's see what you've got."

I couldn't believe he was inviting me to race 100 meters with him! My heart beat wildly as the two of us crouched down behind the starting line. I looked across at him and all I could think of was, Run! Lift your knees up, pump your arms, and run as fast as you possibly can. Chase him until your heart explodes.

Of course, I was no match for the Olympic gold medalist. On the word *go* he left me for dust, but that was the fastest I ever ran in my life. I saw him sprint down the track ahead of me, and I pushed myself to the point where I thought my lungs were about to give up. My feet had never traveled so quickly.

Linford's invitation to race meant something on a deep level. He challenged me to think I was good enough to race against the best. He didn't offer me any kind of head start or advantage. He put me in the top 1 percent and made me a contender. I like to think he saw my determination and connected with it. I have never forgotten that feeling of validation.

Even though he was the fastest man in the world, being the competitive sort, I was pissed off that he beat me by such a distance. Still gasping to get my breath back, I returned the challenge. "Ok, you're fast, but can you play pool?" I asked.

Still smiling, and perhaps surprised at my cheek, he accepted. "Something tells me you're a mean pool player!" he laughed and high-fived me. Later that day, we met at the pool table, and after two hours of play, the score was even. Christie won on the track; Evans won on the table, 3-0. As the saying goes, you have to be in it to win it. Or in my case, once you're in, find a way to win.

Around the same time, I landed my first job. Dad's best friend, Andy, and his wife, Lindy, lived next door to us in Middlewich, and the couple had been like a second set of parents ever since I could remember. Our two families did almost everything together. Andy owned a very successful beauty salon supplies business, and on weekends he ran a stall that sold electrical items at enormous liquidation markets around the country.

Andy was the type of man who'd wake up asking himself, "How can I make a pound?" I knew there was so much to learn from him and his business ethos. He always aimed to make every pound matter, which was a tiny yet essential detail that would stick in my mind forever. There is no question that Andy was integral in showing me the grit required in business.

One evening when we were at Andy's house having dinner, he offered to make me his assistant at the market. I was so excited to be offered my first job! From then on, without fail every Friday after school, I would race across to his house to load up his van with microwaves, televisions, radios, toasters and washing machines. At 5 a.m. the following morning, Lindy would open her front door, yawning in her dressing gown, to find me waiting eagerly with a pack of sandwiches, ready to hit the road.

Every weekend the market was in a different town, and not before long we covered the majority of the north of England. The market doors opened at 9 a.m., and business would be nonstop until they closed at 5 p.m. On an average weekend, 15,000 bargain-hungry customers came through the doors. Andy and I would place bets with each other to see who could make the most sales. Desperate to win, I'd climb on top of a washing machine to see over everyone's heads and hawk our wares at the top of my voice to the passing crowd. I was determined to be the top seller, and each week I'd get closer to the target. At the end of each day, we'd count our takings: 12,000 pounds, 15,000 pounds, sometimes even 17,000 pounds! Andy would proudly hand me my percentage of the profit and holding my wages in my hand, I would feel so grown up. While other kids my age were washing cars or picking strawberries on the weekend for a mere 10 pounds of pocket money, I was raking it in.

Soon I began to see the potential to make money almost everywhere. Influenced by Dad and Andy, I became obsessed with thinking up enterprising ideas. I loved negotiating and the thrill of making a sale and generating cash. The whole process seemed to come naturally to me. One day, a money-making opportunity at school presented itself that was too good to ignore.

During lunch break that day, I couldn't help overhearing a conversation between two boys in front of me when we were walking the short distance from the amusement arcade back to the school gates.

"I've only got a quid left," said one boy, regretting that he had gambled away all of his pocket money.

"My dad gave me a fiver this morning, and now I've only got 30 pence," groaned the other. "I had two watermelons lined up on the fruit machine, and when I hit the nudge button I was sure it was going to be another and then I would have had the jackpot."

"Yeah, me too!" the other boy said, beating the air with his fist. "I put all of my 10 pence coins into the sliding drawer machine. I swear, I just needed a few more and I'd have won them all back. It was so close."

Little did they know, as they dragged themselves back to school with empty pockets, that they had just given me a fantastic idea.

I noticed that the kids who went to the arcade on Monday all had the same financial problem on Tuesday. They always spent all of their lunch money on games and then had no means to buy food for the remainder of the week. I saw an opportunity to solve their lunch money deficit problems.

Most students owned a Parker fountain or rollerball pen. I knew each pen had a retail value of 10 to 12 pounds. So, I offered all those broke students the chance to sell me their pen for 1 pound. They could buy their pen back from me at any time before their parents noticed it was missing, but for 2 pounds. It worked like a treat! Everyone went to the arcade on Monday, sold me their pens on Tuesday, bought them back from me the following week, and I doubled my money. Within a matter of weeks, my school bag was bursting with various styles and colors of Parker pens. With the market sales on the weekends and my pen-pawning business during the week, I was racking up earnings of over 100 pounds every week. Not bad for a 14-year-old kid with dyslexia and a grim future.

However, not everyone supported me or wanted me to succeed. Not surprisingly, Bogarelli was one of those people. To say he resented that a junior student was making 100 pounds per week would be a major understatement. He wanted to take over my pen business and the money that went with it.

But he underestimated me. I had vowed after the last time he beat me up that I would never let him fuck with me again. I had promised myself that I wouldn't curl up in a ball and take another kicking. I was determined to stand up for myself, make a statement and ignore his threats.

Ignoring a person like Bogarelli was easier said than done. As time passed, paranoia set in, and once again I found myself permanently on edge, convinced that he and his gang were plotting to lynch me and steal my bag of pens and money at any time. My nerves spilled over in the final days of term when I boarded the school bus and discovered Bogarelli and some of his mates sitting together at the back. As I sat down they began to chant, "Tomorrow you're dead. Tomorrow you're dead. Tomorrow you're dead...."

I desperately blocked my ears as they chanted over and over again while the bus rumbled along the country road back to Winsford. The name-calling, the bloody playground fist fights, cuts and bruises, fear and agony, and, on top of those memories, the humiliation of their bullying plagued me. Flashbacks of downing pills and my parents' tear-streaked faces, the stomach pump and the nurse's voices whirred through my mind, everything playing like a horror movie on fast-forward, until the bus finally stopped. When the bus drove off, I stood alone on the pavement in a cloud of exhaust fumes and watched Bogarelli's mob, with their brutish faces pressed against the glass, thumping the windows until the bus disappeared out of sight. I couldn't take the bullying any longer and was going to take the law into my own hands.

The next morning was the last day of the school term. I boarded the bus and made the usual journey through the streets. From the window I watched people going about their daily business, walking to school, driving to work, delivering the morning newspapers, and opening their shops. Everything appeared normal; there was nothing out of the ordinary—except for the air pistol that I had sneaked into the side pocket of my school backpack.

The first few classes passed without any sign of Bogarelli or his gang, but I knew I wouldn't have long to wait before I bumped into them. I left the classroom at break time and slipped the pistol into my pocket and, keeping my finger on the trigger, made my way to the playground. I knew that he would be lying in wait for me and the whole school would be watching. I turned the corner, and there he was! He stood in the middle of the playground, puffing out his chest, his arms stretched out and his palms facing upward, inviting me to fight.

"Oi, Evans! You cocky fuck!" he shouted. I felt my heart pound heavily. "Where the fuck are you going, dickhead?"

Instinctively, I turned to walk away and head back to safety, but a voice inside my head told me to stop. "No more," it said. "It's time to fight back!" I had to defend myself. So, I turned on my heels and marched toward him while he stood in the middle of the yard, planted to the ground like a giant.

"What the fuck are you gonna do?" he scoffed.

I stopped 10 feet from him. The noise from the gathering crowd grew louder as they circled around us for the fight. "What am I going to do?" I sneered. "Take a step closer, and I'll show you what the fuck I'm going to do. Prick!"

I pulled the pistol from my pocket and pointed it at his head.

He didn't even flinch. "What the fuck? An air pistol?" he laughed. "What the fuck are you going to do with that?"

"I'll fucking shoot you," I said, trembling, as the crowd gasped.

The moments that followed passed in slow motion. Bogarelli stood secured to the spot, with clenched fists at the ready, but I could hear his gang shouting, "Get him, Boga! Fuck him up!"

I steadied the pistol with both hands and took aim. "Get back, Bogarelli!" I commanded.

Deep down I knew that a 177 air pistol wasn't in the least bit likely to stop a 15-stone bully intent on knocking the shit out of me, but it was my hope that it would be enough of a deterrent to make him walk away.

I didn't expect him to move.

He didn't expect me to shoot.

He lurched toward me. I squeezed the trigger. He jolted backward, holding his hand to his face. Everyone gasped. The pellet hit him right in his eye, and he collapsed to the ground, squealing in agony. I stood motionless. Seconds later, Mr. Little pushed through the crowd and grabbed the gun from my hands.

"Evans, you've got some explaining to do to the police!" he bellowed, grabbing me by the shirt collar.

But I really didn't care. In fact, all I wanted to do was laugh.

I wanted to celebrate like a footballer who had just scored a goal, because I knew they would have to expel me from school on the very last day of the term. That meant I would never have to see Mr. Little, Bogarelli or any other dickhead from that school ever again. I also hoped that Bogarelli had learned his lesson and would think twice before bullying anyone else, and that was also something worth celebrating.

The police and my parents were summoned to the headmaster's office. Mum arrived and saw Bogarelli nursing his face with an ice pack. Without having to ask, she knew what I'd done. Yet, to my amazement, she wasn't in the least bit angry. It turned out that she recognized him instantly. She had seen him before, on the street outside our house, dragging me violently by my wrists from his older brother's car. Now, she couldn't keep herself from telling Bogarelli what she thought of him.

"Well, you asked for that," she said proudly as he sat whimpering, holding the ice pack on his swollen eye. "It's about time you got what you deserved! I'll be telling the police what I saw you do to my boy."

It came as no surprise that I was expelled from Middlewhich County Comprehensive School that day and given a police caution. That was my first brush with the law and the last day I ever used that bloody typewriter.

WAKE-UP CALL 1
THE AWKWARD YEARS

These days I firmly believe that it's better to focus on what life brings you, not what it takes away. As you now know, the dark time I went through in my youth almost drove me to suicide.

Being different is a good thing, although not everyone always sees it that way. The emotional scars of being bullied and humiliated for having dyslexia will always be with me, but I'd rather fix my attention on what good came from all of that.

Take it from me, you don't need to fit in. You don't need to conform. And you don't need a typewriter.

Nowadays, I accept that having dyslexia is a gift. It has shaped many of the traits that I consider to be essential to my success. Here are some of the beneficial traits that I think come from having dyslexia:

Intuitive. Fearless. Persistent.
Lively and creative imagination.
Curious and sees differently from others.
Unconventional without the need to follow the crowd.
Adaptive to change.
Great at problem solving.
Lateral thinking.
Superior verbal communication.

Wake-Up Call 2

LEARNING THE HARD WAY

CHAPTER 5

DAD'S NEW JAG

After being expelled from Middlewich County Comprehensive I was enrolled into Winsford Lodge at the start of the new school year on the condition that I join the class in the year below mine. I became the oldest in the class, as opposed to being the youngest at Middlewich. Winsford Lodge was different in every way. For a start, it was located on the outskirts of town but close enough to my home that I could walk or cycle there each day. The school appeared to be more focused on specialist learning and extracurricular activities than my previous school was, and the teachers at Winsford were much more supportive than the teachers at Middlewich. Within days I settled into school life and felt at ease in my new environment.

It all felt more natural. There was no typewriter, no bullies, no Mr. Little and, better than that, I made friends! I became best friends with a boy called Marcus, and soon we became inseparable. Marcus lived close by, and together we shared all the highs and lows typical of teenage life and all the awkwardness that came with it. Puberty, girlfriends, heartaches, our obsession with Liverpool FC, athletics, martial arts, water sports and anything else that took our fancy.

For a while, I wanted for nothing and felt truly happy. Of course, I was a young teenager, which typically meant that winding up my sister also became a sport and being asked to do chores around the house was like being issued a punishment. Poor Mum was forever lost beneath piles of grass-stained, sweaty sports kit, and I don't doubt that, because I was an energetic teenager,

I drove my parents to the brink of sanity on more than a few occasions—such as the time I accidentally flooded the house.

In my bedroom, I proudly kept my growing collection of sports trophies and athletics medals, including the 100-meter and 200-meter Cheshire County Championship cup, which took pride of place on a shelf above one of my tanks of tropical fish. Because of my love of water sports and the ocean, I began collecting fish, and one day, when I was cleaning out the biggest tank, disaster struck!

Regardless of how well I cleaned the tank and no matter how many times I carefully replanted the various plants and stones, the soil kept turning the water a murky brown color. After 10 attempts produced the same frustrating result, I became so angry that I lost my temper, lashed out and punched the tank, bursting it instantly. I froze in horror as 300 gallons of water gushed onto my bedroom floor, soaking me to the skin and collapsing the ceiling of the living room below.

Once everyone had got over the shock of the how I'd managed to destroy both my bedroom and the living room, thoughts turned to the expense of gutting both rooms, replacing the carpets and repairing the living room ceiling. Dad was fuming. He called a family meeting around the dining table and sternly reminded me that I was not the only person living in the house and that it was about time I grew up. I had never seen him so angry.

"Dad, it was an accident!" I protested, but he was in no mood to listen.

He issued me clear orders. "From now on there are new rules. Number one: clean up your room. Number two: be nice to your sister. And number three: be more helpful around the house. No more of this nonsense!"

I took his stern telling-off on the chin, and when I was finally dismissed from the table, I ran outside to the garden to let off steam. As I kicked my football around, I thought about how much I had upset Dad. I couldn't help noticing that he had seemed a lot more stressed than usual recently. I wondered if there was something else on his mind.

Keen for his forgiveness, I took Dad's advice seriously. I rearranged and organized everything in my room, cleared out all my junk, and painted the walls. And when all the repairs to the house were finished, I gave away boxes of all my old toys and sold the fish tanks. I arranged my clothes in color-coded order and made a cabinet for my trophies. My room became grown up and clutter-free. The only memento I kept was a small model of a black Porsche 911 that Dad had given me. It was my favorite toy, and I kept it under the lamp beside my bed.

A few weeks later, Dad's unusual mood finally made sense. Out of the blue, he came home from work and called another house meeting around the dining table. I was confused and wondered what I could have done wrong? What was the meeting all about? I was sure I had observed the new house rules: I had been kind to Keely, I had done chores for Mum without complaining, and my room was immaculate. We took our places around the table. Dad's forehead was creased with a deep frown. The silence before he spoke made my palms sweat.

"OK, so I have some news that I need to tell you all," he said as he looked at each of us. "There's no easy way to tell you, so I'm just going to come out with it." We waited for his next words as he picked his fingernails in frustration. Something wasn't right. "You know Steve, my business partner?" My sister and I nodded. "Well, the sneaky bugger has done a runner with our money," Dad said with a sigh.

"Done a runner, Dad? What do you mean?" I asked.

"It means, Paul, that he's stolen 750,000 pounds from the company bank account, run up a huge credit card bill, and has done a bunk!" Dad sat back in his chair and folded his arms.

"So what does that mean for us?" I asked, unsure if I really wanted to hear the answer.

"It means that I may have to declare myself bankrupt. In a nutshell, it means we have no money." Dad looked defeated. Each of us sat stunned as we came to terms with the news. My eyes dropped to the floor, and my shoulders slouched under the weight of the news.

"Kids, you're going to have to understand that we are all going to have to make some changes," Dad said. "No more new trainers, football strips and fancy clothes, no more holidays. Paul, I'm sorry, no more trips to LaSanta."

My back suddenly straightened. No more LaSanta?

"We may even need to sell the house," Dad said, his head sinking forward as he struggled to fight back tears.

Mum jumped in and looked at Keely and me. "Your dad and I need you both to understand that life isn't going to be the same for a while, OK? But we'll get through it." she said quietly.

I reached across the table and grabbed Dad's hand. My palm was almost as big as his. I looked straight into his tear-filled eyes as I tried to reassure him with a knowing grip. "We'll get through this, Dad. This is not your fault. You built the company before, so I know you will do it again. Without Steve in the picture you'll probably do it better. We don't need new things. We don't need fancy clothes, and I certainly don't need any more football stuff! We'll knuckle down and pull together. I'll share everything I have, and so will Keely. We'll help you, Dad. I promise!'

"Good lad." he said, nodding modestly.

When I went to bed that night, I lay awake contemplating the thought of no more football stuff and no more LaSanta. I squeezed my eyes tightly as I admitted to myself that doing without was going to be easier said than done. Feeling guilty about my selfishness, I remembered the disappointment on Dad's face and snapped out of it and vowed to sacrifice anything I had to be there for my family, just as they had always been there for me.

It didn't escape my notice that when I had taken Dad by the hand, I had felt myself grow beyond my years. Until that house meeting, I had never seen Dad's vulnerable side, and it was a bizarre moment in our relationship. I felt that our roles had momentarily switched. He had always been my support mechanism. It was a novel experience to step up and offer my support in return.

The next day, I waited for Dad to return home from work. We didn't know if we should expect good news or bad. When he finally pulled up outside, I was surprised to hear him beeping his car horn playfully to get my attention. I raced from my bedroom across the landing to the window, which looked directly onto the driveway. I saw him standing, as proud as a man could be, next to a top-of-the-range bright red Jaguar XJS fitted with the full sports kit. The sports car of his dreams. "Dog-dick red," as he later loved to playfully describe it. I couldn't believe my eyes. Excited but confused at the same time, I bolted downstairs.

"Dad?" I shouted, as I raced outside in a state of confusion. I stood with him, admiring the beautiful car. "I don't understand." I looked up at him. "Did you buy it? Is it ours? You said no holidays, no trainers, no more LaSanta. No more this, no more that."

Still grinning from ear to ear, he paused before responding. "Yes, you're right, son," he said. "Yesterday I did say that. But today I woke up and thought differently. Yes, we could tighten our belts and live more frugally. Or the alternative is that I go out there and make a life for us that I will want to get out of bed every single day to pay for. I prefer the alternative option!"

He smiled at me and opened the car door to reveal the plush leather interior. "I want to drive a nice car," he said. "I want us to live in our house. I want to give you the things you want. All of that is important to me. So by having it, you can be sure, Paul, that I'll get out of bed every damn day to pay for it."

Dad's eyes beamed. "Do you know, today I made more business than I ever have in a single day before, because it matters to live life this way," he said. "Strive for the life you want, not for the life you don't. Remember this, son, whenever you need money, don't cut from the bottom. Always fill from the top."

I didn't notice the effect of any cutbacks that he may have made after that day. I'm not sure he actually made any, and he kept the red Jaguar, number plate Wiji 35, for many years. He never spoke of Steve or being broke ever again, and although I'm sure he spent many sleepless nights worrying about whether he was doing the right thing, he didn't ever show it. He just worked 10 times harder and with even more passion than he had before. He re-built the company and recouped the stolen money and in doing so, he taught me to never be scared of making or losing money. After all, if you look at life from the right perspective, success and money will follow.

CHAPTER 6

CAR BOOT BUSINESS

Mid-Cheshire College,
Winsford, England, 1991

Marcus and I left school and started at Mid-Cheshire College in Winsford at the start of the academic year in September 1991. The college was a bustling modern campus that was home to around 5,000 students, all busily studying a variety of practical, technical and business-orientated subjects—everything from computing and IT to bricklaying. Marcus and I were accepted to join the business and finance degree course. The course was almost full, and we both felt lucky to get in. Being on such a popular course was really important to us, not for the syllabus or the qualification that we'd have at the end of it. What mattered most was that the course would give us access to many people. It was all about our business.

I had just turned 17 and was still working with Andy at the liquidation sales on the weekends. Not everyone at college was making the kind of money I was making, and most kids my age couldn't begin to afford the designer fashion brands that were all the rage. Most students had only enough money to survive on pot noodles and beer. High street fashion and luxury gifts certainly weren't within their budget. I had already flagged up an opportunity in the student market, and getting into the busiest course at the local college was the key.

In the summer before joining college, during my last visit to LaSanta, I was fortunate enough to meet a lady who I'll call Maggie. She ran a very discreet and profitable side-line business in unused warehouse clearance goods that she bought and sold wholesale at bargain-basement prices. The products were sourced from anywhere and everywhere and were extremely popular. You name it, and we were able to supply it.

I knew that the students would return fresh from the holidays with money in their pockets. So just before college term started, I placed my first order with Maggie. When she called me to tell me my order was ready, I persuaded Dad (because his car was big) to meet her at the motorway service station near Birmingham to collect the delivery. When Maggie revealed how much stock I'd actually bought, Dad couldn't believe it. She wasn't exaggerating when she told me that my money would go a long way! The boot, seats and footwells of his red Jaguar were so full that Dad had to drive back from Birmingham with his car seat fully pushed forward and his nose pressed flat against the windscreen. When he arrived home and opened the car doors, waves of stock spilled out like water from a ruptured paddling pool.

"I hope you've done your maths, son," Dad joked before leaving Marcus and me to empty the car and itemize the hundreds of products. There was so much stock that I wondered how long it was going to take us to sell everything. I thought for a moment that I had gone overboard with this first order, but after we had checked each piece for quality, Marcus and I were satisfied we'd be able to sell everything. We just didn't know how long it would take.

When college started, we attended every lecture and every social event with the sole purpose of marketing our wares to as many students as possible. We did try to study a bit, but as the distraction of our enterprise escalated, our motivation in class took a nose dive.

Every day we loaded up the boot of Mum's beige Austin Maestro and parked it in the college car park. At break times we were inundated with students climbing over each other to bag a bargain. We'd go to the pub at lunchtime, have a few pints, come back in the afternoon, and muddle our way through the rest of our lectures until the next break, when we would go back out to the car lot to sell more.

We plowed through the stock much quicker than we expected, and Dad's meetings with Maggie at the Birmingham service station soon became a fortnightly necessity. By November, with the lead-up to Christmas, we were making shit loads of money. We were just having it away, and the other students loved it.

But, of course, there's always someone who wants to ruin everything. In this case it was the head of the business finance degree course, a pushy little man called Richard. He had absolutely no time for Marcus and me. He knew that we weren't interested in his course any more than he was interested in buying a branded tracksuit from us, and he was hell-bent on kicking us off the course. I guess he wanted his students to excel in their exams—which made him and the college look good—rather than demonstrate an actual head for business and finance. I found this to be more than a little ironic. There I was, running a business and demonstrating my financial and entrepreneurial ability—while on a business and finance degree course—but it counted for absolutely nothing!

We continued to flog our goods in the car park until the day came for Richard to call us into his office.

"Ah, the infamous Paul Evans and Marcus Lewis," he sneered as we presented ourselves in his office doorway.

"Pleased to meet you again, Dick, err, I mean Richard," Marcus cheekily replied. I dug him in the ribs to stop his giggles.

"Well, lads, it's clear to me that your active participation on this course isn't your priority," Richard said. "There's a long waiting list to join the class, and I've made the decision to offer your places to other students who are likely to show a higher level of commitment. I have discussed this with the college dean, and our decision is final."

As he spoke, I couldn't help but look out the window and see the line of people forming around our car. My thumbs itched as Richard continued to drone on and on.

"Here at Mid-Cheshire College, we pride ourselves on the high standards and the great results…."

"Yeah, yeah, Dick, err, Richard," I interrupted. "I get it. You want exam results not actual business-savvy students. You've got a line of students, and right now I've got a line of customers."

Richard was stunned by my retort. "Look," I said, pointing to the window and outside to the group growing around Mum's Austin Maestro. "That's a lucrative business out there. We identified the market, we sourced and marketed the product, we control the finances, and we maintain the margins. That's all the stuff you teach on your course, isn't it?"

"I can see that, but it's just simply not on, Mr. Evans!" he fumed.

And that was that. No more business and finance degree.

That afternoon, Marcus and I sat in the college pub and mulled over the day's events with a pint. Leaving college was not an option. We were making so much money that we simply had to find a way to stay. As we thought the problem through and sank a few more pints, we noticed a group of girls giggling in the corner of the room.

"I wonder what course those fitties are on," Marcus laughed, taking a sip of his beer as he caught the eye of one particularly flirtatious girl.

"Probably fucking home economics or something," he scoffed.

I thought about what he'd just said. "Mate, that's it!" I said excitedly.

"What's it?" Marcus looked confused.

"That's the course we'll do. Home fucking economics. It's full of our customers, and they only need to attend about four hours of lectures a week."

"But, Paul, we'll need to cook cakes and sew dresses and shit like that. Are you mad?"

"Yeah, maybe. But four hours a week is nothing. I can do that so we can stay and keep our business going for as long as we can."

"Mate, you're a fucking genius!" Marcus downed his pint proudly. "Let's get the drinks in lad. Here's to home fucking economics!"

The next day, we went to the college office and applied for a transfer to the home economics department. Marcus and I were more than happy to be surrounded by girls and bake the odd cake for four hours a week as long as we continued to flog our stock at every opportunity. With even more time on our hands, our fortnightly orders for stock went through the roof. We began making as many as three trips per week to Birmingham to meet Maggie just to keep up with demand. Marcus and I dated most of the girls on the course, partying and selling our wares and raking in barrow loads of cash for the rest of the year.

All good things eventually must come to an end, however. We knew our luck would run out at some point. At the end of the academic year we were called into the dean's office. We were under no illusion as to what was going to happen, and rightly so; we had milked the system for as long as we could. The dean was in no mood to negotiate and ordered that both our business and our time at Mid-Cheshire College stop at the end of the term. We were told we weren't welcome back for the second year.

"Everyone has enjoyed buying our stuff though, sir," I said. "I even served seven of your teachers yesterday; they bought presents for their parents and clothes for their kids." This remark was met with a stony silence. It didn't make any difference. We were done for, and we knew it. We sold the rest of our stock that afternoon at give-away prices and drove the Maestro out of the car park for the final time.

Driving the empty car home, I reflected on the dean's final words as the conversation played over in my mind: "Paul, isn't it time for you to move on? Isn't it time for you to get out there and get into work? I think you and I both know conventional education isn't going to be your place to excel." He was right. I knew it was definitely time to get a proper job.

Dad, who was sitting at the kitchen table with Mum knew as soon as I walked through the door that I had bad news. It must have been because I wasn't boasting to him about how much money Marcus and I had made that day. "No more home economics next term eh, son?" he asked as he looked at me over his cup of tea.

"Got it in one, Dad," I replied. "The dean told me it was time I got a proper job."

"Well, we'll start tomorrow with a few people I know and see what interviews we can get lined up for you," he said. "The sooner you get started the sooner you'll make progress."

Typical Dad, always quick to find the positive perspective.

After sending my CV to 50 or so names in Dad's contacts book, I was invited to my first interview with a company called Northwest Securities, a personal-loans company with offices throughout the UK. They offered me a job as a telesalesman. Without thinking, I took it straight away.

It wasn't the exciting job I'd hoped for. Every day I'd spend hours sitting at a desk, wearing one of those silly little headphones and cold calling my way through a computer database of 40,000 names to ask them about their existing finances. The script went something like: "Do you need to borrow any money? Do you have any credit cards? Do you have any plans to buy a house? A car perhaps? Any plans to redecorate the living room? Do the garden? Go on holiday? A new kitchen? Upgrade the central heating?" Basically, my job was to do whatever it took to get them on the hook, reel them in, and tie them to a finance package with the most exorbitant interest rates imaginable.

I worked in a division called AA Financial Services and earned a measly annual salary with sales-related commission, but I knew I had to suck it up to gain experience. I had to start somewhere, and it was as good a place as any. So, I kept my head down and did the graft on the corporate conveyor belt.

It soon became apparent that Northwest Securities didn't have a great reputation; most of the staff members were using their employment as a stepping stone to other jobs, so no one stuck around for long. In an effort to tackle their high staff turnover, the company bosses launched a national rewards campaign, the intention of which was to "dangle a carrot" and encourage employees to complete a full year's service and unlock the opportunity to receive a Renault Clio company car.

On the evening of the Your One Year's Service campaign launch party, a thousand members of the sales team from all over the UK, myself included, were invited to a fancy black-tie gala dinner at a local hotel.

Dressed up to the nines, we took our seats, and as the starters were served, the huge video screens all around the ballroom showed the iconic Renault Clio commercial, the one in which a pretty French girl (Nicole) sits with her father in their garden. When Papa falls asleep, Nicole sneaks off in her Clio to meet her boyfriend. When Papa wakes to find her gone, he sneaks off in his Clio to deliver a bouquet of red roses to a mystery woman. The commercial ends with both of them returning to the garden and asking each other the "Nicole? Papa?" line that every Clio owner still remembers.

After a four-course meal and numerous long, boring speeches, the drums finally rolled and the highlight of the ceremony was revealed. Each of the sales team members in the room who had completed more than 12 months was given keys to a new Renault. Music blared, and confetti guns burst from the stage, showering everyone in the room as the CEO of the company stood on the stage and grinned to rapturous applause. We couldn't believe it; it seemed too good to be true. But true it was, and we all went home that night with the keys to a brand-new car and wondered if the novelty was enough to sway our loyalty to the company. OK, the cars had only 1.1-liter engines, which is little more power than a hairdryer has, but a free car was a free car, so it seemed like a fair deal—for now.

At work the next day, my colleagues and I raced our new Clios in hot laps around Chester's town center. By lunchtime the novelty had worn off, because the cars could reach only 80 mph flat out and accelerate from zero to 60 in minutes rather than seconds. To spice things up, we came up with the idea of first-gear races instead. The rules were quite simple: Any race around the city had to be completed using only first gear; the winner was the first driver to cross the finish line outside the office building without blowing up the engine.

Soon enough, the races became the highlight of the day. It wasn't who was atop the sales leaderboard that gripped everyone's attention; it was who topped the first-gear hot laps leaderboard. We spent every lunch time doing very slow, very loud laps of the city followed by celebratory pints and games of pool in the pool hall. I went through three gearboxes in the first six months, before my car was confiscated. I had the first two gearboxes replaced for free by saying it was a manufacturer's fault, but by the third time my boss figured out what we were all up to, and the price of the final gearbox was deducted from my wages. I guess Nicole, Papa and the whole campaign had kind of backfired.

Car-less, I quit Northwest in the winter of 1994 and took a new job as sales manager for Lombard Business Finance. Lombard was the leading personal loans company in the UK at the time—and a place where I was eager to climb the career ladder. I was young, driven and willing to stop at nothing to get to the top. However, the lesson waiting for me around the next corner was not how quickly I could build a career, but rather how easily I could lose it.

CHAPTER 7

ROAD RAGE

Chester, England,
Sunday, October 1, 1995

My usual Sunday habit, upon waking with a blistering hangover, was to sweat out the previous night's excesses at the Chester Ju-Jitsu club and then go for a pint with the lads. This particular Sunday, I was still excited to have earned a brand-new company car, this time from Lombard. It was a Vauxhall Vectra SRI, and I decided to drive home after ju-jitsu instead of going to the pub.

"You sure you won't come for a pint?" My friend Tim asked as I opened my car door and flung my gym bag onto the back seat.

"Nah. You're all right mate," I replied. "I'm going to take this thing for a spin."

By that point I was the sales department's golden boy at Lombard. This new car was a definite upgrade from the Renault Clio that I'd had in the last job just 12 months earlier. I'd smashed my quarterly sales target, which I'm sure had caused much eye-rolling among the rest of the team members, who were all almost twice my age and probably quickly fed up with my youthful arrogance. Anyway, I was on a roll and didn't really give a shit.

I settled myself into the seat, turned the key and blasted two hoots of the car horn. I waved to Tim and my other friend Jason as they disappeared into the pub.

At that time, the streets of Chester were deserted on Sunday mornings. Thinking I was Mika Häkkinen, I tore along the high street, past the shopping center, over the river and past the football ground. Within minutes I was out of town and ripping along the 15-mile stretch of open country roads back to Winsford, with an Oasis CD on full blast.

Coming up to a roundabout on the outskirts of town, I spotted a silver car approaching from the left. It was heading in the same direction, and as we neared each other, it sped past me and cut me up on the inside. Cocky prick! I thought and shifted into a lower gear to catch up and see if I could catch a glimpse of the driver.

The silver car showed no signs of slowing down. Soon we were racing each other along the empty streets toward the town center at high speed. Neither of us was willing to give up the chase, until we were forced to stop at a red light. The light turned green. I floored the accelerator and took the lead, but as we approached the next signal, the silver car nudged in front and then the driver slammed on the brakes. What I had thought was a bit of fun suddenly turned sour.

The silver car stopped. The door flung open, and an angry bald-headed man stepped out. His face was red with rage. He marched toward me, pushing up his shirt sleeves and puffing out his chest. "What the fuck?" I said to myself out loud. "This guy is a fucking nutter!"

I opened my door and stood up to confront him in the space between the two cars. The man's wife got out of the silver car and stood at the roadside, watching us nervously as she tried to talk her husband back. As we faced each other, I could see he was bigger than me, but his thick neck and beer belly showed me he wasn't in particularly good shape. I stood tall as his angry eyes sized me up. Satisfied that he could fight me, he gave me a patronizing smirk, looked back over his shoulder, and said something to his wife that set me off: "This won't take a minute, babe," he tutted confidently.

I saw red.

The confident expression quickly melted from his face when he turned back to face me and saw that I was wearing martial arts bottoms. The tone of his voice reminded me of Bogarelli, which made my blood boil. I glanced over at his wife. My eyes narrowed.

"You're not wrong," I replied in the seconds before rage consumed me.

I left the fat prick lying on the roadside, cradling a broken face, with his wife in tears by his side. Showing no emotion, I got back in my car and drove off. I drove slowly. I didn't want to bring attention to myself, and I was still processing what had just happened. I hadn't killed him. He was still conscious, but I'd made a mess of his face. Medical reports later confirmed that the three strikes I made—two with my elbow and one with my knee to the front and side of his head—left him with a broken nose, jaw and cheekbone.

I drove around aimlessly for a while until the red rage cooled. I pulled up outside my house an hour or so later to find Marcus, who lived with me at the time, pacing around the living room looking rather nervous.

"What the fuck happened, mate? The police have just been here looking for you. Something about a fight," he said anxiously.

"Yeah," I said. "Some fucking dickhead with a bad case of road rage cut me up, and I cracked him when he had a go at me."

As I explained what had happened, Marcus's face twisted with panic.

"They've got your car registration and your address, mate. They said you've got to report to the police station."

"Don't worry. It'll all be sorted," I reassured him coolly. "Yeah, I probably did hit him a bit too hard, but he came at me, and it was self-defense. He threw the first punch. I reckon I'll be slapped with a few hours of community service and a fine for giving him a smack."

Marcus didn't mirror my confidence.

Later that day, as instructed, I reported to the police station. Introducing myself at the reception desk, I explained to the police officer that I wanted to make a statement about an incident I had been involved in earlier that morning. The officer scribbled down some notes and made a phone call before replying dryly, "Mr. Evans, you are to remain here for further questioning under caution. You are entitled to a legal representative and can make one phone call. Do you understand?"

What, no fine? How serious was this? How much trouble was I in? I seriously began to wish I had gone for that pint with Tim and Jason after all. All words escaped me. All I could answer was a simple "Yes."

The officer escorted me to a cell at the back of the police station. "Empty the contents of your pockets onto the table, along with your shoes and belt," he ordered.

As though I were in a bizarre dream, I did exactly as asked and placed my belt alongside my shoes. I realized they wanted my shoe laces and belt to eliminate the risk that I would hang myself. Barefoot and alone in the cell, I finally accepted the grave reality of my situation. This was way more serious than I had anticipated. It turned out that Marcus was right to be freaked out. I needed a lawyer.

After I had spent four hours locked in the cell, a CID officer arrived to interview me. In a harshly lit interview room, I recited the morning's events minute by minute. At first, I tried to make light of what had happened, suggesting it was simply a bit of a fracas. The officer's raised eyebrow suggested he wasn't going to accept my watered-down version of events. "I fought back in self-defense, then he hit the curb. Honestly, I hit him only once!" The officer's face was blank.

"Mr. Evans, while you claim to have hit Mr. Anderson only once, he is presently undergoing surgery in hospital for facial reconstruction. In support of his claims, we also have statements from his wife and two other witnesses, who claim that they saw the assault from their window. All of them state that you used excessive and unnecessary force."

I later found out that Mr. Anderson's wife was a lawyer. The other two witnesses were schoolchildren who had been playing a game of cops and robbers when they saw me from their bedroom window. Regardless of their age or Mrs. Anderson's bias, it was to be my word against theirs as the officer read the formal charge out loud for the record: "Paul Evans, under Section 18 of the Offences Against The Person Act 1861, you are hereby charged with grievous bodily harm with intent; an offense which, if found guilty in the courts of England and Wales, may carry a custodial sentence. You do not have to say anything. However, it may harm your defense if you do not mention, when questioned, something which you later rely on in court. Anything you do say may be given in evidence."

WAKE-UP CALL 2
LEARNING THE HARD WAY

Being an academic doesn't mean you've received an education. I think I learned more about life and business by just getting out there and "doing it." I'll admit, I've probably made more mistakes than your average man has, but I firmly believe that because of that, I haven't lived an average life.

Lessons from my mentors and the school of hard knocks have contributed to my success in more ways than I can imagine:

1. It's meant to be hard. Hard is what makes it great.

2. Building relationships with people is everything.

3. Opportunity is everywhere when you open your eyes.

4. Find mentors and surround yourself with people more experienced than you are.

5. If you do it for money, you will fail. Do it because you are driven.

6. Nothing is ever resolved with violence.

Wake-Up Call 3

IT'S A DOG-EAT-DOG WORLD

CHAPTER 8

JAILBIRD

Chester, England,
Monday, April 15, 1996

We gathered outside Chester Crown Court for the hearing of Ander-son v. Evans. My friends Tim and Jason joined me and my parents for moral support. Over the years, since our college days, the two of them, along with Marcus, had become as close to me as brothers. For Tim and Jason to come to court said everything about how much we relied on each other.

"Don't worry, mate," Tim reassured me as we stood outside the court-house. "A few hours of community service? You can handle that. You've had worse punishments. Your mum's made you do your own laundry before!" He was joking, of course, trying to lighten the mood.

Mum smiled at them. Dressed in blue with her hair styled neatly, she was wearing a brave face as she hugged me. Despite her well-groomed appear-ance, I knew she was worn out and worried about what was coming. Dad took my right hand, and Mum took my left, and they walked me briskly up the steps to the courthouse door.

Dad didn't show any signs of nerves as we were greeted by Mr. Mellor, my lawyer, in the doorway. He and I had spent the last six months building my defense, and we were confident that we had all we needed to present our case in front of the judge. However, in the event that things didn't go according to plan, Dad had my resignation letter tucked away in his jacket pocket, ready to send to my boss at Lombard.

Our best plan to lessen the prospect of jail time was to demonstrate to the judge that I fully accepted responsibility for my actions and to acknowledge my wrongful behavior and apologize most sincerely. By the time of the hearing, my lawyer and I had collected hundreds of testimonials and good-conduct references from friends, colleagues, neighbors and acquaintances who had crossed my path over the last 10 years. Mr. Mellor was confident that he had enough material to present a strong case that would steer me clear of doing time at Her Majesty's pleasure.

Once everyone was seated, the judge called for my lawyer to begin the court proceedings.

Mr. Mellor read my character statements, which described me as a well-meaning and affable person from a good family with a bright future. He summarized my personality as fun-loving and youthful and said that I was well liked by many. My references came from work colleagues, friends, neighbors, teachers from Winsford Lodge School and sports coaches from all over the county, including the Chester Martial Arts club, every one of them applauding me for my outgoing, approachable and friendly nature. By the time Mr. Mellor was finished, I felt sure that the judge would see this as a one-off event that, though it resulted in injury, was not the act of a person who posed a threat to the community.

I knew that the Andersons' lawyer would try to counter that perception and present me as a thug with a wildly dangerous and volatile personality. When the time finally came for the Andersons to describe the events of that Sunday morning in October of 1995, I couldn't believe my ears.

During questioning, the Andersons both denied any involvement in a car race. When my lawyer suggested that Mr. Anderson had been driving provocatively that morning and had become involved in a pursuit, both he and his wife denied all knowledge. "I have no recollection of seeing Mr. Evans' car until we were at the traffic lights and he approached our car," Mrs. Anderson claimed from the witness stand.

What lies! I thought, as I stood in the dock, helplessly listening to her read her statement to the court.

They both suggested that they were driving innocently along the road when I approached them aggressively at the traffic lights. When questioned further, Mrs. Anderson even denied that her husband had been the first person to get out of their car. She claimed he had never once shown any aggression toward me and denied that he had said anything to me or her in the moments leading up to the fight. I couldn't believe what I was hearing.

When the court session ended, it was obvious to me that the Anderson side of the room had lied throughout their witness statements, and to bolster their claims of innocence, they had blatantly played down their involvement. Our side, on the other hand, presented a thorough and detailed account of the events that really took place on a day when two people lost their composure after a silly road prank had escalated out of hand and ended in a moment of inexcusable madness. The guy who threw the first punch was willing to accept, acknowledge and apologize. We thought the truth would win.

The judge looked at me and asked, "Mr. Evans, how do you plead?"

"Guilty," I replied.

The judge continued, "Upon reviewing the case and the evidence presented here today, I will say, Mr. Evans, that you are clearly a talented young man, a man with good prospects and someone who is respected within the community. It is evident from what I have heard here today and my experience of you that there is no doubt that you have a promising future ahead of you."

This is going well, I thought. Maybe it'll be community service after all.

"However," he continued, "I do feel that given the seriousness of this incident, it is not in the best interests of the community and the public at large that a highly qualified martial arts professional does not undertake his obligation to abide by the set of ethics that are entrusted to him by the sport itself and by his own better judgement."

Oh fuck, what does that mean?

"And for that, Mr. Evans, I sentence you to a twelve-month custodial sentence."

His words ricocheted around the wood-paneled walls and hit me like a punch to the side of the head. In an instant my whole world came crashing down. Twelve months! Oh my God! A feeling of terror flooded my stomach as I trembled with nerves. I looked around the courtroom to see everyone's reaction. Tim and Jason had a look of utter disbelief on their faces. They stood up and stared at me, urging me through their body language to be strong. Mum was visibly crushed, her eyes hidden behind handfuls of tissues as she sobbed uncontrollably on Dad's shoulder.

What the hell just happened? I had to look away as Dad's face turned gray. I thought that if I continued looking at any of them I might be sick on the spot.

I felt a tug at my arm and turned to find a gray-haired, heavy-bellied man wearing a police-type uniform handcuffing me to usher me out of the dock.

Is that it? I asked myself. What about the lies his wife told in court? She's a lawyer! Surely that's an offence in itself! What about the two witnesses? They were just kids. What about all my good-conduct testimonials? Didn't they count for anything? My mind was spinning like a washing machine. I'd never been to prison before. I hadn't had any official offenses before, only a rap on the knuckles for popping Bogarelli with an air pistol at school. Surely that didn't count?

There didn't seem to be any point in trying to make sense of it. It all happened so fast, and the reality of the situation was still catching up with me. I stood up with the court guard and could hear my family and friends' gasps and cries of shock behind me. I wiped away my tears with the back of my hand and looked down at my wrists, now locked together with heavy steel cuffs, and took a last look around the courtroom. I took a deep breath. My heart was racing as I saw a door open to the side of the dock.

"Come this way, sir," the guard said flatly, indicating for me to step down and follow him. I felt like my knees might collapse.

I followed the guard through the door from the courtroom. The long chain, bunch of keys and handcuffs hanging from his belt underlined his authority. He was completely expressionless and said nothing as he led me down a harshly lit corridor past a series of locked doors to a room where I was to see my family for the last time.

"Wait in here," he said gruffly. "Your family will come in from the other side."

The small room was partitioned into speaking booths, each with a small metal chair positioned in front of a glass screen punctured with a circle of holes only large enough to poke my little finger through. Mum and Dad entered through a door on the other side of the room, and we sat facing each other through the glass, not knowing what to say.

"It'll be all right, son." Dad's words of encouragement seemed so distant from behind the glass. "I'll look after everything from this side. You just look out for yourself and keep your head straight, and you'll be out in six months with good behavior."

We all touched palms and kissed through the glass as we said our good-byes, our eyes full of tears.

When my parents left, Tim and Jason took their place. Their tone was totally different, and their eyes were burning with rage. "This is fucking bullshit!"

They punched and poked the glass as they spat their instructions at me like coaches preparing a boxer for the fight of his life.

Jason pressed his forehead against the glass. "Here's the fucking rules," he said. "Dry your eyes, mate. Don't let anyone in there see you're scared. D' you hear me?"

Tim fixed his eyes on me. "Listen, Paul. The first person that looks at you badly, you chew their fucking face off. Got it? Take no shit from anyone. You do that the first time then no one will touch you after that, all right? I mean it! Chew their fucking face off!"

I was petrified. I got up from my chair and faced them in silence with gritted teeth. I nodded in agreement and appreciation. I knew they were right. It would be two weeks until the next visiting time. Two weeks until I would see another friendly face. Until then, I was going to show only one side of me.

The gray-haired guard met me at the door and led me from the visitors room through a series of barred doors to a holding cell. He unlocked the door and gestured for me to go inside. "You'll be here until they come for you, so you may as well get comfortable."

I assumed by telling me to get comfortable he meant that I could be in for a long wait, because the room's long, steel bench certainly wasn't designed with comfort in mind. He pulled the door shut behind him and then tested the little hatch in the door to ensure I was visible. I sat on the bench in an eerie silence and contemplated the events that had culminated in my arrival at that particular point. Twelve months in prison? What was going to become of me?

After what seemed like hours of being alone in the cell with my thoughts circling in my head in a repetitive loop, the door was unlocked, and the gray-haired guard re-cuffed me and led me to the rear of the building, where the prisoner transportation awaited. I stepped into the van, which was separated into small cells. I was ordered to sit down in the cell on the left, and then the wire door was locked shut. I was being transported like a caged animal. I was aware of two or three other men in handcuffs already in the vehicle's other cages, and I avoided making any eye contact with any of them.

Tim and Jason's last words were still ringing in my ears when we started to drive away: "Don't look weak on any level, mate!" I had seen prisons only on TV, and now I was in a van with a bunch of convicts in handcuffs on my way to a maximum-security prison. I had no idea what to expect, but I had never known such fear.

When the van pulled into Walton jail, my anxiety and sense of foreboding took on a whole new level. When I first saw the complex that was to be my new home, my chest felt so tight I could barely swallow. The building looked like it had stood untouched since the 19th century and the days of Jack the Ripper. This was a sinister and scary place, old and intimidating. Its stone walls were thick and dark, and razor wire and high security fences surrounded the perimeter.

Once it had passed through all the security checkpoints, the van stopped beside an open steel door. The cages were opened one by one, and I was handcuffed to a security guard and led into a reception area, where I was sternly greeted by more emotionless people clad in black-and-white uniforms.

"Name? Age? Weight?" a man sitting behind a desk asked abruptly as I entered the room.

"Take this!" A plastic bag containing a set of blue overalls was thrust into my hands. "Go over there!" he shouted, pointing to a curtained area. "Take off your clothes. Put them and any other belongings in the bag. Put the overalls on, and then you'll see the doctor."

"Yes, OK," I muttered, still shell-shocked. The guard un-cuffed me so I could undress. He listed each item of clothing that I took off and the contents of my wallet to a man who was filling out my paperwork: "'Brown jacket, black jeans, black socks, white shirt, 45 pounds cash, bank cards, national insurance card….'"

After I was dressed in the blue overalls and my belongings were packed away in the plastic bag, my photograph was taken, and I was led away to a room farther down the corridor. Time seemed to tick by slowly. After evaluating my medical history, with a nurse recording my height and weight, the doctor used the body orifice security scanner to make sure I wasn't smuggling contraband in any hard-to-reach places. I was finally given the all clear and taken to my cell.

The interior of the jail was a vast, echoing hall lined with cells on three levels. A series of barred doors and steel staircases contained each level. I was led to the second landing, where I was given a neatly folded sheet, pillow, blanket, plastic cutlery set, a bar of soap and three packs of cigarettes, which was to be my full allowance. My cell was at the end of a row, directly opposite a set of stairs that led to the floor below. Inside were two sets of bunk beds. Three of the beds were already taken.

I felt exhausted, terrified and anxious all at the same time. I could sense the creepy eyes of my cellmates watching my every move as I placed my bedding onto the top bunk, hiding my cigarettes under my pillow. I glanced over my shoulder at one of them, who was mumbling something that sounded like, "Got any ciggies, mate?"

I could see they were all junkies, skinny good-for-nothing skag-heads who looked like they would trade a hot meal for a hit of heroin any day of the week. I knew I would have to watch my back every minute while they were around. Jason and Tim's advice may come in handy sooner rather than later, I thought, as I lay on the coarse mattress and tried to get some sleep. I wasn't intending to actually fall sleep, but it seemed best to pretend so I wouldn't have to make any conversation with my new roommates.

"Skag-head bastard!" I yelled when I felt a bony hand slip under my pillow at 4 a.m. I opened my eyes and saw that all three men were creeping around my bunk. "Fuck off!" I shouted as loud as I could. One of them waved his hands in my face, while the others pulled at my bedding, trying to reach the cigarettes under my pillow. I leapt off my bunk and stood in front of them with my fists clenched. I was barefoot but on my tiptoes, ready to fight. Tim's instructions to "Chew their fucking face off" raged through my mind.

Within seconds, I was in a blind rage and totally out of control. I kicked and punched them until the guards heard the commotion. Two of the men were out cold on the floor when the third jumped on my back, just as the cell door opened. I hurled myself through the door with him still clinging to my neck. Stopping abruptly at the top of the metal stairs, I had just enough momentum to grab him, toss him over my shoulder, and send him head first over the banister to the floor below.

The guards instantly wrestled me to the ground. "Oi! Take it easy!" they ordered as I wriggled and screamed. "Hands behind your back!" One guard pinned my face to the floor. Another pressed his knees in my back while they cuffed my hands. "OK, slowly stand up." They steadied me on my feet and led me away from the cell. The medics had arrived to tend to my cellmates.

"It's going to be solitary for you, son," said one guard as they led me away.

CHAPTER 9

THE WEAVERS

HMP Walton, Liverpool,
England, 1996

My solitary confinement cell in Walton jail was a damp, smelly, graffiti- and shit-covered concrete cube, just 6 feet wide from wall to wall. If I lay down on the floor with my arms stretched over my head, I could easily touch each side from tip to toe. There was a metal-framed bed along one wall and a stainless-steel toilet bowl fixed to the other wall, in the corner. A small cracked and barred window placed just above eye level provided a sense of the outdoors, although I was granted only one hour in the fresh air per day. That made the light from the window and the constant draft of cold air that whistled though the crack seem all the more cruel.

With no one to talk to and nothing to read, I could only sleep (which I did a lot of), do sit-ups, or lie on the thin mattress and read the graffiti scratched into the walls. I completely lost track of time as the days rolled by. If I'm honest though, I was glad to be segregated, because at least I knew the noises at night weren't monsters coming for me. All I had to was wait it out.

I did know one person in Walton. A senior prison guard named Kenny was one of the senior jiujitsu instructors at the Liverpool jiujitsu academy. He knew that I was in Walton, so he did what he could to make sure I was treated kindly while in solitary. He came to my door every time he was on shift to check up on me. Two weeks had passed when he came to my cell with the news that I was to be transferred that afternoon to Kirkham prison, between Preston and Blackpool, which was a category D open jail.

"It's basically for the people that are at the end of their sentences or the wealthier businessmen that are done for tax evasion," Kenny explained when I asked what Kirkham would be like. "It's not for nutters and psychos, like they are in here, mate. It'll be a walk in the park compared to this shithole."

It was pissing with rain on my last day in Walton. I stepped into the Securicor van with my hands cuffed in front of me. As the electric fence opened, the van jolted forward and rolled through the security gates. The rain pelted against the black-tinted windows of the van as I took one last look at the vast, thick, wet walls of Walton jail. It had to be one of the most oppressive and intimidating buildings in all of England.

As the van weaved through the streets of Liverpool, I stared through the rear window until the Monster Mansion (as it had been dubbed by its most famous inhabitant, Charles Bronson) disappeared from view. I knew these roads like the back of my hand, and by the time we reached HMP Kirkham 40 miles away, the familiarity of the roads and the scenery on the route had helped to calm my nerves and apprehension about where I was being taken. Nothing could ever be as bad as the place I'd just come from.

My first impressions of HMP Kirkham indicated that this would be a much lighter experience altogether. No more grim cells, no more handcuffs and no more prison-issue overalls. The prison building was an old army barracks laid out in the typical formation of single story, modular-unit buildings known as a billet. Each billet probably had 10 twin-bedrooms on one side and 10 on the other side, a little corridor down the middle, a tiny sitting room at the front that had a TV, tea and coffee facilities, and a shower and toilet block at the other end of the corridor.

This place was the opposite of Walton. It was run on the principle of trust and good behavior. They never turned your light off or on, and we had as much fresh air and outdoor activity as we wanted. All inmates were free to come and go as they pleased. The only rule was that everyone had to be inside his billet by 8:30 p.m., when they'd lock the front door. The door was so flimsy that it would have been easy to kick it open. The rule was simple: Inmates not inside their billet at the lockdown time or caught trying to escape were immediately sent back to the maximum-security jail.

Kirkham wasn't a violent place like Walton. Kenny was right: The prisoners in this jail weren't rapists and murders. A small minority were tax-evasion guys or financial fraudsters, but the rest were lowlife scumbags—robbers, thieves and burglars—the sort of horrible people who wouldn't bat an eyelid at robbing a little old lady for her pension money or breaking into a house at Christmas time to steal a child's presents from under the tree.

I shared a room with a guy who was a convicted car thief. He was just like the other 99 percent of the inmates: a lost soul with no home, no family, no role models and a nasty drug habit. He was addicted to heroin and caught up in the downward cycle of repeat offending. This was his twentieth time in jail, and he was only about 23 years old. Whenever he was released, he would have to sleep on the street. So, he'd steal a car, get caught and be put back in jail. For him, Kirkham was the better option. He got three square meals a day, smoked a bit of heroin once a week, and when the drugs wore off, he could sit on his bed and pick at his skin with a paperclip to pass the time. In Kirkham, it was wise to lock away any sharps or razors, not for fear of being attacked with them, but to prevent the self-harmers from using them to decorate the walls with their own blood.

I did sympathize with these guys to some degree, but the sadder the souls I met, the deeper I felt an immense inner sense of gratitude for the relatively good life I knew I had. I realized that I still had opportunities and a loving family and friends waiting for me when I got out. Not like those poor bastards. I vowed that there was no way this place was going to break me in the way it had broken so many others. Men who had turned to heroin out of boredom and depression. If I was going to survive this place over the next six months, it meant keeping to myself and maintaining my wits at all times. I would trust no one, and I was prepared to be mentally and physically stronger than everyone else. The danger in Kirkham wasn't violence; it was psychological weakness.

Kirkham jail ran various vocational programs, NVQs and apprenticeship certifications, and as part of the rehabilitation process, all inmates were enrolled in multiple programs while serving their time. Because Kirkham is in the north of England, it made sense that the main vocational trainings were in textiles or farming. I was assigned to be a weaver. It wasn't a vocation I was particularly familiar with nor one that I was likely to take any further. But Mum was a talented seamstress, and looking on the brightest side possible, I thought that maybe one day I could impress her by being so textile-savvy.

The weaving shed was a large warehouse within the prison compound and was home to about 60 enormous looms. These looms produced hundreds of yards of cloth per day. The inmates generally regarded being a weaver as one of the worst prison jobs because of the noise and dust. When the looms were running, thrashing up and down and spinning the yarn into cloth, the noise was deafening. As the machines clattered away, a fine cloud of dust from the yarn hung in the air and eventually stuck in the back of your throat. From 7:30 a.m. until 4:30 p.m., we'd work the looms, winding, knotting, plaiting and threading the yarn. The main point of the job was to watch the loom until one of the threads broke. Then we would stop the machine, change the thread, and restart it so no unwanted lines or flaws appeared in the finished cloth.

Once you got used to it, the work was therapeutic in a weird kind of way. It helped pass the time and gave you some satisfaction in working at a steady pace and producing a finished product. There was a good spirit among the weavers, but I don't know if that was because the noisy rhythm of the machines sent us all into a kind of trance after a while.

The entire prison routine repeated itself day after day. Wake-up was about 6 a.m., breakfast in the canteen half an hour later, vocational work started at 7:30 a.m. and went until 4:30 p.m., with lunch somewhere in the middle. At 5 p.m., the canteen opened again for dinner, after which you were sent back to your billet for free time until the 8:30 p.m. lockdown. After about a week I began to relax, as I became more familiar with the system, the people and the surroundings, and I had figured out who was who and how things were done.

As a weaver, I was paid 8 pounds per week. In addition to the prison wages, each prisoner could receive a maximum of 10 pounds per week from family members on the outside. Every Sunday was shop day in the canteen, where you could buy groceries at standard supermarket prices. You would present your prison ID at the canteen reception window and then they'd tell you how much money you had in your account. You could use that to buy pot noodles, bread, butter, biscuits, chocolate, toiletries, cigarettes or phone cards.

Phone cards were jail currency. Each phone card was worth 2 pounds and could be used on the prison black market to buy coffee, tobacco, marijuana, heroin, whatever. A pack of cigarettes cost two phone cards; a small bag of marijuana would set you back six phone cards, and so on. I wasn't doing drugs, so I rarely had any need to buy anything on the black market. The only things I bought in the canteen shop were phone cards, and within a month I had accumulated about 40 of them.

Kirkham was like a revolving door, with inmates arriving and leaving on a never-ending cycle. Inmates were assigned to jobs in prison work departments; these were mostly run by lead civilian wardens, better known to us as civilian screws. After only a fortnight of working in the weaving shed, I was considered a veteran because there were so many newcomers. Everyone had to be trained on the looms, so I managed to convince the head screw to promote me to supervise the training. He was a sweet old guy, and I persuaded him that at his age it wasn't right that he should handle all the hoodlums who came to the prison. Instead, I suggested, he would be more comfortable sitting in the office, reading the newspaper with his feet up while I supervised the factory floor. I also managed to negotiate a raise in my salary from 8 to 12 pounds per week. From then on, he sat in his little office doing crosswords, while I supervised the workers and trained all the new inmates on how to use the weaving machines.

It worked like a dream. It took only two days to train inmates how to use the looms. They would make a few mistakes, get upset, then I'd step in and show the technique a few more times, and that was it. It was simple, really. Once a guy knew how to use a loom, he knew how to use it. After that, I would just sit in the little office too, reading the newspaper, chatting to the senior warden about anything and everything, idling away the time until I could go to the gym.

The main benefit of this new post was that I got to meet almost every new person who came into Kirkham. By meeting everybody I could begin doing a little business trading, which is what I really wanted to do. As a supervisor I earned the highest salary in the prison, and I received the weekly 10 pounds that my family sent. I was remembering my school days and my Parker pen pawn business. The opportunity to do the same with phone cards was far too good an opportunity to miss.

I started lending out phone cards to fellow inmates. My terms were simple: Borrow one phone card today, and in a week's time you pay me two phone cards. Borrow two phone cards today, and in a week, you pay four phone cards, and so on. I soon had a group of about 30 customers who would borrow different quantities of phone cards regularly. It was all was highly illegal, of course. So, using fabric from the weavers, I made a secret pouch for my phone cards that tucked safely from view down the inside of my leg. At any time, I could be walking around with more than 100 phone cards hanging down my pants.

Rules are rules, and business is business. The prison had rules, and my business had rules, too: Any loans had to be paid back. Most of my customers played by the rules. My best customer was a very wealthy man who had several women's hair salons across the UK and was in his last year of doing a four-year stretch for tax evasion. Once I had 100 phone cards, I'd sell them to him for double the price. He needed the phone cards to get himself the best cigarettes, nice coffee and decent food. He would pay the laundry guy in phone cards to get brand-new clothes, new shirts, jumpers, jeans, trousers and trainers, and in return for the 100 phone cards, he'd put 400 pounds in my bank account on the outside. I was probably making 600 to 700 pounds per week dealing in phone cards.

One day a big, heavy lump of a lad, who I didn't know that well, came to me looking for a short-term loan. He wanted two phone cards and said he'd give me back three the next day. I agreed to it. I wouldn't normally, but he had said he was good for it. The next day at dinner in the canteen I saw him sitting at a table of about 12 people. I tapped him on the shoulder and asked, "Have you got my cards?" I immediately knew that agreeing to his loan was a bad decision.

He stood up, looked at me and replied nonchalantly, "You're not fucking getting them!" The rest of the men at table stopped eating and froze in silence, waiting to see how I was going to handle him.

"What do you mean I'm not getting them? Where are my cards, dick-head?" I answered, screwing my face into my meanest expression. "You know you owe me three cards!"

The big lad just shrugged and walked off. He knew there were wardens around, and that because the canteen was full, it wasn't likely I would retali-ate. I tried to keep calm, but I knew if I didn't do something there and then, this incident, in full view of everyone, would mark the end of my little busi-ness. I walked to the front of the dinner line, picked up a metal food-service tray and walked back to him with the tray tucked under my arm.

"I'm not going to ask you again. Where are my fucking phone cards?" I hissed.

The big lad leaned toward me and pushed me backward by my shoulders. I waited for his gorilla-like arms to drop to his sides before I hit him in the throat with the side of the tray. He instantly dropped to his knees, gasping for air. Of course, commotion ensued, as numerous security guards tackled me to the ground and led me away to a detention cell, where I remained for the next four days. I was aware of the risk of prolonging my sentence, but for my own security, I had to keep my reputation intact. Fortunately, four days in that cell was considered enough of a punishment and I hadn't for-feited my opportunity to be released after six months instead of 12.

From that day on I counted down the months, weeks and days until my freedom would be finally granted. I made every effort to look as hard as nails; I shaved my head and kept a permanent snarl on my face. It was a look that went with the territory. I trained in the gym and did what I could to get myself through each day. I was 22 years old, weighed 185 pounds, and was training five times a week, so I guess you could say I was in the best shape of my life.

I had to adopt the tough-guy persona because I had no other options. After all, I was in a jail with 800 other convicts, trapped in a place with people who were constantly trying to rob, steal and dominate each other. Like I said, I had to make sure the loans were repaid, so my philosophy had to be, "I'm going to be a horrible bastard. If I'm not, someone is going to be a horrible bastard to me."

So, the time ticked slowly by, and I kept to my routine. I got up in the morning, fed, washed, did my job in the weaving shed, then went to the gym.

In the evenings I ran around collecting my phone cards, giving out new ones, and cracking down on anyone who didn't pay. I repeated the same monotonous cycle, in the same order, at the same time, day in and day out.

Tim and Jason visited every few weeks, which allowed a brief break in my military-style drill for a bit of banter, but Mum and Dad came to see me only three times in total. I told them to stay away; I didn't want them to see me in that situation—in jail. I especially didn't want Mum to see me. It was hard to switch the hard-man image on and off, and I didn't want her to think that I had turned into a thug. More than that, out of selfishness and guilt, I didn't want them to visit because they would leave and I couldn't. It broke my heart every time I had to say goodbye to them and see Mum cry.

Jail time gave me a lot of time to think and reflect on things and decide what changes I wanted to make for myself when I was released. It wasn't the cramped living conditions or the constant threat of violence that really got to me; it was the loss of liberty. Losing the freedom to go to bed when you want, get up when you want, go away for the weekend, meet somebody or not, or to just sit and watch TV was awful. Being away from my friends and family, missing out on weekends and missing out on all the things they would tell me about when they came to see me—that was the hard part of being locked up.

During my time in Walton and Kirkham I witnessed firsthand the real shit that other people had to deal with in their lives, and it had a far deeper impact on me than I expected. I thought about how I'd lost my freedom, but I also reflected on how some inmates had never really known what freedom was. There were so many lost souls in jail who would escape their demons through drink, drugs or self-harm. I didn't like to judge them, but at night when the lights went out, I would think about them and wonder, Fuck, what happened to you? How sad that drugs are the better option, that life on the outside is worse to you than being in here. Where's your father? Where are the people who care about you? What chance have you really got when you get out of here?

I also thought about the consequences of my own actions. I figured my temper stemmed from the bullying I had suffered as a kid. Having been bullied for so long, I was happy that no one was able to bully me anymore.

But even though as an adult I was able to defend myself, look where I ended up. How ironic! Because of one meaningless fight, I'd lost everything I had fought to become. I remembered my old teachers who had forewarned that Paul Evans would have no future unless he completely changed his entire outlook. Well, was it possible that they were right?

On the inside, I made acquaintances with people only because I needed to use them to get by. It isn't normal to be so calculated about people, but during my last days in Kirkham I was categorically clear about those relationships. I let it be known that I didn't want to see anyone ever again. I didn't hand out my contact details; there was no point. I had absolutely no intention of keeping in touch with any of them. And as I left the billet for the last time, I didn't spare a living soul a second look.

I was released from prison on October 17, 1996. After completing six months of my 12-month sentence, I was out and decided to draw a line under that part of my life and move on. Looking back, I don't regret that time in my life. That might sound like a crazy statement. After all, I had worked so hard to get to the point where I was before I went into jail. But there is simply no better way to appreciate what an amazing life you have than to have it ripped away from you.

I've decided that it wouldn't do anyone any harm to do at least two to three weeks in jail. Shitty though it was for me and my family, if I was given the option I certainly wouldn't remove that chapter from my life. It helped shape me and made me more determined, more grateful and compassionate. I saw how fortunate I was. The gratitude that I felt when I hugged Mum for the first time since before my court case affirmed that I was a richer man for the experience.

CHAPTER 10

EYES ON THE PRIZE

Winsford, England,
October 1996

On that miserable afternoon, six months earlier, when Dad left the courtroom without me, he handed my resignation letter regretfully to my boss at Lombard Business Finance. In that moment my career and any previous achievements I had attained were wiped from existence. I had become a number, a prisoner, the "wasted potential" that my school report cards had predicted.

Being locked up for six months gave me plenty of time to contemplate what kind of life I was going to create for myself after my stretch was finished. I'd often lie awake for hours on my uncomfortable prison bed, staring at the naked light bulb dangling from the center of the ceiling while I mapped out my future in my mind. I would visualize myself with a city slicker's job in the corporate world, wearing sharply tailored suits, and with a drawer full of collectable watches and a Porsche Turbo in the driveway. I imagined my success to be the toast of the city and everyone would know my name. I'd fly first class, drink vintage champagne and have a stunning beauty by my side every night of the week. In prison it was vital to have a dream. That visualization of success kept me going as the repetitive daily drill of being a weaver would remind me of the turgid depths of my reality.

After my release and a small, low-key welcome-home party, I preferred to be around only my trusted circle of friends, namely Tim, Gaz, Jason, Marcus and Dad. For the first few days of freedom, I didn't want to be around anyone; everything seemed a little staged and awkward. Mum's fussing felt smothering. She didn't mean it to be stifling, of course, but she'd have wrapped me in cotton wool if she could.

It took time to get used to the calmness of home and the absence of constant surveillance and noise. Out of habit I'd still wake up early, thinking that I needed to beat the line for the toilet and shower before reporting for duty at 7:30 a.m. at the weaving shed. But after a decent amount of Mum's homemade meals, watching footy in front of the telly with the lads, and the warmth and familiarity of family, we all began to relax and enjoy the return to normality.

I was eager to piece my life back together and was determined not to be branded forever as an "ex-con." I had managed to navigate the slippery slope of prison life that forces men with potential to lose their grip on a better future. I knew that the sooner I put the memories and emotional scars of the last six months into a tiny box at the back of my mind, the sooner I could move on.

But finding work after you've been in prison isn't easy. Normally the first question asked in an interview is, "What have you been doing for the last six months?" Well, for me that question was like a gun to the heart. I rehearsed all sorts of plausible answers: "I've been travelling and working abroad"; "I've been volunteering in an old-folks home"; "I've been doing a home-study course."

I thought up anything to avoid the truth. But the fact of the matter was that nobody was interested in hiring a felon. By mid-November, I had applied for every job advertised in the area and hadn't had a single interview.

Being turned down so many times tempted childhood feelings of self-loathing and doubt to resurface. I wondered if I was going to have to start all over again and wash cars for a living. But prison had hardened me. I'd learned a valuable lesson on the inside, that a man will destroy himself when he doesn't strive to better himself. So, rather than becoming consumed by those old, familiar demons, I encouraged myself to believe that I wasn't the issue; the problem was that the jobs I was going for were beneath my capabilities.

I realized that to make any progress I had to change my job-seeking strategy. Instead of applying to every job under the sun, I specified my list of ideal career options and targeted only the UK's most reputable companies. I decided that it would be better to enter the job market and aim high then work my way down, rather than begin at rock bottom and work my way up. Positioned at the top of my list of my dream careers was the largest finance company in the world: GE Capital Finance. At that time, GE was the Rolls-Royce of the finance sector. In fact, GE partly owned Rolls-Royce. It attracted the world's best talent and offered the best jobs and the best platforms for career growth. I knew from previous experience that they had a local division in Manchester, under the leadership of a fiercely brilliant lady by the name of Christine Goldman. My goal was set. There was only one job I wanted. Now I just had to figure out how to make it happen.

I visualized myself becoming Christine Goldman's prodigy. Of course, my immediate reality was quite different, but it felt so much better to have a goal. I imagined in detail how she was going to mentor me and develop me into the finest salesman in the company, and in return, I would work like a Trojan for her and secure millions in sales. I promised myself that my dream career was going to be a comeback story of legendary proportions.

The first step was to get myself on the payroll of a stepping-stone company. So, I posted my CV to every finance company in the north of England until my luck finally broke with a call from Haydoc Finance. My resumé had landed on the boss' desk, and the company had done a little digging. They learned about my work at Lombard and offered to take me on, no questions asked. To my relief, I felt like I was about to get my career back at last.

I seized every opportunity to throw myself like a madman into my work from day one. I was the first man in the office in the morning and the last man to leave. Driven by a burning desire to claw myself back from the shadows, I wasn't fazed one bit by the long hours, cold calls, client visits and ambitious sales targets. Any sort of challenge seemed like fuel to me, and though I was physically exhausted by the time I fell into bed each night, I didn't want to stop.

The first few months at Haydoc Finance whizzed by and after a few paychecks, life got back on track. I moved out of my parents' house and back into my own house on Overdean Road in Winsford. Tim moved in with me, and for the next year I worked my butt off. On the weekends, Tim and I would head out to the local pubs and clubs and try our luck with the ladies with varying degrees of success. Sometimes Tim got lucky; sometimes I did. But as much as I loved female distractions, I was always careful not to fall into the woman trap. I was enjoying life, but working hard and finding a way to get that job at GE someday was my number-one focus.

One evening long after my colleagues had gone home, I sat alone at the sales desk, sifting through a mountain of old business cards when luck struck. Tim had just sent me a message to join him at the pub when a business card caught my eye. It read: "CHRISTINE GOLDMAN, Sales Centre Manager, GE Capital Finance."

I held the card delicately in my fingers like a sheet of paper-thin glass and read the name again in disbelief. I knew that this was my big chance. As when you're in the final stages of a poker game and know you can win, I felt both excited and nervous simultaneously. It was pure fate that her card was in front of me; now all I had to do was play my hand and play it well. This telephone call, if I had the confidence to make it, might prove to be the best phone call of my career. If not, Haydoc Finance and sharing my house with Tim were going to be my reality for a long while yet.

I composed myself, picked up the telephone, took a deep breath, and dialed the number. As the phone rang on the other end, I stretched back in my chair, placed my hands behind my head, and put my feet up on the chair next to me, hoping my confident body language would be communicated in the call.

"Hello, is this Christine Goldman?" I asked, as she picked up.

"Yes." As soon as I heard her voice, I snapped upright in my chair.

"Paul Evans here, from Haydoc Finance."

"Who?" she replied impatiently.

"Paul Evans, Mrs. Goldman. You don't know me yet, but I'm sure you'll remember our meeting well if you are available to meet me for a quick coffee next week. I'm in your neighborhood and would like to discuss a business opportunity with you that shouldn't take more than five minutes of your time."

"Please hold," she interrupted, as the line immediately switched to an automated answer-phone jingle.

My eyes rolled toward the ceiling as I bit my nails and waited for her to return to my call.

"Coffee? I don't do coffee," she snapped as she came back on the line. "I assume this is a sales call, or you're looking for a job."

My heart sank. As soon as she put me on hold I knew I'd blown it, but I decided to continue regardless. "Well, interesting you say that, Christine, I…"

She interrupted again mid-sentence: "What was your last monthly target valued at, Paul?"

"One hundred thousand pounds," I replied.

I could hear her sigh with disappointment. "You sound very inexperienced, Paul, and in all honesty, until you're turning over at least one million pounds and have 10 years of experience under your belt, I'd say you've got some work to do. Thank you for your call. Goodbye." Then she hung up.

"Fuck!" I slammed the phone down.

Damn, she was good! Her ruthlessness only made me want to work for her even more. If she knew that I'd served time and had rejected me for that reason, I may have accepted it. But the fact that she'd rejected me because she thought I sounded inexperienced infuriated me. I was going to have to get her attention another way. I sat for a moment and contemplated the conversation. I needed to make myself stand out.

After flicking the remainder of the pile of business cards across the table while trying to figure it out, the answer finally came to me. When the eureka moment came, I felt like a fucking genius!

It was clear that the only way to impress Christine Goldman was to achieve big sales. I knew there was only one shark in the finance market capable of catching the kind of big fish that she was talking about, and that was GE itself. To get her attention, I'd poach the accounts from her own territory. If I couldn't go to Christine, she would have to come to me! I knew that the next time I spoke with her, we would have a very different conversation. As I switched off the office lights that night, I felt confident that my dream career at GE was one step closer.

In the mood to celebrate, I headed down to the Dog & Duck to meet Tim for a pint. He had been working in Nottingham for the last few days, so I knew we'd have some good banter to catch up on. True to form, as soon as we got the beers in, he started talking about a waitress called Kay, who he'd met at a Hooters bar. According to him, she had the biggest boobs he'd ever seen. Reaching into his pocket, he pulled out a Hooters beer mat; her phone number was written on the back. His face was creased with delight as he recounted his flirtatious encounter with the busty bombshell.

"Mate," I said excitedly, ordering the next round, "send her a message! She's bound to have a hot friend. Let's invite them up to Winsford for the weekend!"

Wasting no time, Tim pulled out his mobile and typed out an invitation promising there would be too much fun for her and a friend to miss. "Sent!" he grinned. Two pints later, a message pinged back: "Sounds good. I'll bring Lexi. X."

"Way-hey!" Tim said as he emptied the last of his pint. "This weekend's entertainment is sorted!" He shook his empty glass toward me to suggest another beer.

And that was how I met Lexi.

She was dwarfed behind Kay's boobs when I opened the door of the bachelor pad to welcome them. She was petite and slim, with bobbed shiny blonde hair and a beautiful, wide smile. Aware that Kay's chest had caught my immediate attention, she giggled and tilted her head sideways to divert my eyes.

"Over here," she waved. "Hi, I'm Lexi."

"Sorry," I said, taking my eyes away from the obvious. "Come in. Do you girls want a drink?"

I couldn't help but think that Lexi looked nothing like a waitress from Hooters. She didn't have the hallmark chest or the shiny, tanned legs on show for all to see. She was unbelievably sexy though, standing there in a T-shirt that hung off one shoulder and a pair of skinny jeans and wearing a pair of boots that defined her slim legs.

"Yeah, why not. I'll have a beer if you're having one," she replied, giving me a cute look that let me know I was in with a chance.

That night Tim and Kay didn't waste any time. They completely skipped the getting to know each other phase and left Lexi and me together to go to the pub on our own.

We giggled and flirted with each other for the whole night, until we eventually staggered home hand in hand in the early hours of the morning. We had hit it off from the get-go, and by the time the weekend was over I knew I had fallen for her big time. By Sunday afternoon Tim and Kay were completely shagged out. They kissed their goodbyes and gave each other empty promises to stay in touch. But I knew Lexi and I had a lot more going for each other than that. She was going to be my girl.

We saw each other at every opportunity. I would make detours on sales calls near Nottingham just to steal a few minutes with her. I'd drive to see her after work when I could, and every weekend we made plans to be together. When we didn't see each other on weekdays, we spoke on the phone until we fell asleep. Three months later she gave up her job, packed her bags, and moved to be with me in Winsford. She got a job as a receptionist at a local car dealership, and soon after that I bought us a house on Gladstone Street.

With Lexi in my life and a goal to work for GE, I felt more driven than I ever had. I was hungry and motivated and had fire in my belly. I spent the next few months targeting every single account that GE had in the local area and made it my business to win over each one. If there was an account that had Christine Goldman's name on it, I went after it. I was on a mission for her to know my name. By the time I took her 18th account, I knew she'd call.

At the same time as all of that was going on in my life, my parents were making some life-changing decisions of their own. Out of the blue one evening when Lexi and I went to their house for dinner, Dad announced that he and Mum were going to sell their house and move to Egypt, to a sea-side town called Hurghada.

At first, I thought he had completely lost the plot and that it was some kind of joke; no one had ever heard of Hurghada, and it all seemed rather sudden. But as the shock wore off and the idea sank in, I saw how excited they were and could see it as a great opportunity for them. After all, until that point, I'd given them both a lifetime of stress, and in all fairness, they had earned the right to do something for themselves and live life on a beach for a while.

It turned out that their plans were well underway. The boat was already being built and scheduled for completion within 12 months, and they had already started house hunting. Before long, it would be time for them to pack up, ship out and set up a new life in preparation for when the boat would be ready. Talk about a surprise.

Ten weeks later, my parents headed to Hurghada on a flight from Manchester airport. We promised not to do the emotional goodbyes at the airport, but of course, the whole family turned up to see them off. We all ended up in floods of tears as we hugged each other and held hands until the very last minute before they had to go through the security gate. Mum cradled my face in her hands as she kissed me on both cheeks. "This is your time, son," she told me. "Look after Lexi. She's a good girl. Be happy."

Dad put his arm round my shoulder and said, "Be good. See you on the other side."

We waved at the plane until it was out of sight. It was a strange feeling to see them go. They had always been around me, and as a family we had always been so close; to see them jet off into the distance was a bit surreal. It's natural for children to flee the nest when they've grown up, but not the other way around. But by then I had gotten used to living an unconventional life. I hoped that Mum and Dad moving to Egypt was going to be another new and exciting chapter for us all.

The sun was just coming up as Lexi and I neared home on the drive back from the airport. The rush-hour traffic was beginning to thicken. I received a call on my mobile from an unknown number.

"Hello, Paul Evans speaking," I answered.

"Yes, hello, Mr. Evans. My name is Christine Goldman of GE Capital Finance. I thought I'd catch you early before the day starts. I am going to be in the area on Tuesday, and I wondered if we could meet. I may have an offer of interest to you."

"Sorry, I didn't catch that. Christine who?" I said with a smirk. Of course, I knew exactly who she was.

"Christine Goldman. GE Capital Finance," she replied.

"Oh yes, Christine. How nice of you to return my call."

"I'm sorry?" she replied, quizzically. "I think you have me mixed up with someone else."

"No, Christine. Actually, I called you some time ago," I giggled. "I said we'd talk again. Maybe you don't remember."

"No, Paul, I'm sorry, I don't."

"That's OK, Christine. I'd be delighted to meet you on Tuesday. Shall we do lunch?"

WAKE-UP CALL 3
IT'S A DOG-EAT-DOG WORLD

The quality of your life is reflected by the quality of your choices. That lesson really hits home when you're sitting alone in a jail cell.

Of course, I sometimes wish I'd never got into my car that fateful day. If I had gone to the pub with the lads instead, then maybe I'd never have ended up in Kirkham. On the other hand, if I had gone with the lads, then perhaps I wouldn't have the life that I have now. It might sound odd, but I'm glad about my jail-time experience. Of course, I'm not proud of what I did, but I think a two-week stint in jail could do a lot of people the world of good. To be stripped of your freedom and left with absolutely nothing makes you grateful for everything. And that's a perspective very few people are willing to experience.

It was the shock I needed at the time to make me look at myself and consider the kind of life I wanted.

Wake-Up Call 4

LIFE'S A BEACH

CHAPTER 11

ESCAPING THE RAT RACE

O ver lunch that day, Christine offered me the dream job that I had visualized when I was jobless after being released from prison. She was furious that she had lost one major account every month for the last 18 months, and when she discovered that every one of those accounts had been won over by me, she knew she had to have me on her team.

Christine was intelligent, articulate and laser sharp, and she ran an extremely tight ship. Her team and I were so dedicated that we were willing to work all day and all night for her if we needed to. And over the next four years, that's exactly what I did, always under the watchful eye of the inspiring yet fearsome leading lady herself. There was no such thing as job security on Christine's sales floor. Every month she unceremoniously axed the bottom 10 percent of the sales team and replaced them with new hungry talent. It was a ruthless tactic that she employed to make sure the gloves were always off. It was known as the "rank and yank" method, introduced by Jack Welch, the CEO of the company. He was known as "Neutron Jack" for his ability to eliminate employees while leaving buildings intact.

She was neat and uncompromising. Her tone of voice always as precise and sharp as her tailored suits and her short hairdo. She meant business, and though she stood only five foot four inches in heels, she towered over everyone in the industry. With ease she out-maneuvered and outpaced every man in the business, and I made it my mission to study and learn her every move and tactic. Watching her at work was like witnessing the conductor of a world-class orchestra. To this day, if I'm ever in need of a second perspective, I find myself thinking, What would Christine do?

Christine had given me a foot in the door with GE when I was just 22, the youngest kid in the office by a long way. By 26, though, I was looking after the largest accounts for the group, earning bonuses big enough to buy myself three houses and build a sizeable bank account. I reveled in the status that GE gave me. Being the sales team's golden boy, I was able to rid myself once and for all of the "stupid dyslexic drop-out" label that my schoolteachers had hung around my neck. I couldn't get enough of the pace, the attention, the money and the buzz that the job gave me. Perhaps I got carried away with it all, because the more my spiral of success continued upward, the more I forgot about what was important in life. The more targets I smashed, and the more bonuses I achieved, the more attention and adulation I got. My head grew bigger and bigger. The company seemed to encourage all of this by bombarding us with propaganda-type encouragement. At GE, simply *wanting* to be the best was seen as amateurish; you either *were* the best or you were nothing.

It took me the same amount of time to get my career on track as it took Dad to build his first boat, which he proudly named *My Rosetta*. By his own admission, it should have taken him only 12 months to complete, but as he noted in his usual jovial tone when he called me from Hurghada to say *she* was finally ready, "Four years to build a boat in Egypt is pretty impressive, considering the pyramids were the last thing to be built properly there. And they were probably put in the wrong fucking place!"

My parents' dive boat business was finally ready to open, and so to help them out, I spent my spare evenings and weekends trawling though the telephone directory for diving and water sports centers across the UK. I made a call to each one to explain the story of the Englishman who moved to Egypt to build a boat and a diving business and that *My Rosetta* was, at last, ready and available to take bookings. After building a database of thousands of names of potential customers who showed an interest in going on a diving holiday to the Red Sea, I was finally ready to make a much-anticipated trip to Egypt. I booked two weeks off to join my parents on the boat and sail down the Suez Canal, past Sharm El Sheik to Hurghada, where the first group of paying guests would be waiting to board. Lexi opted to stay home, as the timing clashed with the plans for her sister's wedding. Time on my own was probably just what I needed.

I hadn't realized how much stress I had been under, but as soon as the plane took off from Manchester, the sheer relief of leaving my workload behind washed over me. Egypt was like another world. Mum and Dad looked years younger, so much more youthful and energetic. After a day of basking in the glorious Egyptian sunshine, we sailed along the beautiful coastline. I missed Lexi not being there to enjoy it. We hadn't really spent any quality time together in ages, and I could sense that a gulf was forming between us, probably due to the pressure at work and Christine's perpetual threat of cutting anyone from the team who fell below her performance expectations. I knew that this extra time together would have helped us reconnect. But when we moored in Hurghada and helped Dad's first guests aboard with a welcoming glass of champagne, I spotted Samantha and instantly knew that I was in trouble.

She was wearing ripped denim shorts cut so high that they barely covered her arse and a slinky bikini top visible under a see-through cotton T-shirt. I could see every contour of her beautiful body, and no matter how hard I tried, I couldn't take my eyes off her. I later learned that she was a model from London. I was pleased to notice that the attraction was mutual, as she coyly smiled at me and raised her champagne glass with a cheeky wink. I looked to the clouds and thanked my lucky stars.

That night, Dad gathered the whole group for dinner and drinks on the deck of the boat to mark the official first night of the first group to sail on *My Rosetta*. The wine flowed well into the night as we regaled each other with stories, mostly told by Dad, under twinkling stars. One by one, as the night wore on, everyone bid goodnight and retired to the cabin, leaving just me and Samantha. The hours of subtle flirting that had gone on all day and throughout the evening meal continued all night. Within minutes of the last cabin light going out, I desperately wanted to kiss her, but somehow I managed to resist.

The rest of the week flew by in a flash, with Samantha and I flirting with each other at every opportunity. From the boat we swam to secret islands and snorkeled among colorful schools of tropical fish. Being with Samantha was exciting, although I knew it was dangerous. Something lurking at the back of my mind wanted to throw everything away and live in this blissful bubble with her. But my sensible mind overruled me. I remained quiet and kept my feelings for Samantha under lock and key. Yet inside, I knew that I wanted more.

After a fortnight, I returned to England, the grim weather and the daily grind of work. It felt like such a comedown after the sun and fun of Egypt. The thrill of my job and the allure of the big bonuses had completely worn off, and I was left feeling empty and uninspired for the first time. Egypt was calling me to go back to the sun and away from the rat race. Also, I couldn't get Samantha out of my mind, and so after a few weeks of resisting the urge, I called her to see if she was still thinking of me.

She was. And that's when my heart overruled my head. An affair began, and over time I made less and less of an effort to keep it secret. I became more and more detached from Lexi. I would drive to London at every opportunity to be with Samantha, leaving Lexi at home alone with some lame excuse that I was working away over the weekend—which she had to know was a lie. If she did, I didn't really care. I was completely absorbed in my own self-indulgence, and it bothered me not a jot if she suspected me. Samantha and I would stay up all night together at wild house parties, hit London's top clubs, and drink bucket loads of champagne with her equally wild friends. Until one night, Lexi had enough. While I was partying in a club, she called my mobile over and over again. Naturally I didn't pick up, but before giving up, she sent me a text message that read, "I know what you're doing. Be man enough to call me."

The next morning, as I pulled my clothes on in Samantha's bedroom, I returned her message with one final lie: "Work is crazy. I'll be home soon." But I knew my time was up.

Unknown to me, the previous evening, while I was partying, Marcus's wife, Becky, was at the house to keep Lexi company. Over a bottle or two of wine, Becky gave Lexi the "It's time to wake up" chat. Becky had known all about the affair for a while and was sick and tired of covering up for me and constantly having to witness Lexi's innocent responses to my lies. So, with a few glasses of Chardonnay inside her for strength, Becky finally told Lexi everything that she knew about Samantha and me.

I drove home, saw the look on Lexi's face and confessed all. I pleaded for one last chance, but she was in no mood to forgive me. She wanted to kill me! What seemed like years of pent-up emotion came pouring out of her. In a blind rage and with tears streaming down her face, she stood on the bed, screaming, "Asshole!" at the top of her voice as she hurled the pillows at me. "Bastard!" as she heaved my clothes out of the wardrobe and threw them over the bannister. "Fucker!" as she kicked my shoes one by one down the stairs. Finally, she flung herself, exhausted, onto the bed.

To my surprise, one of the things she had cried about as she was throwing my expensive suits across the floor was that she hated what we had become. The houses, the cars and all the materialistic bullshit that our lives had become filled with—to her, all of it was meaningless. I had thought it was what she had always wanted, and I was surprised to hear her say that she didn't want any of it.

I lay down beside her and held her gently without saying a word. As I looked at her, tears filled my eyes and I felt the lump in my throat. My feeling of guilt was almost unbearable. I hated myself for what I'd done to her, and as we lay together it dawned on me that I didn't recognize who I'd become. I had got carried away with the high life and was about to lose the best and most wholesome thing in my life.

"Why don't we just get away from all this? Do something different? Make a fresh start?" I suggested, as we lay together, staring at the ceiling. "If this isn't the life we want, then let's break the cycle. Fuck it, Lexi, let's go to Egypt and live and work on the boat!"

We looked at each other's puffy red eyes. "If you can forgive me," I said, "then, seriously, let's do it!"

We spent the rest of the night lying together on our bed, talking openly about how we felt about each other and our lives. There is something to be said for having a row to clear the air, although I knew as usual it was I who had taken things to the extreme. I knew that my affair with Samantha hurt Lexi beyond words, and I was determined to make it up to her any way I could if she would permit me. Deep down I knew it was me who had to change. I had pushed myself to the limits yet again to prove that I wasn't the good-for-nothing dyslexic schoolkid, or one of the men who I'd shared a room with in Kirkham, and in doing so, I'd gone way over the top. I knew I had become so engrossed in the pursuit of success at GE and become so obsessed with power and money that I had exceeded the boundary of who I really was. I had become so arrogant and self-righteous that even I didn't recognize myself anymore, and I wasn't proud of that.

Despite how much I loved my job, and knowing how much it was going to pain me to walk away from Christine's team, I realized that for my own sanity I had to make a clean break. Lexi and I still had a chance, and that was worth holding on to. I made a pact with her that I would hand in my resignation the next morning, and that we could then begin in earnest to rebuild our lives together in the sun.

It was nerve-wracking to stand in front of Christine and break the news to her that after four years I was going to chuck in the towel and go and live on a boat in Egypt. I can't say she made it easy for me as she paced around her office in her usual style, giving the impression that she was only half-listening to me, continually interrupting me to take calls on her headset while I was speaking. But when I eventually got to the point, she froze.

"The fact of the matter is, Christine, and I'm not proud to admit it, I've been caught being a naughty boy, and I need time to sort my life out," I explained as she pulled her headset from her ear to show her willingness to give me all of her attention. "Christine, you have given me the support and resources to build my career in more ways than you can imagine, but I have to build a life to go with it."

Christine looked at me and said, "I can't say I want to lose you from my team, Paul. You have a good future here, together with us. Would you consider a sabbatical? I could transfer you to New York for a year. How does that sound?"

She was bartering, of course; that was her true nature.

I thought about her offer but concluded that if she was willing to propose such an offer, there was a good chance that she'd still want me back in a year or so.

"I really appreciate that, Christine," I said. "Really, I do. But I need a clean break."

We shook hands, and she smiled at me and said, "I took a chance on you, Paul, and I never regretted it. Make sure you never regret this decision."

While I worked my notice for Christine, Lexi and I counted down every day of the next three months, getting more and more excited about our plans to start our new life in the sun. We sold the house, and every night we joked about which household item Lexi would sell next to put toward our "Egypt kitty." Soon enough she would have sold the toaster, the oven, the beds and the cutlery so that our only option would be to leave, as we would have nothing to eat from or sleep in. The day finally came for us to celebrate with goodbye drinks in the pub with all our friends. The following morning, we packed up our last suitcase of belongings and made our way to the airport, Egypt-bound.

And just like that, in November of 2001, our lives completely changed. We were free from the stresses and strains of corporate life, and the UK's gray weather was left behind us. Twenty-four hours later, we were on our beloved boat, *My Rosetta*, with my parents. It was a fresh start for us both, working together in the sunshine, diving all day with the guests, and putting on hospitality in the evening under the stars. It was exactly what we needed. I was like a new man, and I fell in love with Lexi all over again.

CHAPTER 12

OOPS! I BOUGHT A NIGHTCLUB

Hurghada,
Egypt, 2001

A few months passed, and Lexi and I were in our element running *My Rosetta* with Mum and Dad. It was idyllic and worlds away from the life we had left behind. We would start the day at 5 a.m., have breakfast on deck at sunrise with our diving group, then plan our route according to the latest sightings of the best fish.

Every Friday we would collect a new group of as many as 20 holiday makers from the airport and welcome them aboard for a week of jaw-dropping scuba diving in crystal blue water, relaxation in the sun, and fun night-time entertainment. The final night of the itinerary would always include a big piss-up at the bar on the local beach called Papa's Bar. The bar was owned by two affable Dutchmen, Freek (which I thought was a rather strange name until I realized it was short for Frederik and pronounced *Frek*) and Ramon, and I had gotten to know them quite well by being a regular in their place since we'd arrived in town.

When one particular dive safari week drew to a close, I made the arrangements with Freek and Ramon to bring our party of divers over to Papa's Bar for their final night. This group was an exceptionally rowdy bunch who were keen to enjoy every last minute of their holiday and were determined to drink as much beer as they could. So, to keep them entertained, Freek and

Ramon made arrangements for them to have their own beer keg and private area in the corner of the bar. As the night progressed, we all drank so much that a single keg was not enough! We may have polished off as many as three or four kegs! My last memories of the evening were of Freek and me doing whisky chasers at the bar and then staggering home with Lexi under my arm as the sun came up. It must have been nearly 6 a.m.

Of course, I woke up with the most horrific hangover and tried to remember the events of the night before, but it was all rather blurry.

I shuffled into the kitchen, looking like death warmed up, and sat at the kitchen table to check the messages on my mobile phone, while Dad stood at the cooker in his underpants, making breakfast.

"How's the hangover, son?" he joked.

"Brilliant, Dad. How's yours?" I winced in reply.

"I'm sure Freek puts something in that beer, you know. Your mother and I are sure we didn't drink that much," he said, stirring the eggs in the pan.

"Didn't drink that much? Dad, we drank at least three whole kegs!" I laughed.

"Ah, that'll be why I feel like shit then," he shrugged with a comical look on his face. "Do you want some breakfast?"

All the while Dad was talking to me, I was distracted by a text message that I noticed Freek had sent me earlier. It read, "When can I pick that money up? F." I was totally confused. Money? What money? What was he talking about?

As Dad twittered on in the background, asking me about bacon and eggs, he elaborated on his theory that Freek and Ramon had found the secret formula to success in Papa's Bar. Their customers got so pissed and had such a good time that they completely lost track of time. Dad suspected this was a ploy to make people spend far more than they normally would.

Just then, a vague memory came back to me, fleetingly. I recalled that at some point between 4 a.m. and 5 a.m., the whisky chasers we were downing were in celebration of our becoming business partners. I had agreed to invest 10,000 pounds.

I sat at the table scratching my head. I attempted to piece together the drunken conversation we'd had at the bar.

"I think I've invested in a bar, Dad," I said, still staring at Freek's text message.

"You what? A bar?" Dad replied, with the same confused expression on his face that I had.

"Yeah, I think I agreed to lend Freek and Ramon ten grand last night to finish the beach club they're working on," I mumbled.

Dad looked at me skeptically as he placed a plate of bacon and eggs in front of me. "What do you know about building bars?"

"Fuck all," I chuckled. "In fact, I know as much about building bars as you know about building boats."

Dad laughed as he filled our coffee cups. "Yeah, you're probably right there. Fair point."

We ate our breakfast and slurped down gallons of strong coffee and agreed that despite it being a drunken decision, it might be an exciting opportunity.

"Freek and Ramon are decent guys," Dad concluded. "Nothing ventured nothing gained. Just make sure you get it all down on paper."

I finished eating the rest of my hangover cure and downed another cup of coffee before replying to Freek's message: "I'll pop into Papa's later and we can discuss the details. P."

At this point, Lexi staggered into the kitchen. "I smell coffee," she groaned, rubbing her eyes sleepily.

"Paul's bought a bar," Dad announced.

"What do you know about running a bar?" Lexi laughed with a shrug, unsure if she should believe him.

"Yeah, Dad and I've already been there. Let's not get into that again." I kissed her forehead. "Coffee's in the pot, babe. I'm off to see Freek."

Dad and I drove to the foreign-exchange counter at the Sheraton Hotel to withdraw 10,000 pounds, which in Egyptian pounds was a real pile of cash. Manhandling a mountain of Egyptian bank notes, the teller eventually gave up trying to fit it all into the bags that I had given her and put the remainder into a black garbage bag. With a rucksack on my back, a large hold-all in one hand, and the black garbage-bin liner slung over my shoulder—all stuffed full of cash—I left the bank looking like I was committing a robbery.

I arrived at Papa's Bar soon afterward, and as I was still rather hungover and unsure whether I was going to do the deal or not, I asked Dad to stay in the car with most of the cash and took only the smaller rucksack of money with me. I walked through the main entrance and into the bar. "Has anyone seen Freek?" I asked the barman.

"Yeah, man, he's out there on the beach," he replied.

I walked outside, and as soon as I turned onto the beach, I spotted Freek.

He was quite possibly the coolest guy I'd ever met. His chiseled, tanned, surfer-dude good looks, along with his laid-back accent, made him effortlessly, well, Dutch. I stood watching him for a while as he made himself busy on the beach. Totally absorbed in his own world, he was unaware of me watching. He was outlining a shape roughly the size of a football pitch in the sand with a large bag of white flour when I tapped him on the shoulder. It startled him.

"Hey, mate!" I smiled. "What're you up to?"

"Ah, Pauly," he beamed, pushing his sunglasses up onto his mop of messy blonde hair. "How are you, man? I'm just measuring out the beach club we're gonna build together."

"What, with a bag of flour?" I quizzed.

"Yeah, well, it's a rough drawing maybe, but I can see it." He said with a twinkle in his eyes. "The bar will be here," he said, pointing to a square of flour in the sand, "and the terrace over on that side."

I absolutely loved his passion for something that he could visualize. "We'll have a stage over here, and the DJ booth over there," Freek said as he continued marking out the floor plan with such excitement that I didn't want him to stop. It was like watching an artist at work, and you wouldn't dare interrupt an artist.

"OK, man," I said after he'd finished giving me the grand tour of his imaginary club. "Let's go inside and talk money."

Ramon, Freek's business partner and the crazier of the two, was in the Netherlands at the time. His wife was about to give birth any day, so Freek and I sat down in his cluttered office at the back of the bar and made a call to him on speakerphone.

"Hey, Pauly," boomed Ramon as he answered the call. "Two pieces of good news, eh? I'm becoming a dad, and you're becoming a business partner, right? How cool is that?"

"Yeah, slow down, mate. Do I get to see any accounts and numbers first?" I asked.

I could hear Ramon pause to draw on his cigarette before he replied, "Aw nah, mate, it'll be alright. It'll be fine! We don't have shit like that!'

I didn't know much about numbers anyway. Frankly, if Freek had produced a profit-and-loss account there and then, I'm not sure I'd have known what to look for. I didn't know anything about balance sheets, EBITDA, amortization, etc. In fact, to tell the truth, I didn't know much about running a business at all. All I knew was how to lend money and how to make money. That was pretty much it.

Before I made my decision to hand over the cash, though, I did some math quickly in my head. I worked out that if Lexi and I were to remain in Hurghada for the rest of the year, we had 35 weeks left in Egypt. My weekly tab in Papa's Bar multiplied by the remaining weeks of the year meant I would be spending more than 10,000 pounds, even with the freebie drinks Freek and Roman bought. I figured that this could be the best investment I'd ever made. So, I asked the two Dutchmen, "OK, as an owner, do I get to drink for free?"

Freek looked at me casually and nodded while Ramon shouted over the speakerphone, "Yes, sure! That's the biggest perk!"

I smiled and opened the rucksack stuffed with bank notes and slid it across the table. "Then you have yourselves a deal, gentlemen," I said. " Dad's outside in the car with rest of the cash. I'll go and get him. You better get the beers in because you'll be counting cash for some time."

It was the start of our business partnership, and yes, he's still the coolest guy I've ever met.

CHAPTER 13

BULLDOZER

Aside from being excited by the deal I'd just done that would secure me a bottomless supply of free booze for the rest of the year, I was thrilled to be part of Freek and Ramon's business. Of course, I was a salesman by trade, and at the time I didn't know a thing about bars or nightclubs. Until then, my closest experience to working in the hospitality industry had been my time aboard *My Rosetta*. To this day, I don't think I could pull a pint or fry an egg, but Freek was a creative genius when it came to design and architecture, and Ramon knew all there was to know about music and the club scene. It seemed that by putting our heads together we could create the best bar business in town.

Since coming to Hurghada, I had noticed that most hotels sold their holiday packages as "all-inclusive," which meant their guests would obliterate their buffets and bars like swarms of locusts all day and all night. This type of offer maybe meant large occupancy levels for the hotel, but the downside was that it ate up large chunks of the profits, especially if the guests never left the hotel. Low on available budget, most hotels were reduced to offering evening entertainment that was nothing more than a cheesy disco. I assumed that a large percentage of hotel guests would appreciate something a little more exciting. We were more than happy to offer all hotel guests free entry and non-stop live music on the beach at Papa's Bar. It was simple really: The hotels gained greater margins on their all-inclusive packages, the guests got to let their hair down until the sun came up, and we made money. I made arrangements with as many hotels as I could to ensure that hundreds of their guests would stop by Papa's Bar every night. As the word got out that Papa's Bar was the place to be, as many as 50 or 60 busloads of tourists were turning up every day.

Soon our name was on everyone's lips, and Papa's Bar became synonymous with the nightlife scene in Hurghada. I became good friends with Colonel Hindawi, the manager of Hurghada airport and a very useful person to know. Together we formed a marketing company with his business partner, Jürgen, that enabled Papa's Bar to be advertised on huge billboards all over the airport. Every tourist who arrived in Hurghada received an invitation to join us on the beach for our free live music sessions. As a result, Papa's Bar rose to iconic status. We had found the sweet spot just as the tourist scene in Hurghada was taking off, and in less than two years Freek, Ramon and I were living the high life and making so much money that we didn't have enough space in the safe to store it all.

Not everyone was welcome to join in on the party, though. Another Dutch guy, called Ruben, never saw eye to eye with me. He rented a bar farther along the beach called the Shack. The venue, like its tenant, had seen better days. It was weathered and run down. Ruben sat at the bar all day, smoking weed and drinking beer, so it was no surprise that the Shack attracted a dodgier clientele.

One night, I was sitting on the couch in Papa's Beach Club, having a few beers with the lads. Around 2 a.m., Ruben walked in as pissed and high as a man can could be. As usual, he was behaving badly, bouncing off the walls and deliberately bumping into the ladies on the dance floor. Initially, I decided not to get involved. I hoped that the bar staff would refuse to serve him and that he would leave on his own accord. Failing that, it was only a matter of time before the bouncers would throw him out. Instead of making it my issue, I decided to turn a blind eye and continue to enjoy drinks with my friends.

About an hour later, however, Ruben was still staggering around and causing trouble. My eyes followed him as he pushed clumsily though the crowded dance floor toward Lexi, who was ordering a drink at the bar. By that point I was quite drunk myself, so I thought it was better to sit back and see what he did next rather than cause a scene myself. I contemplated leaping over the couch and tackling him to the ground, but I decided against doing that in front of a venue full of my own guests.

In his drunken stupor, Ruben tripped and staggered as he tried to get closer to Lexi. When he did get close enough, I saw him slur something in her ear and grope her bottom. Alarmed, Lexi turned with a look of horror and threw her drink in his face, pushed him away, and ran to the other side of the dance floor to be with her friends.

I was outraged. I rose quickly to my feet and ran over to her to find out what had happened. At first, she refused to tell me, probably because she knew I was drunk and didn't want me to start a fight.

"Baby, what did he say to you?" I asked.

She shook her head and replied, "Nothing, Paul. I'm OK." But her body language said otherwise. It was obvious that whatever he had said really upset her.

I wouldn't let up. I had to know what he had said to my girlfriend. So I asked again, "Lexi, what did that prick say to you?"

"Nothing. He's just a creep. I'm alright," Lexi sobbed.

I could feel myself getting wound up.

I'm going to kill him! I thought. I put my arms around Lexi and asked the waitress to bring her a drink from the bar.

As she took a sip of her vodka and coke, Lexi blurted out, "OK, if you must know, he asked me, 'When do I get to fuck you?'"

Without hesitating, I steamed across the dance floor to where Ruben was leaning against a cocktail table. I pushed him off balance. "Where the fuck do you get off talking to my girlfriend like that?" I spat at him.

Ramon did his best to hold me back.

Ruben looked at me nonchalantly and joked, "Hey man, don't be so fucking uptight. What's the problem? We can all share. We can just be Dutch."

Had Ramon not held me back, I probably would have done Ruben some real damage. Luckily for him, Ramon was as solid as an ox, and no matter how hard I tried, I could not shake him loose.

The bouncers escorted Ruben off the premises. Ramon released his grip on me after I calmed down and regained my composure. As Ruben was being dragged away, I made a point of calling to him, "You've made a big mistake. Trust me, this will come back at you!"

But Ruben just flapped the air with the back of his hand to signal that my threat made no impact on him whatsoever. That was a mistake he would later regret.

I never did forgive him, and my chance to settle the score finally came about a year later. While in my office in Papa's Bar, I received a phone call from a local businessman called Farris, who owned the Tabia Hotel. The Tabia owned the Shack. The call was music to my ears.

Farris was a chatty man and always took ages to get to the point. Finally, he came to the subject of his call and asked if I'd be interested in renting the Shack. I sat upright in my chair and replied without hesitation, "Fuck yes. I'm interested in renting that shithole. What's the deal?"

He explained that Ruben's contract was due to expire at the end of the year, and he felt it was an appropriate time to invite new offers on the tenancy, as the site was probably in need of some new investment.

The rent was 20,000 Egyptian pounds per month, Farris explained. Without batting an eyelid, I put the phone down, reached into the safe and grabbed 50,000. With the cash stuffed in my pocket, I raced down to the end of the street to the Tabia Hotel and knocked on the door to Farris's office.

"OK, What's the situation, Farris? What do you want to do?" I asked. "Shall we have coffee and discuss this properly?"

Farris could see that I meant business. "Well, look," he said, "Ruben and I have a good relationship, but I think I can get a little bit more for the place. So I'm thinking of opening up for bidding on the rent and see who offers the most money."

Keen not to let Farris skirt the issue, I got straight to the point. "Look, Farris, I'll make this dead simple. If I walk out of this office today without renting the Shack, the reality is I'll never rent it. I'm only going to discuss this one time. I have no intention of entering into any kind of bidding competition." Farris took a sip of coffee and tried to look composed. "I'll give you the rent you want," I continued, "but on one condition, that I'm the one who gets to tell Ruben that you aren't renewing his lease." I smiled wryly. "That's my offer, Farris. We either do a deal today, or we don't do a deal at all."

Farris sat back in his chair to consider my offer. I could tell he was feeling faintly guilty about stabbing Ruben in the back, but I knew his guilt would be short lived. I could see his brain ticking back and forth, as he muttered something about ethics under his breath.

Eventually I interrupted him and said, "This is well and good, Farris, but you rang me. I expect that you rang me because you know we'll build a great place. We'll pay the rent on time, and we'll pay you more than Ruben. So go ahead, take your time, but I won't wait all day!"

"OK, Paul. Let's discuss the numbers," Farris answered coyly. "Ruben currently pays 25,000."

"No, he doesn't, Farris!" I laughed. "I know he only pays twenty, not twenty-five. And I also hear that he's two months behind on rent."

Farris conceded. "So, what's your offer, Paul?" he asked, raising his thick eyebrows.

"I tell you what, Farris, just so you'll never regret this decision, I'll pay you double what Ruben pays you, and I'll give you 50,000 as a deposit right now to seal the deal—provided I get to tell him. That's my offer. It doesn't get any better, doesn't get any worse." I slapped the palms of my hands down on his desk, making his pens do a somersault.

Farris huffed and puffed and muttered more concerns about ethics to himself until he was satisfied that he had put up a good performance of appearing to be a concerned landlord. Then, comically, he stopped his act, leaned over and opened the top drawer of his desk to produce a pre-prepared tenancy contract for me to sign.

"OK, deal," he said. "I just had to make sure."

We shook hands enthusiastically, and I put the contract in my bag. I wandered back to Papa's Bar feeling extremely pleased with myself, knowing that come January 1, the Shack would be mine.

For the next few months, I didn't tell a soul about the new tenancy agreement. I couldn't wait for the sweet moment to arrive when I could knock on Ruben's door, say hello and remind him of the day he insulted my girlfriend in my club. Then I would wave my keys for the Shack right under his nose!

As Christmas passed, the anticipation grew. I quietly finalized my plan. The only person I confided in about the plan was Saeed, our maintenance guy (and I use that title loosely!). I initially hired Saeed to help build the extension to Papa's Bar, but let's just say building-and-maintenance work wasn't his forte. But because he was so lovable, I couldn't bring myself to fire him, and so he became my odd-job man, my translator and my driver. To be fair, he helped me in almost every aspect of my life in Egypt. He was a jolly little guy and always wore a smile. He was unwaveringly loyal and incredibly useful: He could source anything, would go anywhere, and knew everyone. What he lacked in intelligence he made up for in humor, and when he made mistakes, as he inevitably did, he usually made me want to laugh rather than kill him.

"OK, Saeed, listen. We're taking over the Shack," I told him carefully.

"OK, boss," he smiled vacantly. "What you need me to do?"

"First of all, don't tell anyone, Saeed. This is just between you and me, OK? It's a surprise," I explained. "I just want you to round up everybody and tell them to meet me on the beach on January 1 at 3 p.m. OK?"

"No problem, boss," he replied confidently.

"Oh, and Saeed, I almost forgot, I need you to be there with a bulldozer."

"Bulldozer? No problem, boss. I will bring one," he said, grinning.

As planned, around 3 p.m. that New Year's Day, my team congregated at the beach club. I announced that the space known the Shack was now ours and that we were going to go and take possession of the place. Then, to everyone's astonishment, Saeed drove around the corner honking the air horn of an enormous bulldozer and parked the vehicle in front of us.

"Wow, Saeed! You didn't muck about when I told you to bring a bulldozer, did you?" I laughed.

"I found a good one, boss," he said proudly.

"OK, Saeed, lead the way!" I cheered.

We all walked along the beach behind Saeed's bulldozer toward the Shack, where Ruben was sure to be sitting, smoking some grass, completely unaware of what was about to happen.

When we arrived at the front of our new bar, Saeed blasted the horn, and Ruben appeared from the shadows with a spliff in one hand and a can of beer in the other. His hair was matted and wiry, and as I approached him, I could smell from 10 yards away that his skinny body hadn't seen soap in weeks. "What the fuck do you want?" he shouted, shielding his eyes from the sun as he squinted to look at me.

"Ruben, about a year and a half year ago you asked my girlfriend, 'When do I get to fuck you?' Do you remember that?"

"Jesus Christ, man! Paul, that was years ago!" he said. "What's wrong with you?"

He spotted Saeed in the bulldozer and realized that things were about to go horribly wrong for him.

"Listen," I said, "I have a long memory, and you never did apologize for what you said to her. I promised you that night that it would come back at you. So today, Ruben, I get to fuck you."

I pulled the lease agreement from my pocket and showed it to him.

"There's the contract," I said. "Now get the fuck out of my beach club!"

Ruben exploded into panic. "You fucking psycho!" he shouted. "You can't do this! This is my club. This has always been my club. Get these people off my property."

He tried to summon his bouncers, forgetting, through his haze of alcohol, that he hadn't had any bouncers, or even customers, for weeks.

"Saeed, drive the bulldozer through it!" I shouted, reinforcing my instructions with hand signals to make sure Saeed understood above the noise of the roaring diesel engine.

Grinning widely, Saeed shoved the bulldozer into gear and drove it straight through the middle of the Shack, while the team behind me roared and cheered.

"Cheers!" Lexi and I each cracked open a bottle of beer and stood on the beach while we watched Saeed flatten the Shack to dust and rubble.

We didn't see Ruben again after that day. I heard a rumor that he left Egypt after Farris had tried to collect what he owed on the Shack rent and that he ended up falling into bad company and setting up a meth lab somewhere in Europe. But that could be just a tall tale. The Shack, on the other hand, was reformed into a beautiful new club that would be popular for years to come and eventually be renamed the Ministry of Sound The Bar.

REFLECTIONS

WAKE-UP CALL 4
LIFE'S A BEACH

When I first moved to Egypt, you could say I was running away from something. A fast corporate lifestyle, money and materialism, a rocky relationship, and the boozy lifestyle all contributed to my decision to give it all up to go and live in the sun. I think many people could relate to that.

Yet, although I had relocated, my problems came with me, and I didn't listen to the wake-up call when my mental demons showed up again. I pushed the people closest to me away and got closer to work and the bottle. It's clear as day now that I had a vicious cycle to break out of. I found myself on a path to self-destruction. I was out of control, and instead of tackling the elephant in the room, I believed happiness could be found in vodka and the party after the after-party.

I only need to look at the photographs of myself at that time to see how much I needed a wake-up call. I had ballooned in weight and was barely recognizable. Taking my mental and physical health for granted was a reckless gamble. Never in my wildest dreams did I think that at age 28, I was about to be given the wake-up call that came next.

Wake-Up Call 5

LIFE SAVERS

CHAPTER 14

METAL

Hurghada, Egypt,
June 23, 2003

There was nothing out of the ordinary about this particular day. The folks out sunbathing were soaking up the last few rays, and the scuba-diving boats were bringing the last divers back to shore as the day was drawing to a close. I sat with my usual bottle of house red under the palm trees at Papa's Bar and watched the sea sparkle as the sun went down. I emptied my bottle, stubbed out my cigarette, jumped in my Jeep, and headed home to freshen up before the night ahead.

The only thing that was different about this day was the odd taste in mouth. No matter what I ate or drank, nothing took away the taste. I realized that the taste had been there for few days, but I had just shrugged it off.

It was like the taste of metal.

Until that day, I'd always thought I was in good health, despite the obvious weight I'd gained from my constant partying.

I'd had reason to visit the doctor only once, maybe twice. Even then, any visits to the doctor were never serious and were probably due to Mum's overreaction to my having a snotty nose. Previously if I ever I'd felt unwell, I never questioned it. I'd always just tell myself to give it time, and it'll go away.

So, true to form, I ignored the metal taste in my mouth and continued as normal. How could I know that this decision was about to backfire in dramatic style?

After a quick dinner, a shower and change of clothes, I headed back out to meet the lads. I kissed Lexi goodnight, leaving her curled up on the sofa with a glass of wine and a movie, which in Egypt meant a pirated DVD with Arabic subtitles. She knew that when I returned home in the early hours of the morning, I'd be shit-faced and have a noisy group of party people in tow, and that we'd continue partying in our pool and on the beach until the sun came up. Bizarrely though, she never complained. I don't know why she tolerated all the drunken craziness. Maybe she liked that side of my personality, or perhaps she was waiting to pick her moment to leave me. Or maybe she thought that someday I'd change? Either way, it was clear to everyone but me that I was completely out of control.

I was well aware by then that owning a chain of a bars and nightclubs was the perfect occupation to mask my growing alcohol problem. Endless drinking and partying went with the territory. After I'd maintained a rock 'n' roll lifestyle for 18 months, the tolls on my relationships, my business and my body were obvious. The life that I had dreamed of creating with Lexi in Egypt was slipping further and further away. I looked awful. I was overweight, sluggish and permanently either drunk or hellishly hungover. But rather than straighten myself out, I just wanted to keep partying with the lads and keep the bars pumping to avoid the comedown.

When I talk about the lads in Egypt, I'm referring to Ramon, Freek, Gaz, Nathan, Jason. These guys were the real-deal, proper, relentless party people. Mental! There are so many stories I could tell you about these guys, but I don't know who's listening, so I'll keep it clean. Ramon and Freek, as I've mentioned, were my business partners and were two tall, good-looking crazy Dutchmen. Ramon was slightly crazier than Freek, but both were equally amusing and typically Dutch. Nathan and Jason were newcomers to Hurghada; we met them through a shared love of diving. They had just set up their own diving safari business, and Gaz, well he was the craziest of the lot, a friend from UK who lived on my sofa every summer until he was partied-out and would have to return home to recover. Together we made one hell of a team when we hit the town.

That night, we all met as usual (minus Freek, who had gone with his wife to Aruba) at Papa's Bar 1 to get the drinks flowing, the tills ringing, and the punters on the dance floor before heading downtown to Papa's Bar 2 and later to Papa's Beach Club to do the same. The tourists in Hurghada wanted good music, good drinks and a good time. So that's exactly what we made sure they got. Our business formula was simple: Give them what they want! It went without saying that each night, as the music got louder, the better the vibe became. And as the party got started, the dance floors would be jumping, the booze would flow and the fun would explode, and our tills would ring with cash all night. There were many nights when the party never seemed to end.

But that night the vodka and Red Bulls weren't taking effect. I wasn't getting the buzz I was used to, and the metal taste in my mouth was making the whole night something of a chore. So, feeling a little fed up, I went home early, leaving the lads to carry on without me. Although that was a very unusual thing for me to do, they were all too far gone even to notice anything was wrong. But then, looking back, I didn't think anything of it either. But something was wrong. I just didn't know it yet.

The pain woke me the next morning at 8 o'clock. It started in my abdomen and radiated up my back. I put my hand to my forehead and felt it was blisteringly hot. The metallic taste was now so strong, and I felt like I was going to throw up. My pulse raced uncontrollably, and my head was pounding. Everything in the room was spinning, and I felt hot and dizzy. Shit, I thought. Something is wrong. Very, very wrong.

The pain on the left side of my stomach was excruciating. I crawled to the bathroom. Gripping the edges of the sink, I managed to straighten up and look in the mirror. My face was red but white around my lips, and my eyes were bloodshot. My skin was glistening with sweat, and glancing down nervously, I was horrified to see that my stomach looked like a giant hunk of blue-veined cheese. Bright blue lines were creeping up my side, and my abdomen was so bloated that I looked as if I was nine months pregnant. Fuck me! This is not right!

The pain intensified by the minute, while the blue lines grew darker and my stomach continued to swell and expand in front of my eyes. I knew that I needed help, but I couldn't see anyone around. I called from the bathroom for Lexi to wake up, but I couldn't hear her as the pain sharply stabbed my sides. I staggered out of the bedroom and onto the poolside decking to see if any of my friends were there. I looked around, cradling my stomach in fear that it might burst like a water bomb, my eyes searching for someone who would be able to help or know what to do.

Some bodies were lying around outside by the pool, on sunbeds and couches in various stages of undress—the detritus of the night before. Not likely anyone here is going to be of any use, I thought. I spotted Ramon propped up against the wall in the shallow end of the pool, a glass of wine still in his hand. Seeing me in the doorway, he waved his hands in the air, gesturing for me to join in.

"Hey, Pauly, you're up. Come on, let's have a drink," he joked.

"No, mate," I replied. "I think I need to go to hospital."

Sensing something was up, but still oblivious to the urgency of the situation, he eased himself slowly out of the pool, slid on his flip-flops and shuffled toward me in his usual laid-back fashion, the glass of wine still in his hand.

"Hey, Pauly, you look like shit, man," he slurred in his Dutch accent and looked at me though glazed eyes. "Hey, have a coffee. Have a cognac. You'll be fine."

He shrugged and slapped me on the back. That was Ramon's normal response to most things. He always had a lighthearted way of dealing with anything serious: Just chill, have a coffee, have a drink. "No need to panic," he would always say. In this instance, I doubted it was the right advice.

I couldn't bear the pain any longer. I scrunched my eyes tightly and fell to the floor, letting out the most agonized scream. Ramon reacted like he had been zapped with a cattle prod and instantly straightened out. The drunken haze from the night before vanished with the sight of me writhing in agony on the floor at his feet. The sense of urgency suddenly dawned on him, and panic took over.

Lexi heard me howling and ran outside to see what all the commotion was about. She screamed at the sight of me and ran back inside to grab the phone, quickly returning with the handset. Her fingers shook profusely as she dialed the emergency numbers.

"What's wrong with him, Ramon?" she demanded. "What the hell has happened to him?"

Ramon stooped to pick me up off the floor.

"We have to get him to hospital!" Lexi cried.

We all knew the ambulance was going to take ages. One of the few drawbacks with beautiful Hurghada was that the nearest hospital was 45 minutes away in El Gouna—a very long time when your stomach is a 20-pound hunk of blue cheese. There was no time to wait. Between us, we decided Ramon would have to drive.

I should point out that I've never known anyone able to hold their drink the way Ramon could. I'd seen him drink non-stop for three days and still never seem drunk. He wasn't normal. He never seemed to get to that crazy out-of-control drunk stage like the rest of us. So yeah, at that time in the morning, he was still pissed. He had been drinking all night and still hadn't been to bed, but that was nothing out of the ordinary for him. So, in his permanent cool-as-a-cucumber state, he finished his glass of wine, took a shower, got changed, and drove us to the hospital.

Ramon drove like a lunatic at the best of times, and that morning was no different. He drove like Ayrton Senna along the dusty, pot-holed roads to get me to the hospital in El Gouna as fast as he could.

During the drive, Lexi kept looking at her watch, watching the minutes tick by. She looked like she was about to burst into tears at any moment. Between panicking about Ramon's crazy driving and worrying about me, she grew more anxious with every minute that passed.

Although Ramon's foot was rammed to the floor, the 45-minute journey seemed to stretch to eternity. I was huddled in the back of the car in the stifling, 110-degree heat, my knees scrunched up to my chest, howling with pain.

I didn't know why I was in so much pain. Had my appendix burst? Had my liver packed in? I definitely thought that whatever it was, it was sure to be alcohol related. Why else would a man of my age be so unwell? All I knew was that I had never felt pain like it in my life. It was as if a red-hot poker was being driven through my side or somebody was performing surgery on me while I was still awake. Lexi tried her best to comfort me as we drove, but only one thought consumed my mind: This. Fucking. Hurts!

Because we weren't in an ambulance, Lexi knew we'd have to pull some strings to ensure our arrival at El Gouna hospital would be treated urgently.

As Ramon sped along the highway, Lexi called General Hindawi, the manager of the airport. He and his business partner, Jürgen, were good friends of ours and were collective business partners in our advertising company. Lexi was sure they would have phone numbers for everyone at the hospital, as they managed the advertising account for it. Hindawi promised to call the hospital's general manager immediately and tell him to be ready for us. It so happened that Jürgen was nearby, and he promised Lexi that he'd meet her at the hospital to offer her help.

We finally reached the hospital in El Gouna at 11 a.m. I heaved myself out of the car and limped, with Lexi and Ramon under each arm, into the hospital. Lexi filled in my paperwork hurriedly at the reception desk, while I was stripped down and dressed in a hospital gown by a nurse. I lay down on a trolley and was pushed into a side room, where the nurse pulled a curtain around my bed. Then, just as I thought I was about to see a doctor, the receptionist blurted out from her kiosk that all the doctors were busy and that the hospital staff were all going on their lunch break. Without further explanation, she slammed the reception windows closed, and the nurses, one by one, disappeared on their lunch break, leaving me writhing in agony on my trolley and the others with me in stunned silence.

But that was typical of life in Egypt. Let's just say that things aren't done quite the same as they are in Europe or America. Everything in Egypt is significantly slower and infinitely more laid back, and most things seem illogical or lost in translation. So, for everyone to go on lunch break at the same time in a hospital didn't come as a surprise to anyone but us.

I badly needed something to numb the pain, but an hour later, when the nurses returned from their break, they rejected my demands for painkillers. However, because I made so much noise, a nurse eventually poked her head around the curtain, and speaking haltingly in broken English, she tried to explain. "Doctor only, sir," she said. "You make scan and test first. Then painkiller. Doctor coming."

But still no doctors came. The pain continued to intensify as I lay there waiting.

Finally, at 1 p.m., the general manager of the hospital arrived and offered some words of comfort. But I couldn't listen to anything he said. Instead, I reached out in desperation and grabbed his arm. Lying on my back, my hand gripping his forearm, I begged him, "Please, just stick a needle in me! Put me to sleep! I can't bear this any longer!"

Just as the nurse had explained, he said that despite my pain, all medication was forbidden without a doctor's prescription.

"You're the boss! Get a fucking doctor here then!" I yelled.

I've never wanted anyone to show up in my life as much as I wanted that elusive doctor to appear right at that moment. Everyone around me felt helpless. The general manager was pacing back and forth, speaking frantically to people in Arabic on his phone and issuing orders to the staff, trying to try make things happen.

After two hours of unbearable agony, the doctor arrived. He reviewed the information that was hanging from a clipboard at the end of my bed and checked me over, prodding here and there, pressing my flesh. After a thorough examination, he wrote up his diagnosis on the clipboard, and in a very matter-of-fact way, he turned to me and finally told me what was wrong.

"You have pancreatitis," he said coldly.

"Pancre-what?" I said, frowning. I'd never heard of it.

"We can give you some pain relief now, and we'll see how you develop over the next twenty-four hours," the doctor replied.

"Twenty-four hours?" I gasped.

"Don't worry. At this stage, it's not acute. Not particularly serious," he said with a shrug.

"You're telling me this pain isn't serious?" I asked in horror. "Tell my fucking stomach that!"

The doctor finished his examination and pronounced nonchalantly, "Nil by mouth. No food. No water. Nothing."

The nurses agreed to his instructions and wheeled me out from behind the curtain. They pushed me down the corridor into an unwelcomingly sterile treatment room, which felt a little more permanent. It was certainly more private and was furnished with more medical equipment. It appeared that I was going to be staying for a while.

Everyone had followed the gurney and now stood beside my bed. Lexi held my hand and told me gently that she had called my parents and informed them that I was in hospital. Ramon stood silently to the side, probably trying to figure out where he could get a coffee and cognac. He was with Nathan and Gaz, who had also come to the hospital as soon as they had heard the news. They all stood around me, watching me and feeling just as useless as I was.

I remember looking out the window a few hours later and seeing it was starting to get dark. Sun-downer time, I thought. My friends had remained by my bedside and looked wearier, minute by minute, as their hangovers kicked in. My pain had subsided a little, no thanks to the doctor whose cold words "not particularly serious" were still ringing in my head. What the hell did this guy consider to be serious if this wasn't?

I had been under observation for a few hours when I suddenly felt my chest start to tighten, and within seconds I couldn't breathe. No matter how much I gasped, I just couldn't get any air into my lungs.

I began to feel faint. The last air drained from my chest, and my face turned a deep bluish-red as I battled for air.

Was it serious enough now, Doctor Motherfucker?

My eyes searched frantically around the room for a nurse, but there was none. There were only my mates, my hungover and, by now, totally freaked-out mates. Desperate to help, Gaz inspected all the available medical equipment as I gasped for breath. Grabbing the oxygen canister and mask in the corner of the room, he wheeled it over to my bedside, turned on the tap, and placed the mask over my face.

As his shaking hands pressed against my face, we both knew that the whole thing was absurd. It was like some kind of dark comedy. It turned out the oxygen mask was for a little kid. It had teddy bears on it, and it hardly fit over my nose. It was so ridiculous that I would have laughed if the situation wasn't so serious. But like I said, this was Egypt, and so it was completely normal. It didn't feel weird that my mate was giving me life-saving oxygen out of a gas mask with teddy bears on it. It was just one of those things.

Hearing the commotion coming from my room, a nurse arrived and popped a little pain-relief capsule into the oxygen mask.

So, I drifted off with the teddy bears.

When I woke up, despite my efforts to quench my thirst by drinking from the taps and then the toilet, the burning cold ice cubes were my only source of water. Now, as I lay in bed, with my lips cracked and bleeding and the insides of my cheeks and my tongue blistered with cold burns, the thirst continued. I was still obsessed with water, but this was about to become the least of my worries.

As time passed, I could feel my lungs tightening again. By the afternoon, I was struggling to breathe, so Gaz, sensing my discomfort, put the teddy bear mask back on my face. But as my lungs grew heavier, no matter how much air I tried to gulp, nothing was going in. I knew I was deteriorating quickly. I could see the panic in his eyes as Gaz ramped up the oxygen valve, but still nothing happened. I felt like I was suffocating. What the fuck was going on? I was terrified as I drifted in and out of consciousness.

Flashes of light, blurred images, then darkness. I would pass out, wake up, pass out, and wake up God knows how many times. My mind was completely tripping. The last thing I heard was Lexi shouting for the nurse. Then I disappeared into complete darkness.

I don't remember being moved.

When I came around again, I could see through the haze that the room was different. Lexi was beside me and told me I was in the intensive care unit. I was connected to three machines, and I could hear my heart beat coming from bleeping monitors behind me. My face was completely covered with a ventilator mask. There were no teddy bears on this one; it was the big kahuna of masks. I had a drip in each hand, one for pain relief and the other for fluids.

"Babe, the general manager of the hospital is going to call your mum and dad. I think you're going to have an operation," Lexi explained.

"Are they coming?" I asked drowsily.

"They're in the UK, at your sister's wedding, remember?" said Lexi.

Oh yeah. I'm supposed to be there, I thought, too feeble to talk.

Then my eyes grew heavy, and I disappeared into the darkness again.

The next time I opened my eyes, there was a hive of activity in the room. Lexi was being pushed backward through the door, screaming my name through trembling hands. There was a palpable sense of alarm in the room as four or five nurses scrambled urgently around my bed. What the fuck was going on? What was happening to me? What were they doing? No matter how hard I tried, there was simply no air to breathe.

I was certain this time I was dying.

The nurses rolled me over and started tugging at my gown. Why are they doing that? I don't need to be rolled over. Leave my gown alone. I can't breathe! Do something about my breathing! I thought. Why is no one talking to me and telling me what's going on?

I was confused and in a state of total panic. I didn't know that my lungs were collapsing. My pancreas had swollen to the size of a watermelon and was putting pressure on my lungs, causing fluid to build up and stop me from breathing.

All I could hear were the loud noises of the hospital equipment and the sound of the nurses talking rapidly in Arabic. I couldn't understand one word of what they were saying, but judging by the shrill of their voices, it didn't sound good. Everything was happening so fast.

As I lay on my side, completely paralyzed and gasping for air, I could see the doctor approaching in my peripheral vision. He had a long metal spike in his hand and was bringing it toward me. What the hell was he planning to do with that? Whatever he was going to do, I didn't want to see it.

I scrunched my eyes tightly, too frightened to watch. I couldn't breathe, and I couldn't talk, so when I realized what was about to happen, I couldn't tell him to stop. The next seconds ticked by in slow motion. I felt a heavy, piercing pressure against my skin and heard two loud bangs as he drove the spike between two of my ribs. Fucking hell! He was cutting into me like a butcher hammering at a carcass, and I could feel every grim sensation of it as the spike plunged into my lungs. And just as it did, I opened my eyes and sucked in a huge gulp of air.

The massive rush of oxygen was an overwhelming relief. As I lay there on that butcher's block having just been saved from death, all I could think was, That fucking hurt, but at least I can breathe! I wanted to touch the spike or pull it out. It's not natural to have a thing like that sticking out of your ribs. Why had I been awake throughout the whole ordeal? I wondered. Surely, they would have administered enough anesthetic to knock me out before they began banging a gatepost into my ribcage like that? Obviously not.

I caught the eye of one of the nurses. Her eyebrows climbed into high arches, and her eyes bulged. I saw a look of surprise on her face as she peered at me over her mask and realized I was awake.

She quickly pierced my buttock with a sedative, and within five seconds I was out cold. I plunged into the darkness again. That was to be the end of my life in Egypt.

If I was going to survive, it would take a miracle. In the end, it would take two.

CHAPTER 15

TWO PROBLEMS, TWO MIRACLES

England,
July 25, 2003

While I was drinking water from the toilet bowl in Egypt, Mum and Dad were drinking champagne in England. They were toasting the bride and groom. It was my sister, Keely's, wedding day.

I had intended to turn up at her wedding ceremony unannounced, as a surprise on her big day. My pancreatitis put an abrupt stop to that plan. I'm not sure if she knows that I had planned to be there. Even if Mum and Dad had been in Egypt, I'm not sure I would have rung them; I wouldn't have wanted to worry them.

Earlier that morning, the phone had rung in my sister's house. She lived in Queensferry, a small town on the edge of Chester, about a 40-minute drive from Liverpool in the north of England. Dad answered it. Lexi was on the other end of the line.

"It's Paul," she said, faltering as she tried to speak.

"What's wrong, Lexi?" Dad asked.

"He's in hospital," she said.

"What's wrong?"

"We're not sure," said Lexi, trying to control her voice. "They're doing tests. Something to do with his stomach."

At that point, no one knew how seriously ill I was. However, Lexi thought that my parents should at least know that I had been taken to hospital. As it was my sister's wedding, she didn't want to cause too much alarm, so she probably played it down a little.

"OK, love," said Dad. "I'm sure he'll be fine, probably just something he ate. Thanks for letting us know, and keep us posted. He'll be all right once they've got some fluids into him."

Lexi said Dad sounded confident as he hung up. He must have thought it was probably just a bad case of gastroenteritis. Tummy upsets were a common occurrence in Egypt. No doubt Dad thought that in two days, three days at tops, I would be back on my feet. He decided not to worry Mum.

Late the next morning, Dad's mobile phone rang again. He was in Andy's car at the time, with Mum and Lindy, on the way back from the wedding. While the rest of the family had been celebrating, things in Egypt had become worse. Much worse.

This time the caller wasn't Lexi. It was Jürgen, who was with the general manager of the hospital in Hurghada. By that time, the doctor had driven the metal spike through my ribs, and I had descended into a coma, and it was unclear if I was going to pull through. El Gouna hospital was ill equipped to treat me, and the hospital staff were at a loss as to what to do next.

The tone of this call was very different from that of the previous one. Mum and Lindy were giggling together in the back seat, still giddy from the fun of the wedding. Dad struggled to hear clearly over their laughter and weak phone signal. They were on the motorway, just about to drive through the Mersey tunnel, where the signal would be lost completely.

"Hello? Hello, can you hear me?" Jürgen stuttered.

Dad turned the volume down on the radio and pressed his finger to his ear to block the background noise. He flapped his hand at the ladies in the back to silence them. "Shush!" he commanded impatiently. Mum's face froze instantly and turned pale.

"Brian, I have some very bad news." The phone line crackled. Dad shifted his head position to try to stop the signal from dropping out. "Paul," he could hear Jürgen say. Then a second's silence. "Coma." The line broke in split-second intervals. "Critical condition."

"Andy, stop the car!" Dad yelled, grabbing Andy's arm. "Now!"

Just before the entrance to the tunnel, Andy slammed on the brakes, stopping the car abruptly in the middle of the road. Andy read the shock on Dad's face and pulled at the steering wheel, turning the car sharply across the lanes to get to the hard shoulder as quickly as he could. Cars braked and swerved, honking their horns all around them. Mum gripped Lindy's hand as time stood still.

Dad leapt from the car and paced up and down the side of the road until he found a signal. Everyone in the car sat silently, trying to hear what Brian was saying over the noise of the traffic zooming past.

It was the type of call that every parent dreads.

Jürgen handed the phone to the hospital general manager. "Mr. Evans," he said, "this is a very serious, life-threatening condition. We're doing the best we can for your son, but we don't have the capability to look after him here. We can't keep him alive much longer. If he stays here, your son will be dead in four days."

The general manager's cold words echoed down the phone, chilling Dad to his core.

A long silence followed. The phone shook in Dad's hand as his throat tightened. He was in utter disbelief. The last he had heard it was just a tummy bug, and now this. Really? How come?

"What do you mean you can't keep him alive for more than four days?" Dad snapped. "Twenty-four hours ago I thought he had a bad case of gastroenteritis."

"Oh God!" Mum wailed as she broke down in tears, shell-shocked by what she had just heard.

"Mr. Evans, sir, what we initially thought was pancreatitis has now become acute pancreatitis," the manager explained. "I am sorry to tell you this, but we do not have the facilities in our hospital to keep him alive much longer. We can send him to Cairo, but if you want my advice, I recommend immediate evacuation to England."

Maybe the general manager was genuinely concerned for my well-being, or perhaps, he just preferred that a British citizen die in a British hospital. Either way, it was clear that I needed better care than he could give.

Dad leaned against the car to steady himself. He thought he was going to vomit. He felt Andy's hand on his shoulder. His stomach lurched as he continued to process the words that had just come through the telephone: "Son. Coma. Evacuation."

He felt like he had been hit with a sledgehammer.

Jürgen returned to the call. "Brian, I need you to take my number. I am here. You can call me anytime. I will help to get Paul home to you."

"Yes, Jürgen. Thank you, I appreciate that." Dad wrote down the number and ended the call after telling Jürgen he'd call back in a few hours with the next arrangements.

He got back in the car and looked squarely at Mum. "We have to find an air ambulance and get Paul the hell out of there, Barb!" he declared. He wasn't about to let me die. He knew that to hesitate would be fatal.

But the big question was, how was he going to get me home? How do you get hold of an air ambulance on short notice? The contact details of such things aren't exactly close at hand. After numerous calls and enquiries, Dad sourced the number for an air ambulance service in Switzerland.

Problem one: The air ambulance cost 25,000 pounds. Up front.

Problem two: Air ambulances are kind of busy. They aren't just sitting on the tarmac at your local airport, waiting to rush to the aid of sick party boys in Egypt. The air ambulance was fully booked. Apparently, the next available window for a flight to Hurghada was in five days. As the doctor had told my father, I would be dead in four.

Let's go back to problem one: money. Dad didn't have access to that amount of money. I did, but obviously I wasn't going to be handing over the passwords to my online bank accounts anytime soon. So, my money was unreachable. And as bad luck would have it, my medical insurance had lapsed a week earlier, so it wouldn't cover any of the cost.

The only way for Dad to raise the funds in such a hurry would be to call every loved one, friend and other contact in his phone book. I can only imagine now what that was been like: Dad, sitting alone, making call after call after call.

Dad has a lot of friends; everyone loves having Brian around. The friends he called that day must have been torn apart to hear his voice. It must have been crushing for them to hear his news about me and not be in a position to help. That must have felt awful. I'm sure everybody wanted to lend him some money, but wanting to and being able to are very different things.

I'm also sure some people were concerned that they might never get their money back. It seems harsh, but that was the reality. There was the unmentionable concern: If Paul doesn't wake up, how will we get our money back?

"No, no, I fully understand. It's OK. Yes, give the family my love. Oh yes, I'm sure he'll be fine. It's no problem. I understand. I just had to ask. Thanks anyway. Bye then." Over and over again, Dad managed to keep his composure, smiling and saying thank you, when all the while he must have been screaming inside, biting his knuckles, holding back from shouting, "Just give me your money! I need to save my son!"

By 7 p.m., after hours of calls and countless rejections, Dad had managed to secure the support of three friends who could raise the 25,000 pounds needed to pay for the air ambulance. I would be coming home, provided a plane was available.

The following day, miracle number one happened.

Late Sunday evening, Dad's phone rang. It was the air ambulance company. A young man had been badly injured that day in an avalanche while skiing in the Alps. The air ambulance went to collect him, but he died on the runway. As there was nothing more that could be done for him, the pilot, a man who shall forever be one of my all-time heroes, made the decision to offload his body and to head to Egypt for me.

It was unfortunate for the man in the avalanche but fortunate for me. May that poor young man rest in peace.

I often think back and wonder what would have happened if that pilot hadn't decided there and then to fly to Egypt. Was that the wrinkle in my destiny that made the difference between my living or dying? There's no doubt in my mind that his decision to fly to Egypt is a major reason why I'm here today. What if instead he had chosen to knock off early, go home, cuddle his wife, and put his feet up? Would I be dead? Am I alive because that man decided to put in the extra hours?

The air ambulance landed in Egypt in the afternoon on Monday, July 28. The British embassy had to get involved to process my paperwork quickly and grant my special permissions to exit the country. Jürgen and General Hindawi ensured that all of the required immigration information was prepared promptly. With a few phone calls and the rubber stamp of the general's authority they made hours of paperwork-related delays disappear. Of course, because of my condition, every minute saved was crucial.

As Ramon would later tell me quite comically, when I was wheeled from the airport terminal along the gangway to the ambulance it was like trying to shove a baby elephant through the tiny door. Due to huge water retention, I had ballooned to 275 pounds. After much shoving, tilting and pushing from various angles, I was finally squeezed in. Lexi climbed in next to me alongside the two ambulance medics and held on to my hand, and Jürgen called Dad to tell him we were on our way.

When the pilot received the "cleared for takeoff" instruction from air traffic control, I was on my way home, where miracle number two was waiting for me.

For the rest of my life, I'll be grateful to the people who were part of the team that saved my life.

But time was not on our side.

CHAPTER 16

ARRIVAL IN THE UK

Manchester airport,
July 29, 2003, 8:15 a.m.

Made it!

The air ambulance doors opened, and four strong men carried me out of the plane and rolled me onto a gurney, which almost buckled under my weight. The wheels wobbled as they pushed me, without a second to spare, into a private ambulance that was waiting to rush us all to the nearest hospital.

The ambulance pulled up 45 minutes later at the hospital accident and emergency department, where my parents were anxiously waiting to see me. Of course, they got the shock of their lives when they saw me. Bloated, pale, swollen, being kept alive by a multitude of machines, and breathing through a pipe that was sticking out of my throat. Nothing could have prepared them for the sight of their dying son.

Arriving on death's door, in an air ambulance from Egypt, I definitely wasn't the usual patient at the local general hospital. We soon would discover that my arrival was a break in hospital protocol, and because I had no medical referral and no report from a local doctor, and I hadn't lived in the UK for five years, the hospital refused to admit me.

Standing helplessly at the doors of the hospital, Mum looked frantically at Dad for answers. Lexi, having held my hand on the plane for six hours, was totally exhausted and sat sobbing on the edge of the pavement. With the breach in protocol preventing me from being admitted, the nurses inspected me inside the ambulance and listed their observations, noting that I had a punctured lung, acute pancreatitis and E. coli and that I was breathing from a ventilator. I'm sure that after encountering a patient with those kind of symptoms, they were wishing they had taken the day off.

"I'm afraid, sir, that without the proper paperwork clearance, we can't treat him here," the nurse explained to Dad as she made her final assessment. "You can try taking him to another hospital."

"Another hospital?" Dad was about to explode. "This is ridiculous! Have you seen the state of him?"

He hadn't let me die in Egypt. He hadn't let me die on the runway or in the air ambulance, and he certainly wasn't about to let me meet my fate in the car park of our local hospital.

"If you lot don't admit my son this minute I'll bloody well admit him myself," Dad said. "I don't give a shit about your fucking red tape and protocols! There isn't any time for that now. This is the UK. This is what the National Health Service is all about! He's traveled far enough, and as far as I'm concerned, his journey ends here, and someone in this hospital is damn well going to treat him. Now get a fucking move on!"

A male nurse could see that Dad had reached his breaking point and stepped forward to volunteer his help. He must have understood that there was no other option. This was a matter of life or death, and protocol would have to be followed later.

"Right, c'mon," he commanded, encouraging the other nurses to help him. Stepping up into the ambulance with his colleagues, he pushed me and my wobbly trolley off the wagon and into the hospital.

Flanked by Mum, Dad and Lexi, they raced me through numerous double doors along the corridor. Meanwhile the nurses scurried around anxiously as they attempted to alert the doctor on duty and the hospital management of my unannounced arrival. My details still hadn't been properly processed when I was whisked through the hospital and through a set of doors marked with the letters I-C-U.

"Please, save my son!" Dad shouted in the general direction of the ICU reception desk. He was out of breath, and his shirt wet with sweat.

That's when miracle number two happened.

A tall man in blue scrubs appeared from around the corner. "Hello," he said calmly, "I'm Doctor Stevens. How can I help?"

Dad wanted to leap at the doctor and drag him over to my side. Instead, he pleaded, "Please help us. Read his case file. He's going to die if you don't do something."

Dr. Stevens gave a reassuring nod of his head, ordered his nursing team into action immediately, and checked my vital signs. Protocol or no protocol, I was now officially his patient.

The miracle was that Dr. Stevens was precisely the person I needed. Dad would later discover, when he finally had the chance to catch up with the doctor later that day at the coffee vending machine in the ICU reception area, that he was the number one pancreatic expert in the UK. By some amazing coincidence he was at that particular hospital at that precise moment, conducting research on the latest techniques for pancreatic surgery and post-pancreatic recovery. If I wanted to pick any doctor in the world to be there at that moment, it would have been Dr. Stevens.

Quick medical lesson: to the best of my knowledge, the pancreas regulates our blood sugar by releasing insulin and glucagon into the bloodstream. It is a large, cone-shaped gland located behind the stomach, next to the small intestine. It sits horizontally across the backbone, and everything sits on top of it: the liver, the spleen, even the stomach. So, to get to it, everything has to come out, and when they do that, it leaves quite a hole.

So, Dr. Stevens, intensive care unit, I'm Paul Evans, here fighting for my life, and I'm all yours.

Dad held Mum and Lexi in a huge embrace. Their thumping hearts could finally resume a regular beat. They had rescued me.

Now it was up to Dr. Stevens to fix me.

WAKE-UP CALL 5
LIFE SAVERS

I truly believe there are people walking among us who are angels on earth. They are the people who have helped me when I was close to death, and they are the people who have guided me through life. In my darkest moments, they have been there, often appearing like miracles. They are my family, my children, my friends, my colleagues, mentors, doctors, nurses, pilots, teachers and childhood heroes.

Some of them I have never met.

Wake-Up Call 6

PARALLEL LIVES

CHAPTER 17

LIFE IN SINGAPORE

My body may have been in a coma in the hospital, but not my mind.

Sure, my body was in Manchester, lying in a bed, wired to machines, breathing through a tube, and struggling for survival, but my mind was off in a faraway land; I was living a dream life on the other side of the world, in, I believed, Singapore.

In this Singapore life, I was fit and well and fully aware of my senses and able to feel, see and hear just like I was used to. I had a job, a car and an apartment and lived much as I would have in normal life. I ate in restaurants with friends and shopped for clothes and groceries, took a shower every morning and spent time with my parents. Like I said, it was real life. Or so I thought.

Yet it wasn't like the dreams that everybody experiences, the kind that happen when you go to bed at night, fall asleep, experience something, and wake up feeling out of sorts or even a bit confused, because for a moment you thought your dream was real. No, my dream life was different. I didn't ever know that I was dreaming, and to this day, I can't be sure that I was.

It was like I had been born into my life in Singapore. I had no concept that there was another version of Paul on the other side of the world, in a coma. Today, my Singapore life is more like a memory than a dream. I can recall it in the same way I can recall the fish tanks in my bedroom in Winsford or meeting Lexi and falling in love for the first time. To me it was every bit as real.

I can't explain why I was in Singapore. I'd only been there once, when I was 12 years old. Dad took me with him on a four-day business trip. The only thing I really remember about that trip is that I wore my bright yellow Liverpool Crown Paints–sponsored football strip the whole time. I never took it off. Other than that, it was just a nice few days with Dad. So why my sub-conscious focused on Singapore as the location for my dream life, I have absolutely no idea. But Singapore it was.

I lived in a very sleek, modern apartment in a high-rise overlooking central Singapore. Though the apartment had two bedrooms, I was definitely single. I didn't live with any family or friends; I lived completely alone. In fact, the feeling of loneliness was a constant presence.

Every morning was the same. I would wake up, open the curtains, stand in front of the floor-to-ceiling windows, and look out over the tops of tower blocks and the city skyline. I'd have a shower in my stylish, black-tiled wet room and then, from the many tailored suits hanging in my orderly wardrobe, I'd select what to wear for the day. I'd have breakfast in my kitchen, which had a central island (I'd always wanted one of those in real life). Then I'd leave my apartment and drive to work.

My commute took about half an hour. The roads were not like British motorways; they reminded me more of the six-lane freeways in America. I drove a black Jaguar XJS, registration WIJI 45. That license plate is interesting because when I was a kid, my father had almost the exact same registration (WIJI 35) for his red Jaguar. I had found this funny, because *wiji* was a local slang term for a little boy's willy.

Every day in Singapore, the sun would shine on me and my black Jaguar as I drove along the vast freeways and over a series of impressive bridges. I don't know whether they have those kinds of roads and bridges in Singapore, but perhaps I'd seen them on television at some point and recreated them in my dream.

I worked in a very modern business village occupied by many technology firms. Each building was a beautiful, mirror-tinted tower more than 30 stories tall. I'd drive up to the entrance of our tower and go through the security gate. There was a landscaped roundabout in front of it, with flowers and plants and a fountain in the middle. I'd take the first exit from the roundabout and drive into the underground parking. I had my own allotted space, the last in the row, number P499. This number may have been another unconscious connection to Dad, whose lucky number was 49. Considering my situation, I definitely needed a bit of luck.

The company was called Virtu-Game, and it occupied five stories of one of the shiny, mirrored buildings. We employed approximately 500 people and specialized in the design, manufacture and sale of virtual-reality games. I was the manager of the sales team. Our office was located on the first floor, a huge, open-plan space with glass partitions around the perimeter. My office, exactly like Christine Goldman's, was positioned right in the middle of the floor, so I could see everyone on my team as they worked.

I was fit, healthy and in super shape, so when I needed to go to one of the other floors, I never used the elevator; I always took the stairs. I never seemed to be still for long; I was always zipping around, keeping busy, buzzing from one floor to another, up and down the stairs multiple times throughout the day.

Virtu-Game created the ultimate virtual-reality experience. They made it possible for the user to live vicariously through the mind and body of almost any person they could think of.

For instance, if you wanted to be an astronaut, you could purchase the Astronaut Pack, sit down at your computer, put on the virtual-reality goggles, and you'd be able to experience life as Neil Armstrong. If you wanted to be a Premier League footballer, no problem. Just switch on and witness life as Diego Maradona. Or maybe you want to be Muhammad Ali. Simply download the pack, and within minutes, you'd be eating your breakfast like you were The Greatest. You could train, box, talk—do just about anything—as Ali.

My job, with my team, was to sell as many of these virtual-reality experiences as possible. And, true to form, I pushed myself and the team to exceed our targets. Considering the nice car and fancy apartment that I had, I assume I was reasonably successful. Strangely though, I don't remember the names or faces of any colleagues. They were all just bland, faceless people. I'm pretty sure I had a boss; I remember hosting regular meetings in the conference room, where an authoritative figure would sit at the end of the table, listening to my presentations and making the odd comment. But other than him and a secretary, who would take the minutes, the rest of the team was simply a group of sales people, engineers and software geeks. There were no characters in Singapore who I can describe as being my friends. I couldn't say, "Oh, that was Mark. He was the funny guy from next door," or, "David was the boss I admired," or, "Claire, the hotshot from the legal department...." Everyone was amorphous.

The only people in my life in Singapore with any real significance were Dad and my granddad.

As a boy I got to spend only a relatively short amount of time with my granddad. He died when I was nine years old. At the time, nine years seemed like forever. When I think about how quickly time flies when you're an adult, nine years is just a flash. I'm curious to know why my granddad came to me in Singapore so many years later. I'll always remember the respect and love I had for him, and sometimes I can still feel him with me, so I like to think that's the reason.

I've always been incredibly close to my parents, so there's no surprise that Dad was with me in Singapore, too. When I was growing up, Dad and I were almost inseparable. And when I first moved to Egypt, aboard *My Rosetta*, he and I would go diving together two or three times a day. I absolutely loved those days; there was no better way to spend time than with friends and family by the ocean. But as time passed, I spent less time on the boat, because my days became filled with work and my nights were spent drinking in the clubs. I felt guilty about that. It was time wasted that I'll never get back.

However, we always made a point of making Saturday a family day. We would get together for a bite to eat by the pool or on the beach. Mum would sit on a lounger and watch and giggle at us, while Dad and I would play around, throwing a ball to each other as we chatted in the water.

These days, I'm aware of getting older myself and my own sense of mortality. I can see my parents' time on earth passing by so fast, which really bothers me. But slowing down time isn't possible. So instead I've decided not to waste a second of it. I focus on making the precious minutes of life matter most and cramming as much goodness into the life we are given. After all, I think I can say that I've had enough life experience to afford that perspective.

Time flies even faster when you're in a coma. I've formed the view from my experience that "coma time" passes even faster than time in the real world. While days and weeks passed in real time for those sitting at my bedside, for me, in coma time, a full year or more passed in Singapore. One week in coma time was equivalent to about a day of real time. A year of coma time, therefore, equates to only a few real months.

Just as in my real life in Egypt, I'd work all week and go to the beach with Dad every weekend in Singapore. It was the only time in the week that I would get to see him. It was our time to relax and shoot the breeze. The beach in Singapore was crystalline and pure. There was no greenery, no shrubbery, just a turquoise sea split by a white sandbank that stretched far into the deep blue ocean. The water twinkled where it reflected and blended with the sky in the most gorgeous sunset. For hours, Dad and I would walk along the sand and throw a ball to each other as we talked. The only noises were our voices and the roll of the gentle waves.

Then one weekend, everything changed. I went to the beach as usual, but this time Dad wasn't there. He had been replaced by my granddad. Although I was confused at first, I was so happy to see him that I didn't think to ask where Dad was. We walked along the beach together, exactly as I usually did with Dad, and as we passed the ball to each other, he told me thrilling stories of his time in the army during the war and how he had survived air raids and enemy gunfire. I walked by his side through the shallows, listening to him reminisce about his friends, all fallen heroes immortalized through time.

When we reached the end of the beach, we stopped. My granddad turned to me and looked straight into my eyes. I could sense he was about to tell me something serious, and I could feel my heart sink in to my stomach. Behind him I noticed the colors in the sky changing into a vivid orange and violet sunset, which turned the ocean into liquid gold. He took me gently by the wrists, and in a soft voice said, "Paul, it's important for you to know that your mum and dad are so proud of you."

"Now, don't be sad," he continued, as a single tear slipped from the corner of his eye down one of the deep creases in his face. "But I have to tell you something. You have to understand that the end eventually comes to everyone. It's now time to let go of your dad. I'm sorry, son, but he's very sick, and soon it will be his time to say goodbye."

My granddad's words made my entire body convulse, and I collapsed to my knees as my lungs let out a desperate howl from the depths of my soul. I was inconsolable, the grief almost too much to bare. I looked up again to cry out to him, but he had vanished, leaving me all alone on the beach, where I sobbed at the beautiful sunset until I had no more tears left.

It was customary on a Saturday evening for Dad and me to go to our favorite street-food market. But I dreaded seeing him later that evening. Having been told the devastating news that he was terminally ill, I didn't know what to expect. I was deeply apprehensive and so desperately wanted it all to be untrue.

We shuffled our way together through the busy market, weaving past noisy stalls and food carts that billowed clouds of fragrant steam into the humid air. In true Singaporean style, we ate chicken robata, a local dish, served straight from our favorite hawker stand, and sat at a table on plastic chairs among the hustle and bustle of the street. But Dad looked bizarre. He looked like a wax-work version of himself. His skin was orange and plasticky, as if his face and body were made of the same hard, shiny, waxy material as the orange plates that our food was served on. I wanted to touch him to see what he felt like, but I hesitated to because I knew he was so sick.

While we ate, we talked about life and cherished memories. We talked about family time mainly, about me and my sister growing up, about the day I flooded the house with my fish tanks, about learning to water ski, overcoming many difficult school days, our happiest days at La Santa, and family holidays together. But all the while I knew we were building up to a subject that I wanted to avoid at all costs.

When the waiter cleared our plates away, the moment came that I had been dreading. Dad drew a breath and began. "Son, I have some news. There's no easy way to tell you, so I'm just going to come out with it."

He paused. I held my breath. I knew what he was about to say.

"I have cancer, and they say nothing can be done." He gripped my hand. "You have to promise to be strong for me, son. I'm going to need you to look after everyone."

He looked at ease as he told me he was about to die. I wanted to protest and tell him that I didn't believe him; after all, he didn't look real. I wanted to prove him wrong, that the whole scenario had to be some sort of trick. Instead, no words came out.

He looked at me lovingly and said, "You know, you don't ever have to try to make me proud of you, son. I'll always be proud of you. No matter what you do, no matter where you are, or how far you go in life, whether you chose to do anything or nothing, I love you. You are my son."

I could feel the seconds ticking by, and I knew that our time together was running out. This isn't right. I need more time! I sobbed. Hearing him say those things didn't bring me any joy. I didn't feel relief or even forgiveness. I felt only regret. Regret for how much I'd fucked up. Regret for the mistakes I had made and who I had become. We were out of time, and I hadn't shown him how much I loved him and that I could become a better person. I desperately wanted the chance to make everything right before he was gone. But this was the final moment; his time was up.

He smiled at me and stood up from the table. "Goodbye, son. I love you," he whispered as he took a few steps backward toward the roadside and, in the blink of an eye, was swept away into the crowded street. He was out of sight in an instant, sucked into the thick, stifling mass of people and traffic. My eyes searched rapidly to catch a glimpse of him amid the throng, but he had vanished without a trace.

Of course, I was oblivious to the fact that it was me who was sick. In the real world my father was alive and well and permanently at my bedside. He was there every day from sunrise to sunset, reading books, telling me the news, recapping the football scores and sports results, and writing a daily diary, all while I lay unconscious.

It was really me who was disappearing into the darkness of death. I would learn much later that one particular night, I all of a sudden became intensely restless and woke Dad, who had been asleep in his chair beside me. To his horror, my face and neck had swollen massively and were turning purple. He alerted the nurses, who rushed to me immediately and recognized the urgency of the situation. I had developed an embolism in my carotid artery, which was potentially fatal. In a professional manner, the ICU nurse informed my parents that there was every possibility I would be left brain dead or worse. There was a high risk of death, and she recommended that the hospital chaplain be called straight away.

I'm told that when the chaplain arrived moments later and stood at my bedside to offer a prayer, Dad refused to let him speak and sent him away. "My son won't be dying today!" he said defiantly. "He won't be needing prayers, and nor will I, thank you."

Upon reflection, it's possible that back in Singapore, where reality was flipped, I was interpreting my own death as my father's demise. Dad's saying "good bye" to me in Singapore was actually happening the other way around. And although Dad refused to believe it, I was the one who was slipping away and dangerously close to the end.

One of the hardest things about death is recognizing that the person is actually dead. I thought about Dad's death every day. I missed him so much and couldn't believe he was gone. The guilt of not having the opportunity to go back over all the things I'd done wrong in my life and correct them gnawed away at me. It wasn't merely sadness; I felt fragile and lost. At any time I could break down. I had a hard time sleeping or focusing on anything but my memories of him. I worried that I'd never recover. The profound loss left me emotionally paralyzed. I was deeply changed by his death, but in the way a tree is changed by having to grow around an obstacle, I began to piece myself back together after months of struggling. Although Dad's presence was always missing, I began to breathe, to sleep, to eat, to go for walks in the sun, and finally I went back to work.

Back to work, in my Jag, along the highways and over the bridges, with the sun shining over the city skyline, to my virtual job, in my virtual world. I'd park my car in the customary spot and go up the stairs in my usual way, I'd buy coffee, have lunch. I'd have team meetings and attend product briefings. We'd have the odd work or social occasion on the weekends, anything to keep me busy and my mind focused.

Our latest game was in the final stages of development. Following several months of design, trials, feedback and relentless re-testing, our new virtual-life experience game was as close to perfect as we could make it. It was a full virtual-body-transformation device, programmed to literally teleport the mind and soul of one human being into the body of another. We were ready to run the first live test with a living subject: me.

I sat back in the pod, a sleek silver capsule fitted with a very plush leather sports chair. I pulled on the shiny motorbike-style helmet. Then an engineer plugged a connector into the side of my neck. I shut the visor, which automatically triggered the device to start.

Neon lights and digital icons flashed and bleeped in front of my eyes. Everything happened in sequence, as the engineers explained it would. I experienced the sensation of weightlessness, tingling in my fingers and toes, and the heightened sound of my heart beat as I started to go under.

I was excited; this was going to be an exceptionally cool ride. I was being teleported into the mind of Jack Welch, chairman and CEO of General Electric.

I could faintly hear my colleagues outside the capsule running through their checklist. "Heart rate monitor: check. Pulse: check. Eye movement and pupil dilation: check. Blood pressure: check. Computer systems live. Power in all ports."

All the while, I could hear the capsule's bleeping, sucking and whooshing noises. Bright colors and hypnotic swirls spun faster and faster around my head as I was sucked out of the capsule, through the vortex toward the second dimension, leaving my "body" behind.

Then something went wrong. The game stopped abruptly, and the lights went out. I could hear alarm blasts echoing far off in the distance. The sound of the capsule bleeping in a fast, high-pitched sequence, urgently calling for someone's attention.

I waited silently in the darkness and tried figure out what the developers were doing and what could possibly have gone wrong with the software. I could hear the echoing sound of fingers slapping against their keyboards, tapping in codes and passwords, overwriting formulas and frantically trying to re-route the program. Nothing appeared to be working, I could sense the developers' panic. As much as they tried to divert me back, I was trapped in the space between two dimensions, unable to return to my body in the capsule. The door back to "reality" had already closed behind me. I was locked out. There was no going back and no going forward. I would have to sit and wait for the team to fix the glitch, and I had no idea how long it was going to take.

I was alone in absolute nothingness. It was as though I was suspended in a deep, dark void. I couldn't see or feel anything. Was I in a room, a bubble or even outer space? I felt like I was floating. Was there anything above or below me? It was hard to figure out where I was, because I was completely blinded and disorientated by the utter blackness.

I knew the situation wasn't good, but I was confident that it was just a glitch. I had every faith that it wouldn't be long before the team on the other side got me out. I could hear echoes of them calling to me, "Don't worry, Paul, mate. We'll get you out! We just have to write some extra codes to change the formula."

Hours passed, and I could hear them continuously trying to correct the defect. "Hey, buddy, we're almost there. We'll have you out in no time. Just sit tight and relax in there. Hold on."

I kept nodding off as I waited for them to fix it, but every time I woke up I found myself still there, and they sounded like they were drifting farther away from me. But I could still hear them trying, so I'd wait a little more and fall asleep again.

Days went by.

As time passed, I began to lose confidence. Their rescue effort seemed to be slowing down. Maybe they didn't know what they were doing after all? Maybe they had run out of ideas? But there was nothing I could do, so I just waited, wearily, in the darkness and continued to drift in and out of sleep.

Days turned into months, and still I remained suspended in nothingness.

Eventually they stopped talking about re-programming the console altogether. There was no more mention of fixing bugs, re-routing the software, or changing plugs and ports. More often than not, they just chatted idly, discussing football scores, what was for lunch, or current affairs. From time to time they'd even sing to me. However, they said nothing to me about the game or the program. I was so exhausted from waiting that I longed to just sink into a long sleep that I'd never wake up from. But every now and then they'd wake me up with their chit-chatting about what was on the telly. And

I'd scream at them to hurry up and get me out of here! But it was clear they couldn't hear me.

After what seemed like six months, a strong, strange voice from the depths of the darkness started calling to me. From the bones of my body I could feel it urging me to wake up and fight my way out. "They aren't going to save you, Paul," it said. "Wake up! Think about it! They can't fix this. That's why they're just reading nonsense to you. You have to save yourself."

Why have they given up on me? I asked myself. What if they really can't fix it? Why had it taken them so long? If they can't fix it, will I be here forever?

Until that point I had allowed the team and the console do all my thinking for me, but after the voice had urged me to wake up, I knew I had to take control. I wondered if this dark place I was trapped in had a deeper meaning. Why was I really here? I had a funny feeling that the answer to that was a lot deeper than I could explain, and I didn't want to find out.

The voice continued to encourage me. I felt my strength returning. The more I focused on escape, the more I felt my energy build. My thoughts became clearer. There would be no more sleeping the endless hours away in the dark oblivion. I couldn't afford to wait any longer for them to restart the console so they could reach in and pull me out. I couldn't count on anyone else to save me.

The voice had started as a gentle whisper but was becoming louder and louder to the point where it was deafening and insistent that I had no time to waste.

"Just do it! Find a way out, Paul!" it demanded.

With my hands stretched out in front of me in the darkness, I frantically tried to feel above me, below me and all around me. I didn't know if I was shut in a box, enclosed in a long tunnel, or suspended in infinite space. There didn't seem to be any beginning or end to the obscure place I was in.

I rotated in all directions in midair, with my fingers spread wide, flapping my arms around and kicking my feet, hoping to kick or hit something. Hours later, I finally did. I bumped into a smooth-surfaced wall. It felt like some kind of membrane or an endless wall of stretchy material, like the side of a never-ending tent in the pitch dark. I scanned the surface like I was reading braille, trying to find an opening. But there was nothing. The membrane went on forever, and it had no edges, no holes and no imperfections. I tried to kick it, stab it, punch it, bite it, but I couldn't get through it. It was totally impenetrable.

But the voice didn't let me rest at all. I relentlessly searched for just one tiny flaw in the material, and I refused to stop until I found it. I was on the brink of madness when at last, a tiny flaw appeared in the fabric above my head.

I began scratching at it manically. "Damn it! Why the hell do you bite your fingernails, Paul?" I cursed at myself as the smooth ends of my fingers struggled to get some purchase.

I scraped and rubbed at the little flaw until after days of picking, a pin-hole of light suddenly beamed through the hole like a laser beam. It was the first element of light I had seen in over six months. I couldn't believe it. "Yes!" I cheered at the sight of it. "I'm going to get out of here!"

Feverishly I kept picking, over and over again—picking, pulling and tugging at the hair-thin threads, a slow and frustrating process when you have short, soft nails like mine.

The more I picked, the more light came through, bit by bit. I poked my finger through the hole, twisting and wiggling it, trying to perforate it further. With more effort I ripped the hole big enough to squeeze a second finger through. I tried to prize my fingers apart and stretch the fabric. I could feel the edges slowly beginning to peel and tear. The material was almost self-repairing, and I found myself having to work quickly to fight against it. It didn't want to let me escape. I ripped at it until the gap was big enough to get my whole hand through. Then my arm. I yelled and screamed as I peeled and pulled at the black material. I forced my arm through up to my elbow. Then twisting into contortions, I folded my other arm and both shoulders through the opening as the material tried to suck me backward. I took a deep breath, and in one desperate heave, I forced the weight of my body upward and maneuvered my head through the hole and into the light. I heard the release as my head popped though the fabric and knew instantly I had arrived somewhere. But I had no idea where.

I opened my eyes. What the fuck? I appeared to be in a hospital bed, and my family and friends were standing around me, singing happy birthday. Right in the middle of everyone—very much alive—was Dad.

It was my 29th birthday, and I had woken up.

CHAPTER 18

HAPPY BIRTHDAY TO ME!

Manchester hospital ICU,
August 31, 2003

I looked around the room and saw familiar faces looking back at me. As I blinked, under the bright light of the room, everything slowly came into focus. The body I was in was thin and bony, with no muscle. It looked pathetic and frail, with skinny arms and long fingernails. This obviously wasn't my body. I could make out Lexi, my sister, my nan, Mum, Andy and Lindy and someone who looked remarkably like Dad, which totally freaked me out. Dad was dead and had been for a long time. Surely the man in front of me had to be some kind of ghost or imposter, yet no one else thought it was strange that he was there, which confused me even more.

They were all around my bed, holding blue helium balloons and singing happy birthday to me. There was an over-bed table in front of me that was full of birthday cards and colorful paintings, which a child must have been made for me. Amber, my niece, I thought. I began to appreciate that these people were more real than the people in Singapore, yet I couldn't be sure.

I definitely knew who they were, but still, Dad was the only one of them who had been with me in Singapore. I couldn't fathom why they all seemed so familiar, considering, to my mind, I hadn't seen any of them for years. I was so confused. They were standing closer to me than any of the people in Singapore ever did, close enough for me to see their eyes looking back at me. Mum was gently rubbing my feet. I couldn't remember the last time I had really felt my skin being touched like that. I thought that if I reached out and touched anyone in the room, they would feel more solid than any of those friends and colleagues in Singapore. Come to think of it, I don't recall anyone in Singapore ever touching me, apart from when my grandad held me by the wrists on the beach—the day he told me that Dad was going to die.

I inspected each person in the room, as I did, I noticed that they appeared more lifelike than my team and the technicians and engineers from Singapore, although they were real to me, too. Or were they?

To my surprise, I had wires and tubes stitched into my wrists and a plastic clamp on my finger. What the hell had happened to me? My whole body ached and felt unbelievably weak. The back of my head was numb from lying against the pillow. I moved my head and was shocked to find that a tube bypassing my voice box was sticking out of my throat. Things were getting weirder by the second. Was I still inside the game? Had I arrived in a new dimension, or was I still in Singapore? Was I dreaming? Was I even alive?

The tracheotomy meant I couldn't speak, so I didn't try to say, "Err, what the fuck's going on?" That's the strange thing about having a tracheotomy: You know you don't have a voice in the same way you would know after an amputation that you didn't have an arm or a leg. So, I didn't try to talk and instead I just stared at everyone, imprisoned in a body that could barely move. In addition to the cables inserted into both wrists, I could feel a tube stitched into my nostril, and could hear machines behind my head, beeping on the left and right. I wondered how on earth I was going to get out of this body.

As far as I was aware, I had just fought my way through the black membrane after picking away at it for months. I'd been alone in a black void for so long that it was just a relief to finally have some company. So, I looked around and attempted to make eye contact as I tried to work out why I was in a hospital. But after everyone finished singing happy birthday, they turned away and began talking among themselves, or watching the TV as if I wasn't in the room. They weren't aware that I could hear them until Mum noticed that my eyes were following her around the room.

I was later told that, while I was in my coma, I sat up occasionally, opened my eyes, and stared at someone or something. Everyone understood that I wasn't conscious when I did this. So, the fact that my eyes opened while they were singing to me didn't give them any reason to jump up and call for a nurse.

But Mum suddenly stopped rubbing my feet. She sensed something was different about the look in my eyes. "Shhh, everyone! I think Paul can hear us!" she said excitedly. Keely, my sister, turned off the TV and rushed to the side of my head, and I turned to face her.

"Oh my God! Paul, can you hear me?" she asked.

I nodded my head.

"Do you know you're in a hospital?"

I nodded my head.

"Do you know why you're in a hospital?"

I shook my head. The questions kept coming.

"Do you know who we are and that we all love you very, very much?"

I nodded my head.

My brother-in-law, Gareth, squeezed my sister's hand and said, "Look! Your brother's coming back to us."

It was the first time that they'd had any conscious response from me, and quite understandably, they all immediately burst into tears—happy tears and tears of relief. But I was still totally bewildered by the whole scenario.

Showing tenderness and care, yet with mounting curiosity, they asked more questions. I continued to nod my head, shrug my shoulders, or shake my head to communicate with them as best I could.

"How do you feel?" Keely asked.

I shrugged my shoulders.

"Do you know why you're here Paul?" Mum wondered gently.

I shook my head.

"Do you know what's happened to you, my love?" Her voice was soft.

I shook my head.

"Do you know who we all are?" Andy asked, pointing at everyone in the room.

I nodded my head.

"Do you know it's your birthday?" Lindy said with a smile.

I shrugged my shoulders.

"Do you remember how you got back from Egypt?" Lexi asked sweetly. I shook my head. Egypt? I thought. When the hell was I in Egypt?

Perhaps they could see that I was becoming stressed by their questions. It was a lot to take in, but none of them asked if I knew what day it was, what time it was, or whether I knew how long I'd been in a coma. I guess they didn't want to freak me out any more than I already was.

"Don't worry, Paul. You're in good hands," said the man who looked like Dad. "The doctor's going to look after you. You're going to get better, and we're all here to look after you."

I didn't move a muscle as I looked at him. You can't be alive, I thought. I buried you. I've mourned your death. You're not real. You're not my dad! What the fuck is going on? I couldn't make sense of any of it, so I closed my eyes and prayed to whoever may have been listening that next time I opened them, I'd be back in my own body and back in my normal life in Singapore.

My name is Paul Evans, I prayed. I've lived in Singapore for nearly two years. I have a mother and a sister, but my dad very sadly passed away about a year ago. I drive a Jaguar. I go to work every morning, and I sell virtual-reality computer games. About six months ago, while testing the latest game, just as it was teleporting me from one dimension to another, something went wrong. Before I was able to enter the body of the person I was programmed to become, the damn thing broke! I was lost in a dark void between two dimensions until I finally managed to pick my way out. I appear to have picked my way into some seriously fucked-up reality, where I'm lying half dead in a hospital. My family is here, but Dad's back from the dead. Please, Singapore, if you're there, if you can hear me, please get me out of here!

CHAPTER 19

SAY HELLO. WAVE GOODBYE

Whoosh! I was gone again.

I didn't go back inside the black void. This time I was splashing my way through an enormous fish tank. The waves crashed down on my head as I gasped for air. The water smelled like bleach, and between the cycle of the waves, as I surfaced, I could hear Puff Daddy's "I'll Be Missing You" playing in the distance. Then another wave came and forced me back under the water, where I held my breath among the bubbles until it was safe to surface.

Eventually the storm calmed, and I found myself washed ashore in what appeared to be a vast, derelict multi-story car park. It looked like a bomb had just detonated. It was a dark and treacherous place that didn't seem secure underfoot. The roof of the building had caved in, and the walls were crumbling and looked like they could collapse any minute. Rubble was littered everywhere. I got to my feet, dusted myself off, and walked toward the open staircase in the corner of the building.

The staircase was never ending. I grew increasingly irritated as I looked for an exit. No matter which way I went—up or down—the stairs, as in Escher's famous drawing, led back to the same point.

In the distance I could still hear a combination of Puff Daddy and a running commentary of the news playing on a loop through a loudspeaker. I could make out the distinctive medicinal smell of the water lingering in the air. Then I heard a mobile phone ringing. I couldn't see where the handset was, but I could hear that the sound was coming from the floor above. Maybe it was Singapore trying to get through to me. Maybe it was my family or someone who could help me find the exit from this car park. I had to find it.

I ran up the stairs toward the ringing, but before I could find the phone, a nurse wearing a uniform from the 1940s appeared and stood in front of me. Her young face was expressionless as she held the ringing phone in her hand. Being from the 1940s, she didn't know what a mobile phone was. When I reached to take it from her, she shook her head and switched it off.

"What the fuck, woman?" I yelled.

She turned and stepped away from me.

"Why did you turn my phone off?" I shouted, my voice echoing around the building.

She glanced back at me over her shoulder, and then she disappeared like a ghost, up the stairs, taking the phone with her.

A powerful gust of wind blew through the building, dislodging more rubble and throwing up large plumes of sand and dust. Within seconds, rain was pelting the building. Raindrops the size of water balloons smashed on the ground all around me, each one big enough to knock me off my feet. The medicinal smell filled my nostrils. I turned around and saw a tidal wave twice the height of the building approaching with gathering speed. "Fucking hell!" I screamed as I scrambled to find a safe place to hide.

I lay behind a wall, hoping it would protect me, but as I braced myself for the wave, I felt the whole building rise and turn 90 degrees forward. I slid helplessly across the wall as rocks and bricks thundered past my head and dropped off into the void beneath me. I came to a halt perilously close to the edge. I clung to the wall in desperation until the building finally came to a standstill. How can a whole building rotate like that? I asked myself. But before I could give it much more thought, the giant wave came crashing through the car park, washing away everything in its path. I closed my eyes and held on to the edge of the wall for dear life as the water swirled around me.

The wave passed, but then the building again began to shake violently as it rotated back to its original position. I was swept back across the floor in a tide of water and rocks. Landing in a heap on my back, I gasped for air and groaned in agony.

I was dazed but came to my senses after a few seconds. Seeing the staircase in the nearby corner, I got to my feet and waded through the waist-high water. I had to get to higher ground as quickly as I could, before the next wave came or before the building moved again.

After I found a safer position, the storm calmed, and then the sun came out. Puff Daddy and the news echoed again in the distance, and I heard another mobile phone ringing on the floor above. I ran upstairs to find the phone, but to my horror, the same nurse reappeared. Once again, she was holding the phone in her hand. I realized I was trapped.

The nurse switched off the phone and slipped up the stairs in the same ghostly manner as before. I sensed the wind howling and beginning to blow up the dust, and I knew another torrent of giant raindrops was imminent.

After my birthday, the nurses had knocked me out with some sedatives and morphine, putting me into a drug-induced sleep for the next four days. During that time, I opened my eyes only intermittently; I might respond if someone touched me, or if the machinery at my bedside made noises loud enough to stir me, but I was so heavily sedated that I recall hardly anything.

Under sedation, I was given daily bed baths by a rather heavy-handed male nurse. He didn't intend to hurt me, of course, but he had a job to do and did it in a very unapologetic manner rather than use the gentler touch that I would have expected from Lexi or Mum. I faintly recall that, aside from feeling embarrassed about being washed by a man, I didn't like when he rolled me or moved me. Mum told me later that every time he entered the room with his basin of antibacterial wash and towels, I would sense he was there and open my eyes widely and scowl at him.

I also took huge offense to any nurse who attempted to turn off any alarms that the machines behind my bed were making. An orange bag of intravenous fluid hung permanently behind my head, the purpose of which was to squeeze anti-MRSA medicine continuously through a central-line catheter in my chest. Every hour, the bag emptied, and the machine would bleep loudly.

Every day that I was in my coma, my family held vigil around my bedside. For the 77 days that I lay in the hospital, Mum and my sister massaged my feet, played puzzles, listened to their favorite songs (including Puff

Daddy's "I'll Be Missing You"), and watched television programs, pretending that I was awake and watching with them. Dad never left my side, either. All day and all night, he read to me and kept me updated on the daily news and sports from around the world, hoping that the day would finally come that I'd wake up and Dr. Stevens would deliver the news that I was stable enough to go for surgery.

WAKE-UP CALL 6
PARALLEL LIVES

I began to live the day I died.

I don't believe it was my time to die. Having been given a second chance at life, I'm making sure I really live and make the most of the time I have.

All the wake-up calls in my life led me to this one. People say life's too short. Unless you have been to life's cliff edge, you don't know how true that statement is. When I died, I was full of regret for the things I hadn't done and the wrongs I hadn't put right.

Since then, I've thought a lot about the concept of time. Time is a perception. We may not be able to turn back time, but I believe we can lengthen our future by filling the seconds of our lives with the things that matter. To me, that is the best use of the time. The most effective way to stretch time is to never waste a second of it.

Wake-Up Call 7

YOU DON'T KNOW WHAT YOU'VE GOT 'TIL IT'S GONE

CHAPTER 20

OPERATIONS

From the day I was admitted into hospital, the doctors and nurses cared for me 24 hours a day, seven days a week. Their sophisticated machines breathed for me, medicated me, fed me and monitored my heart, my temperature and my blood pressure. Multiple times throughout the day and night they took tests of my fluids, my urine and my blood and interpreted the daily function of my organs.

The nurses continuously took biopsies of my pancreas by fine needle aspiration. I'm no doctor, but basically, they were measuring to see when the fluid in my pancreas would reach a certain dilution marker, which would indicate that it was safe enough to open me up, remove all the nasty stuff, cut away the part of the pancreas that had died, cauterize it, and stitch me back up.

Dr. Stevens was a man of few words. He was often curt and to the point, and as he guided my parents and friends expertly through my treatment, he made no attempt to sugarcoat my chances of survival. At times, I believe, he delivered news that was hard for my family to hear, but even then, he offered very little sympathy. Perhaps it was his professional opinion that it was best to present worst-case scenarios, so that if I performed better than predicted, the news would be that much sweeter.

Yet, to the man's credit, Dr. Stevens' prognosis and predicted recovery timeline was accurate to the millisecond.

On September 4, when the final pancreas test came back, Dr. Stevens pronounced me ready for surgery and said he would perform the life-saving operation within the next 24 hours. In his consultation room, he told my parents brusquely, "We got yesterday's results, and as we had hoped, the levels are where we want them to be. We believe Paul is in a stable enough condition to have the operation, so tomorrow morning he'll go for surgery. It's around a four- to five-hour operation, and then he'll be back in the ward."

Everything about Dr. Stevens was matter-of-fact. There was nothing more to be said. The sooner my pancreas came out, the sooner I'd be on the road to recovery. I just had one more hurdle to overcome—the small matter of a life-saving operation.

Dr. Stevens had instructed the nurses to reduce my morphine dosages to prepare me for surgery. As the effects of the morphine wore off, I was finally able to get past the phantom nurse, answer the ringing mobile phone, climb to the top of the stairs, and find the exit from the carpark.

I opened my eyes. I was still in the hospital, and all the wires and machines were still there, too. Dad and Tim were at my bedside. No one else was in the room, just them.

"Hello, Paul. Can you hear me?" Dad asked.

I nodded.

"Remember I told you that you're going to have an operation?" he asked as he gently patted me on the arm.

I shrugged my shoulders. I couldn't ask him why I needed an operation or what was wrong with me. I could only shrug and hope that he might tell me.

He looked at me and softened his voice. "Son, one of the organs in your body has had an infection, and that's why you're poorly. So they have to take it out. After a few hours you'll be back in the ward, and you can start getting better. OK?"

He made it sound so simple, but his face was telling me another story. I remember the haunted look in his eyes; I could see he was trying to mask his fear. Yet I wasn't frightened at all. I had no concept of about how sick I'd been, and I had and no comprehension of what the operation actually entailed. Looking back, I'm glad Dad didn't tell me the details.

I may not have been so relaxed had I known that that they were about to open me up from side to side under my rib cage, lift out all my innards, and place them one by one on my chest to gain access to my diseased pancreas, which lay across my backbone. Following that, they would clean up the horrible mess that they found, remove the pancreas (saving any of it that they could), and then, if I survived all of that, they'd place my organs back inside my body and attach huge drainage pipes on both sides of me that would remain there for the next eight weeks. These would constantly flush me with saline fluid to keep my organs clean and suck out the pus, blood and any other nasty stuff.

Had I known any of that, I may have understood his concern.

"Don't worry, son. A team of the best doctors and nurses are going to look after you. OK?" Dad continued, but he stopped when his voice began to break. He wiped a tear from his eye, while Tim shuffled in his chair and let out a little cough.

"It's OK, Mr. B," Tim said encouragingly. "Paul's a fighter. Aren't you, mate?"

I nodded.

Dad stood up, took a tissue from his pocket, and dabbed his eyes and cleared his throat. "I'll just go and get a coffee, son. Tim's got some stuff he wants to say to you. I'll be back with your mum in a minute."

As he left the room, I thought I could hear him sobbing. Maybe this is more serious than he would have me believe, I thought.

Tim pulled his chair forward and sat close to my head. He looked at me with the familiar cheeky glint in his eye, and with a wide smile, he pulled a yellow envelope from his jacket pocket. He rubbed my arm affectionately while he opened it and said, "Mate, I'm going to read you a letter."

I nodded.

He took a deep breath and started reading the letter to me:

Paul,

Thought I'd leave you a note, because I won't be here when you wake up or when you go into and out of theatre.

Just a walk in the park, mate. Go in, you'll feel a slight nip from the needle, your arm may feel a bit cold, your eyes will feel heavy, and the next thing you know you'll be back in your room—walk in the park.

Then you can start recovering. Best be quick though, because a best man has a lot of duties to take care of before a wedding (10 April, remember).

So, don't be scared, mate. It's the best thing to happen, and I'll be there for you tomorrow night and the night after that, and the night after that, etc., etc.

You'll be fine. Be strong for your mum and dad and Lexi, and I'll see you when you've finished your little op.

Luv you man,
Tim

Tim folded the letter and placed it carefully on my overbed table. "You keep hold of that, mate," he said.

I nodded. I could see he was finding it hard to look at me as he struggled to fight back his tears.

If I had been able to speak, I'd have said, "Oi! Are you really asking me this now? I'm about to have an operation! Don't fucking ask me this now! Don't ask me to be your best man while I'm lying here like this. Are you taking the mick? We should surely be in the pub celebrating when you ask me that!"

But of course, Tim couldn't read my mind, so instead I had to lie there and watch my best friend battle with his emotions as he hoped to heaven that it wouldn't be the last time he'd see me.

Mum and Dad returned with coffee from the vending machine. "There you go. Get that down you," Dad said, passing the plastic cup to Tim. "The doc says Paul's going to get some rest for a short while and then the nurses are going get him ready. Mate, you best be getting on the road before the traffic backs up."

Tim agreed. They gave each other a big hug.

"Call me as soon as he goes in. OK, Brian?" Tim said firmly.

"I will, mate. Of course I will," Dad replied reassuringly as he patted him on the back.

"See you tomorrow, Barbara," Tim said as he hugged Mum and smiled at her. "He'll be fine. I know he will."

Before he left, Tim turned to me and whispered in my ear, "Love you, man."

After he left, Mum and Dad settled down beside me. I could feel my eyelids growing heavier, and as they chatted, I must have drifted off. I had no idea that the next time I woke up I'd be on the operating table.

I woke up, and from my position high in the corner of the operating theater, I had the perfect panoramic view of the entire room. I looked down at a team of surgeons and nurses working calmly around the operating table. It was a wide-open and windowless space lit brightly by huge lamps positioned above the operating table, which could turn and tilt in any direction.

At the head of the operating table were various machines and screens displaying pictures, numbers and readings. The ventilator machine made a loud and repetitive thumping and sucking noise as it fed gas into my lungs through two long tubes connected to my tracheotomy. Next to it was a computer that was recording my heart rate via the small, sticky patches on my chest. I could hear it bleeping as I watched the rhythmic beat of my heart peaking across the screen. Other machines recorded my blood pressure and oxygen levels, and looking at myself, I thought I resembled a puppet connected at every extremity to tubes and wires. Catheters, pipes and drains were inserted into veins in my wrists, ankles, chest, nose, stomach and lungs. Even my dick had a tube in it.

Everyone in the room was wearing blue masks, caps, gowns and gloves. The drape that was placed over my body had an opening where Dr. Stevens was working. I could hear his monotone voice issuing clear and precise instructions while his team navigated elegantly around him, supplying him with whatever he required from the selection of sterile surgical instruments positioned neatly on a steel table near my head.

I was high above, in the left-hand corner of the room, about 15 feet away from the foot of the bed, watching every detail unfold. What I was experiencing was like watching my twin brother being operated on—if I'd had a twin brother. It was like I was watching another version of me, a replica.

I had an overwhelming sense that someone had put me there to watch what was going on. I have no idea who that was or why I sensed that. Why was I being shown this? I wondered. What purpose did it serve?

I was mesmerized by the spectacle in front of me, by the computers, the technology and the intricacy of the work they were doing. The operating table itself was surprisingly pleasurable to watch, too, as Dr. Stevens swiveled it and spun me around gracefully as he operated.

There was no blood anywhere. It wasn't like the chaotic scenes you see in the movies, with arteries spurting over the doctor's face and a nurse hopelessly mopping up bucket loads of blood from the floor. No, the procedure I was watching was clean and clinical, and as my liver, intestines and other organs were lifted out of my body they looked like the plastic models used for surgical demonstrations. They didn't look at all gory, and they slotted together perfectly on the tray that was perched on my chest.

It was all rather serene as Dr. Stevens calmly conducted his team. "Retractor. Flush. Suction. Sponge…." The team of nurses obliged dutifully, carrying out his requests without saying a word, following a well-rehearsed dance that they had performed a thousand times.

About half an hour into the operation, the mood suddenly changed. Dr. Stevens became fractious, and the nurses scurried around as beeping alarms from the monitors grew louder and louder. I watched from above as the situation intensified. This looked serious.

The heart monitor was the only thing I could focus on. As I stared at it, everything else paled into the background. I could hear the sound of my own heart slowing down: beep, beeep, beeeeep, beeeeeeep, beeeeeeeeeeeeeeeeeee….

Panic set in as it dawned on me that I was watching myself slipping away.

Hey, you lot down there! Do something! I yelled from the corner of the room, as the heart monitor displayed a continuous line across the screen.

The nurses quickly moved all unnecessary equipment out of the way, leaving room for only the important kit. Meanwhile the doctors interpreted the readings on the monitors to ensure Dr. Stevens had precisely the information he was asking for. Whatever was going on, it didn't look good.

I begged, pleaded and prayed into the bright lights of the surgical lamps to anyone who could hear me: Please. This isn't my time. Not now. I can't go. I've got so much to do and so much to say. I have things I need to put right.

Please! This shouldn't be happening to me. I have people to talk to; there are things I need to tell them. I want to show my parents I can be a better man; I need more time to show them the real me. It's too early to say goodbye. Please don't let this be the end.

The monitor continued to display just a single flat line and to screech one long, continuous sound. The medical team took a step back from the operating table.

Fuck. That's it. Game over.

I felt a cold chill all over my body at the thought that my life had come to an end. There was no chance to say goodbye. No apologies. No forgiveness. No last hugs. No final kisses. I'd had my turn at life, and now it was over.

Everything seemed to be happening in slow motion. I watched a nurse preparing the defibrillator as another pulled away the drape across my body and placed two large patches over my heart.

I heard Dr. Stevens call out, "Run the fluids wide open!"

At the same time, the nurse, with a paddle in each hand, informed everyone, "Charging to three hundred and sixty. All clear!" Then she placed the paddles on my chest and zapped me.

I saw my body shake as the electricity buzzed through me. It felt like I'd eaten something too hot, as if I'd taken a gulp of tea before allowing it to cool down. Or when you've eaten a curry that's been warmed too much in the microwave, but by the time you realize it's too hot, you've already swallowed it, and you've got to just sit there and deal with that burning sensation in your tummy. I felt like I was slowly burning from the inside out.

As the defibrillator shocked me, I saw all 10 of my toes spread apart in a spasm and then twitch as the electricity pulsed through my body.

I heard the nurse call out again, "All clear!" The voltage jolted me for a second time, making the warm feeling in my stomach fill my entire chest.

Yes! Come on! Fix me! I cheered, realizing that the surgical team wasn't prepared to give up on me just yet. I rooted for them even more than I'd ever cheered on my beloved Liverpool FC. Come on, Team Doctor! Fix me. Wake me up again! I yelled with all the passion I could muster.

"All clear!" The nurse jolted me for a third time and then stepped back. During the long pause that followed, I watched my toes stretch out and lock; everyone in the room held their breath, waiting for signs of life.

The milliseconds ticked by like minutes.

I clasped my hands and closed my eyes in prayer: Come on, Team Doctor! You can do it. I know you can! Please, Team Doctor, restart me!

Then my toes wiggled.

Followed by the glorious sound of beep, beep, beep....

I'm alive. I'm fucking alive!

Dr. Stevens wasn't messing around and certainly wasn't in the mood for celebration. There was a lot of the operation still to perform, and he wanted to get it done, make me stable, and get me back into the safety of the ICU as quickly as possible. After a final check of the readings from the machines and monitors, he ushered the team back into position to proceed at pace.

"We need this pancreas out, and we have to have him closed up before we lose him again," he said to the team. "We don't have much time. I'm going to remove as much of the pancreas as possible, but I'm not going to keep him in here any longer than necessary."

The operation was scheduled to last for another four hours or so, and during that time, my pancreas, spleen, gall bladder and a length of my small intestine were all scheduled to be removed in a "total pancreatectomy." However, because I had flatlined, time was of the essence, so the doctor switched to a less severe option that would leave a small part of my pancreas intact. This meant that my gall bladder and intestine would survive to see another day. Dr. Stevens knew this decision would save my life there and then, but that it could heighten my risk of a relapse later. Only time would tell.

Regaining their composure quickly, the medical team got back into their flow. They sliced, cut, cauterized and stitched as the hours ticked by. Sensing the strong smell of burning flesh as they whipped out a large chunk of my pancreas and all of my spleen, I decided I'd had seen enough hospital drama for one day, and so I closed my eyes and offered my thanks for Team Doctor one final time: If you can hear me, thank you for Team Doctor. Whatever and whoever decided I should witness all of that, I get the message loud and clear. Thank you for giving me a second chance. You won't regret it. I promise. You'll see the new Paul from now on. It might take me a while to get back on my feet, but believe me, when I do, a day won't go by that I don't remember this lesson.

CHAPTER 21

THESE FEET WERE MADE
FOR WALKING

When I woke up, I felt like I'd been hit by a bus. I opened my eyes and turned my head slowly to the side. As I focused, I thought I saw a ghost. The man who resembled Dad was sitting at my bedside, holding my hand. I diverted my eyes and pulled away quickly. I must be dreaming, I thought. Dad can't be right here next to me. He's dead! The man could see that I was freaked out, so he smiled kindly and said, "The operation went well, son. You're going to start getting better now."

Hang on a minute, I thought. What operation? Where the fuck am I? Why can't I move? My mind raced as I struggled to comprehend what was going on. You can't be Dad. I buried him six months ago. This is impossible.

The effects of the morphine continued to play havoc with my mind as I drifted in and out of sleep. I didn't have a clue what was going on, and the next two days passed by in a blur. Each time I opened my eyes, the man was sitting in the same spot next to my bed, reading me the newspaper.

I had vivid flashbacks of picking my way through the black wall. I could see that my room was festooned with birthday cards and balloons, and I could feel that my torso was heavily bandaged, yet I had no idea why. All I knew was that I felt like I'd been used as a wrecking ball.

A few days later, my grasp on reality slowly began to return. It eventually dawned on me that perhaps Singapore had been a dream all along, and

163

that the man at my bedside could actually be Dad. I turned toward him and studied the details of his face. I could see the laughter lines framing his bright blue eyes, his sun-streaked hair, tanned skin and familiar smile. Cautiously I crept my fingers toward his hand until I could feel his fingertips. I examined his hands, touching his skin and turning the gold wedding band on his finger. It was enough to convince me it really was him. My heart filled with relief as I clasped his hand tightly.

"Hello, son. Yes, I'm here," he said with a soft giggle.

He found a notepad in the pile of puzzle books Mum had left on the side table and then gently arranged my fingers around a pen. "I know you can't talk, Paul, but maybe you can try to write something if you like," he suggested and slipped the notepad under my hand.

Still feeling a bit unsure, I looked across to the other side of the bed, where Mum was sitting. I needed that extra reassurance. "Yes, love. Try if you can," she said, smiling tenderly, encouraging me to make the pen move.

I twitched my fingers and wrote, "Are you my parents?"

In the days that followed, I made use of the notepad to try and find out what had happened to me. It took a few days of asking questions and recounting my bizarre stories of Singapore and all the other adventures for me to be able to differentiate between what was real and what I had imagined.

"What day and date is it?" I wrote on the notepad.

Mum explained it was September 8, 2004.

"I have the strangest feeling I have lost the last six months," I wrote.

"You've been asleep for a long time, my love," she explained.

"Where is my mobile?" I jotted down slowly.

"You don't have a mobile phone here, Paul. Perhaps all these beeping noises sound like your phone," Dad suggested.

"I went to Singapore," I informed them.

"No, son, that was all just a dream. You've always been here in the hospital in England," Dad said. "We've all been here every day with you."

"Ice," I wrote.

"Yes, Paul! Ice cubes were the last thing you ate in Egypt!" Lexi said.

Then came the big question. "Tell me about the accident. I bet I'll be shocked," I scribbled.

It certainly came as a shock when they told me there had been no accident. That all the time I lived in Singapore were a dream. That I didn't have a job as a computer-games salesman, and I hadn't been trapped inside a broken game for the last six months. Lexi reminded me that I had lived with her in Egypt before I suddenly became ill and was evacuated by air ambulance to Britain.

I so desperately wanted to talk to them and reply with my own version of reality, but I couldn't. Yet part of the beauty of being unable to speak was that I was forced to listen. All I could do was listen, digest and think.

As my parents and Lexi sat around my bedside and tried to interpret my scribbles, I was trying to comprehend what it all meant. Was it the morphine? Had I really had an out-of-body experience? Was it possible that I had been to a place in another dimension where a greater being or a godly presence was keeping me safe while my body took the time it needed to recover? I wanted to understand the reasons why I had been given so many second chances at life.

As I lay there, I reflected on the sequence of events that had unfolded during my ordeal: the doctor in Egypt who had told my father to evacuate me, the air ambulance pilot who had made the life-saving decision to collect me from Egypt, finding Dr. Stevens in the one hospital that I needed him to be in at the time. I'd survived acute pancreatitis, E. coli, MRSA and an embolism in my neck. A priest had even been called to read me my last rites, and I'd flatlined on the operating table and been resuscitated, Yet I was still alive.

What am I going to do with this second chance I've been given? I thought. Looking back on my life, it seemed I'd come full circle yet completely missed the point of what it meant to live. I was so grateful that I was able to begin again, but it would take a great deal more time in intensive care before we were sure I was going to survive.

The only time I'd seen Dr. Stevens was during my operation, when I watched him from the corner of the operating room. Dad told me that he'd come to see me a couple of times to check my vitals after surgery. I was asleep, so I never met him face to face. When he came into my room for the first time after I'd woken, I wanted to reach out, throw my arms around him, and show him my gratitude for saving my life. Dr. Stevens, however, was less enthusiastic.

"Paul is awake today," Dad said, with a hint of pride in his voice.

Dr. Stevens picked up the clipboard that hung on the end of my bed. His white coat, tall and thin silhouette, gray hair and glasses presented the perfect image of a doctor, along with a distinctive air of superiority.

Unwilling to afford me the luxury of any small talk, he responded as if I was of great inconvenience. "Yes, Paul, nice to meet you." He looked directly into my eyes and raised one eyebrow. "You've been a very lucky young man. If you drink again, you'll die."

He put the clipboard promptly back on the hook at the end of my bed, nodded his head firmly in my direction to confirm what he had just said, then turned on his heels, and walked straight out.

I was lost for words. I'd been waiting nervously to meet this man, and that was it? That's all he has to say? So much for bedside manner. He left no opportunity for questions and was clearly in no mood to mix his words. No more alcohol, was his message, shot directly from the hip with absolute accuracy.

I like to think I'm a personable guy, and that I can make friends easily, but Dr. Stevens was completely disinterested in getting to know me on any personal level. His rejection really stung. As he had saved my life, it was important for me to be able to show him how much I appreciated everything he had done. I didn't want him to think that I was a drunken bum or that I was a drain on hospital resources because I had drunk myself into near oblivion. But Dr. Stevens was indifferent to what I wanted. He'd probably seen enough patients like me in his career that he didn't feel like he needed us to be friends. He looked at me over his spectacles in judgement, as if to say, "You're another one of those dickheads who drinks themselves to death, and I'm tired of fixing you. I'll fix you because that's my job. But will you people ever fucking learn?"

Regardless of what he thought of me, though, I will hold the highest respect for that man until the day I do eventually meet my maker.

By the end of September, I had made enough progress that it was finally time for the tracheotomy tube to come out. It would be the first time I drew breath on my own since the doctor in Egypt drove the spike into my ribs when my lung had collapsed.

"Not long now and we'll be hearing you chatting all day long, Paul," the nurse said jovially. But I knew she really meant that it was only a matter of time before I'd be moved out of the ICU and into another ward. That thought terrified me. I had become so emotionally attached to the ICU and the machines that had kept me alive that the idea of their being removed and my being downgraded to a recovery ward filled me with dread.

You want to remove the machine that has kept me alive for so many months? I thought. What if something happens later, and the machine isn't available?

A while later another doctor arrived. He swabbed my throat and said, "I want you to close your eyes and take a deep breath." I heard a pop as the tube came out. He quickly placed a sticker over the hole in my neck. "Don't try to talk for a minute," he said and patted my chest with his hand. "Just give it a little bit of time. It's going to feel quite awkward when you talk for the first time. OK?"

I nodded.

So I lay and waited in silence. When Lexi, Mum and Dad were relaxing quietly, reading books, doing crosswords and watching television, I mustered up the courage to test my vocal chords.

"Hello, Mum. Hello, Dad," my little voice whispered.

Mum burst into tears, while Dad jumped up and threw his arms around me. Lexi came over and kissed my cheek.

"Hello, princess," I said with a smile.

Being able to talk and to tell people how I felt and to express what I was thinking, as opposed to being locked in my own body of silence, was such an emotional release. Being silent when it isn't a choice is such a curse; having a voice—wow, what a gift!

The days after my tracheotomy tube came out rolled by, and my progress picked up. Soon enough I was able to sit up in bed, and glimpses of the old chatty Paul emerged. But physically this version of Paul was virtually unrecognizable. I was nearly 90 pounds lighter and looked like a bag of skin and bones. My leg muscles had wasted away so much that Dad could put his hands around my thigh and overlap his fingers. My ankles were as thin as my wrists. My fingernails had grown beyond the end of my fingertips, and my normally short hair was long enough to curl behind my ears.

When I say progress, I mean small progress. I had to learn all over again to do the things we take for granted, like being able to breathe on my own. I don't think I'd ever stopped to consider how amazing it is just to have lungs that can breathe unaided until the day I was taken off the ventilator. Today, I often tell myself that as long as there is air in my lungs I can achieve anything, but no one should have to go through what I did to gain that perspective.

I could feel my body was starting to wake up albeit slowly. The first time I tried to sit up after the operation, Dad had to put his arms under my shoulders and haul me up. It felt like my body had been pulled apart like a Christmas cracker. It took one month just to be able to rearrange my position in bed without someone's help. Gradually the numb sensation in my lifeless limbs and spine began to subside.

But there were still some things I couldn't do. I couldn't walk, wash or control myself when I needed to go to the bathroom. Those three things put together made for some fairly cringeworthy moments. There's not a lot to protect your dignity when you're a feeble ICU patient. There were times when I really had to dig deep to keep my sense of humor and save myself from heart-stopping embarrassment. One such example was when the nurse came into my room pushing a crane on wheels, like the hoist used to lift an engine out of a car, and said, "Right, Paul, it's time for a bath."

Baffled, I wanted to respond, "And how the fuck am I going to do that?"

In no time at all, I was fully naked, apart from a tiny towel across my privates. I dangled from the enormous sling while being wheeled down the corridor and lowered into a bath, where I had to endure the humiliating experience of a male nurse cleaning my arsehole with a scrubbing brush.

Then there was the time when I accidentally messed the bed while watching a movie. Mum called for assistance to help clean me. To my horror, I recognized the nurse's voice as he called into the room before entering it. "Come on," he said. "Everyone out. Someone's got to get cleaned up and ready for the party."

I cringed, because I knew that something especially unpleasant was about to happen. I looked up, and the nurse was waving a can of spray soap in one hand and a wedge of paper towels in the other. As I feared, it was John Spander.

I had known him as a kid at Middlewich School, and he was possibly the only boy who was bullied and harassed as much as I was in the classroom. The difference was that he was teased for being gay. I hoped he didn't recognize me.

"Had a little accident, have we? Don't worry about that I'll sort you out," he said, grinning.

Oh my God! Johnny Sparkle-Pants is about to squirt my bum with soapy foam, and there's nothing I can do about it! I thought with impending dread.

"Right," Johnny explained. "I'm just going to roll you over so I can get at the problem. OK?"

With every second that passed, I died a little more inside. This was karma on a whole new level. Johnny rolled me on to my side. Unfortunately, that meant my body weight pressed against my drainage pipes and made me groan with pain. I prayed for the whole episode to be over and done with as soon as possible.

"Oh, come on now. Don't complain, sweetie," he joked as he squirted me between my legs with his can of foam. "Oh dear! We've got a big job on here, eh?"

He's absolutely loving this, I thought as I buried my face in the pillow.

Time ticked slowly as he squirted and wiped and did what was necessary to clean me up. When he had finished, he announced joyfully, "That's you all done, my darling!" He patted me on the butt cheek and rolled me back over.

Forget the coma. Forget the lung puncture. Forget being craned naked across an intensive care ward. Not one bit of it was as bad as having Johnny Sparkle-Pants slap my bare butt cheek and call me darling.

Putting personal humiliation aside and looking for the positives, I made a little more progress each day. Every Monday, the doctor would remove the stitches in my sides, pull the drainage tubes out an inch, and then sew them back in. Three times a day I'd receive a visit from a diabetic specialist who tested my blood to decide what food my body could cope with. For an hour every morning, another nurse would come and shove a suction pipe up my nose, bang on my chest, and empty fluid from my lungs, which was pretty horrible. Once all that was finished and various tests and readings taken, I would spend two 30-minute sessions each day with James, a physiotherapist and all-round nice guy, whose sole aim was to get me walking.

On my first attempt to stand on my own, James and Dad carefully swung my legs around, placed my feet on the floor, took hold of an arm each, and lifted me slowly upward. "It's OK, Paul," James said. "We're both here to steady you. We're going to slowly let go and see how long you can stand."

As my legs straightened, I tried to lock my knees. I was so weak, though, that I couldn't find the power in my legs to support myself. As soon as James and Dad let go of me, I wobbled uncontrollably, and they had to catch me before I fell.

Day after day, we'd try again. Each time I was able to stand for a few seconds longer. Finally, after a week of painstaking efforts, James and I were making some headway. I was able to put my feet on the ground, stand up and remain upright (albeit wobbling like a new-born giraffe) without his help for nearly a whole minute.

James' sessions were the only item on the day's agenda of treatments that I actually looked forward to, but when he boldly announced, "Now you've mastered standing, it's time to take a step on your own," memories of the day I raced Linford Christie at LaSanta flashed through my mind. I pictured myself walking on the beach and kicking a ball and felt intensely frustrated at my current situation. Just putting one foot in front of the other was such a hard thing to do. Sweating profusely and exhausted, I screamed with anger.

James calmly reminded me, "Just focus on what you can do today, Paul. Soon you're going to walk out of here and leave all of this behind you. That day gets closer starting from today."

"Yes, come on, Paul," said Lexi, as she rubbed my shoulder. "Don't be too hard on yourself. Give it another go. Just push your foot over this line." She drew an imaginary line with her toes on the floor in front of me.

"OK, I'll do it!" I confirmed, gathering my willpower.

Mum, Dad and James looked on keenly as I slid my right foot forward. They cheered and clapped as I dragged my left foot over Lexi's line. I'd taken my first step.

Each day after that, James set me new goals: "Walk four steps to the end of your bed." "Walk ten steps to the door."

By the time three weeks had gone by, James was so impressed with my shuffling that he proudly presented me with a Zimmer frame and announced, "Well done, Paul. Now you're ready to come out of your room and walk around the whole of the intensive care unit."

I froze and shook my head. I can't possibly go that far, I thought.

James read my mind. He looked straight at me and said, "Yes you bloody well can! Now come on! On your feet!"

I stood at the door to my room, clutching on to my Zimmer frame for dear life and peered down the corridor. I was as terrified as I might have been if I was about to parachute jump out of an airplane at 30,000 feet. My parents, Lexi and two nurses followed a few steps behind me, pushing the trollies with the various drips, hanging pouches, tubes and drains that were still connected to my body.

"We are going to do this in stages of 10, Paul," James said firmly. "The ICU is a perfect square, so first, you're going to walk to the nurses' counter and then take a rest. Then you'll go from the nurses' counter to the entrance door and rest again. And so on, all the way around until you arrive back at your room. OK?"

"OK," I said, nodding and white-knuckling my Zimmer frame's handles.

Noticing the event unfolding in front of them, a group of nurses came out from behind their counter to encourage me. "I can't quit now. I've got fifteen women watching me," I said, giggling nervously.

I could hear Lexi behind me, laughing with joy as she watched me shuffle. One step, two steps, three steps…until I reached the counter and took a rest. The nurses cheered me on, smiling and clapping.

"OK. Next, we go to the entrance door," I said, beaming with pride. "Ready, Mum? Ready, Dad? Follow me! On your marks, get set, go!"

The whole ICU team counted my steps with me: "One! Two! Three! Keep going, Paul! You can do it!" they cheered as I hobbled and shuffled in my gown and slippers while dragging my machines and equipment behind me.

By the time I arrived at the entrance door, the buzz in the ICU had peaked. There was such a level of excitement that one of the nurses jumped for joy and cartwheeled the length of the corridor. As I turned the final corner into the home stretch back to my room, you would have thought that a major sporting event was taking place in the corridors of the ICU. It had taken me almost two whole hours to walk just about 100 yards, but as I got back into bed, I felt as proud and as happy as I would have if I'd just run a marathon.

CHAPTER 22

EAT YOUR CAKE AND HAVE IT

It took three days for the nurses to convince me to give up my bed in the ICU. Dr. Stevens, my parents, Lexi and Jan, the head nurse, all did their best to assure me that I was well enough to be moved to the surgical ward. Yet, despite the obvious progress I had made with James, I was constantly plagued with doubt and an overwhelming fear that my body was deceiving me. I was convinced that the little piece of my pancreas still inside me was like a dormant volcano, ready to erupt again at any moment. ICU was, IN my mind, the safest place I could be, and I was terrified at the thought of moving.

"No, I don't want to move!" I argued with Dad.

"Son, they need the bed," he said. "This is intensive care. You don't really have a choice mate. We've been saying this for three days now: You're getting better; it's time to move. You'll still get great care in the other ward."

"I don't care. I'm not ready to leave!" I protested. "There are nine beds here in the ICU, and only five are taken. So why do they need my bed?"

No matter how much I put up a fight, it was going to end only one way. Jan finally put her foot down. She'd had enough. "Sorry, Paul, but that's it," she said. "No more negotiation. Today's the big day. You're going to have your own room on the ward right next to the nurses' counter, so you can see them all the time. OK?"

I could see by the look on her face that arguing any further would be pointless, so later that afternoon, I said my emotional goodbyes to the amazing team of ICU angels who had cared for me every day since I'd arrived three months earlier. I had grown so attached to them that I didn't think it would be possible to survive without them.

When I arrived in my new room, I was stunned by how quiet it was. I'd become so accustomed to the size and noise of the machines in the ICU that this space sounded silent and empty by comparison. Of course, there wasn't the privacy I'd been used to; in the ICU, my room was concealed, whereas on this ward, large windows along the corridors opened up the space and exposed all the activity that was going on inside.

From my room, I could see into all of the other wards. I watched as patients dressed in pajamas and dressing gowns made trips back and forth to the canteen. I could see visitors coming and going and the medical team purposefully going about their work. The whole place was busier but surprisingly quieter than the ICU. In fact, I can't think of many other places in the world, apart from the ICU, that get louder the quieter their customers become.

After a reasonable night's sleep, I woke the next morning around 6:30 a.m. and could hear a nurse at her desk making phone calls to other departments within the hospital. Her tone expressed a mixture of concern and humor. "Yes, we're looking for Gladys," she sighed, as if she was tired of repeating herself. "Do you have her down there? She's gone for a walk in the night again.'

Amused, I sat up in bed and wondered who Gladys was. I turned on the television to pass the time until Mum and Dad arrived. While I waited, I had the chance to have another good look at my new surroundings. From my bed I could see the main entrance corridor, the nurses' reception desk, and the waiting area. To my surprise, I saw a man walking past my door with his arm missing. All that was left below his shoulder was a stump with a bandage on it. Poor guy, I thought. But I reminded myself that I was in hospital, so I thought nothing more of it and continued to watch television.

A few minutes later, I was distracted by a slightly older gentleman hobbling past my door in the other direction. He was on crutches and had a leg missing. This is getting weird, I thought. No sooner had I looked away than a woman limped past. She was missing her right foot. By this point I was horrified. Something terrible must have happened, I thought. I buzzed the bell quickly to ask a nurse and put my mind at rest.

"Nurse, what the hell's going on? Has there been an accident? Has something happened?" The shock and concern was obvious in my voice. "There must have been a big car crash. I keep seeing people with missing limbs!"

The nurse sighed and replied sympathetically, "No, Paul, there hasn't been an accident. These amputees have diabetes; you're in the diabetic ward."

I had no idea what diabetes had to do with amputation, so in a state of alarm and in defense of my own limbs, I shrieked, "I'm diabetic! What the fuck has that got to do with anything?"

"Well, one of the complications of diabetes is amputation," the nurse explained.

"What the fuck? No one told me that!"

I was preparing to head for the door just when my parents arrived. "Dad, they're going to cut my hands off or chop my legs off!" I yelled in distress. "I've got diabetes! In the ICU they told me I had to take insulin, but they didn't say anything about chopping my legs off!"

"Woah, chill out, mate," Dad said as he sat down on the edge of my bed to pacify me. "No one's cutting off any of your limbs. Don't worry. Calm down."

The nurse finished her explanation, which Dad translated into layman's terms for me. "Basically, son, if you don't monitor your insulin properly, or worse, if you abuse it by drinking alcohol and testing your blood sugars then continuing to drink, before you know it, your blood vessels will clog up, and then—whoosh—off goes a limb."

I raised my eyebrows in shock and remembered what Dr. Stevens had also told me: zero alcohol.

"But you're not going to do that, Paul," Dad said, tapping my knees. "So you'll be fine! These legs are going to be carrying you around for a long time yet. Don't you worry, son."

"So there's no chance I'll be walking past here on a pair of crutches then?" I asked, looking for reassurance from everyone in the room.

"No. As long as you look after yourself properly, there's no reason to see you back in here at all," the nurse confirmed, shaking her head.

"Thank fuck for that," I said, letting out a loud sigh.

I was down to my final week in the hospital. In total, I'd spent 100 days under close supervision. In that time, I'd seen a lot of people come and go. In the early days, beds became free for heartbreaking reasons. As time went on, I saw people recover and be given the all-clear to go home to their families. I knew soon it would be my turn.

With each passing day I gained weight and gradually shed most of my catheters, pipes and drains. I was now able to administer my own medication, and in the last few days, I'd had been able to visit the café on the ground floor of the hospital without the need of the Zimmer frame. James, Jan, the team of nurses, and my family began a seven-day countdown to the day we hoped Dr. Stevens would discharge me. Every night before I went to sleep, I scratched off another day from the calendar I had stuck on the wall.

Just before I was discharged, something really weird happened.

At night, hospitals can be creepy places, and on my final night, I woke up at about 3 a.m. to a chilling sight. A ghostly figure stood, completely still, at the foot of my bed. It was the silhouette of a gray-haired old lady. She looked ancient and wore a floaty white nightgown. Her straggly gray hair hung down over her pale, bony face as she stared at me without blinking. Her frail shape was lit by the moonlight.

I was frozen with terror.

"What do you want? Why are you here?" I stuttered, but the gray lady didn't flinch. She just continued to stare at me, as if she could see right into my soul.

I fumbled furiously behind my head to find the call button on my headboard and raise the alarm. There were so many buttons, and I couldn't see which one was which in the darkness. In my despair, I hit the wrong switch and mistakenly activated the electric bed's pre-programmed upright position. The bed began to fold upward, edging me helplessly closer to this terrifying apparition. Her wide-open pale eyes remained fixed on me. I pushed myself backward, into the mountain of pillows behind my head, trying to look away, while my fingers searched in vain to find the reverse button. The bed continued to push me toward the creepy ghoul.

In utter distress and panic, my whole body trembled, until finally my shaking fingers located the alarm bell. When the bed came to a stop, I was sitting fully upright and face to face with the scary old woman.

"Quick, there's a ghost! Turn the light on!" I yelled to the nurse who had rushed down the corridor to come to my aid. She flicked the light switch to reveal what all the commotion was about: A little old lady in her nightgown stood at the end of my bed, looking completely lost. I grasped my hand to my chest and took a long breath.

"Jesus, she nearly gave me a heart attack," I said. I realized that this must be the missing sleepwalker who I'd overheard the nurse talking about. Gasping with relief, I lowered my bed back down to its proper position.

"Oh, Gladys!" the nurse said, chuckling. "Look where you got to this time. Did you come to say goodbye to Paul, love? Come on, let's get you back into bed, shall we?'

As the nurse carefully guided Gladys out of my room, she said, "Sorry, Paul. She's a sweet old lady, but she's got Alzheimer's and likes to go on walkabout. Don't you, Gladys?"

As Gladys shuffled out of my room she asked the nurse, "Is it time for cake now?"

"You must have got a bit of a shock," the nurse said apologetically before leaving.

"Yeah, just a bit," I joked. "Don't worry, Gladys. I'll bring you some cake later." I felt slightly embarrassed that I'd been scared shitless by a 90-year-old woman.

In the morning, my parents, Lexi, Andy and Lindy all arrived just after breakfast. They presented big bunches of flowers and a large cake to the medical team to mark their appreciation. Then it was time to take one last look around my room before zipping up my bulging bag of medication. It had been 107 days since I'd been rushed to the hospital in Egypt, and I was finally being discharged in the UK.

A brief consultation with Dr. Stevens confirmed I was free to go, with mandatory bi-weekly follow-up appointments for the next month. I'd be convalescing at Andy and Lindy's house, just a five-minute drive away. After lots of hugs and well-wishes, my discharge papers were finally signed. I headed out of the ward arm in arm with my family, but not before making sure Gladys got her big piece of cake.

WAKE-UP CALL 7
YOU DON'T KNOW WHAT YOU'VE
GOT 'TIL IT'S GONE

I thought going to prison and being deprived of simple luxuries was a good lesson in gratitude, but I had more to learn than that. Without meaning to sound clichéd, I am grateful for so many things in life, simple and complex.

I lost the ability to speak, the ability to walk. I lost my dignity and my confidence, and thought I'd never get any of it back.

I lost my grip on reality, and I nearly lost my life.

Waking up after 77 days in a coma and then going through months of rehab changed me mentally and physically.

I'm grateful that I was able to rebuild myself from scratch. The old Paul was gone. The new version of Paul was a blank page.

Looking back now, I can say that being given a second chance at life was worth every bit of the pain that I endured. However, if I could, I'd remove all the pain that I caused my friends and family; they didn't deserve any of it. We all woke up to what life is really all about, and we all paid the price for that gift.

Wake-Up Call 8

FATHERHOOD

CHAPTER 23

NEW HIGHS

Saying goodbye to the staff at the hospital was a bittersweet experience. Some of them were among the finest people I have ever met, and I will always be grateful to them. However, I still hoped that I would never see them again, apart from a quick social call during my check-up visits to see the doctor. I don't mean that in a bad way, of course, but by that point I was desperate to get back to Egypt and my business and to living life normally. Moreover, I wanted nothing more than to relieve some of the stress that the whole episode had put on my family—especially my parents, who both had aged visibly during the episode.

I have never been able to fully forgive myself for the incredible stress I put everyone through during that time. For a while, everybody's life was turned upside down, and plans were put on hold. *My Rosetta* was docked in the marina for five months while Mum, Dad and Lexi held vigil around my bedside—all day, every day.

My sister had barely tied the knot with Gareth when I fell ill. They spent the first months of their married life traveling from Wales to the hospital to see me every weekend. Meanwhile, my best friends, Tim, Gaz and Marcus, juggled their work and their own family lives around my visiting times to do what they could to keep my spirits up. And then there's Freek, who dropped everything and returned from Aruba to Egypt to run the business when the news first broke that I was seriously sick. He and his wife were in Aruba to explore the possibility of expanding our business into the Caribbean, but all of that was tossed aside when I disappeared down the rabbit hole and into my coma. And, of course, there was the unfailing generosity of Andy and Lindy, who opened their house to anyone and everyone in need of lodgings while visiting me, and who hosted me at their house for six weeks while I recuperated after being discharged.

Just in time for Christmas, Dr. Stevens finally granted me the gift that we'd all been waiting for: I was given a clean bill of health to fly back to Egypt.

Because I was still rather frail, my good friend Gaz insisted that he accompany us. We agreed that he would live with Lexi and me for a few months to give my parents and her a well-earned break and eventually help me get back to work.

So it was that we all boarded a flight back to Egypt in late December 2003. As each day passed Gaz helped me with my physio exercises, took me for walks on the beach, and helped Lexi with life's daily routines. As I gained strength, I gradually returned to work, steadily attempting an hour or so each day until I had fully regained my energy.

Gaz has been my friend since I was 18. I met him when I worked for Northwest Securities. He ran a few car dealerships in town, so our paths crossed regularly, and we became close friends. He was a colorful character then, and he still is. There's never a dull moment when he's around; he's a lovable rogue.

As soon as I was fully able, the first thing Gaz wanted to do was to throw a celebratory welcome-home party at the house. It was the first time I'd ever hosted a house party (or attended any kind of party, for that matter) where I remained completely sober for the duration and ended up partied-out and tucked up in bed before midnight. Certainly not like the old Paul. Gaz, on the other hand, wasn't quite so well behaved.

All of our friends and neighbors were invited to the house to celebrate my homecoming. It was a low-key affair in comparison to the wild parties that we were accustomed to, but then I wasn't quite the same person either I used to be. Nevertheless, it was great to see all our friends from Hurghada again. We fired up the barbecue, put some music on, chatted on the terrace, and had a few drinks—until Gaz decided to take things a step further.

Unknown to me, he had been given the necessary ingredients by a "new friend" that he had made since his arrival in Hurghada to make "special" brownies. So while everyone enjoyed a civilized evening sipping chilled cocktails and chatting on the terrace, Gaz busied himself in the kitchen, making an enormous batch of what turned out to be super-strength brownies. Then he offered them out as canapés to all my unsuspecting guests, deliberately excluding me, of course. It wasn't long before everyone was completely wasted, spaced out and talking absolute gibberish. He managed to get the entire neighborhood so stoned that one by one they either passed out or staggered dizzily home. As guests left the house that night it must have looked like a scene from a zombie movie. Perhaps Gaz realized he may have gone overboard with the brownie recipe when he was the only person left standing. Before he keeled over himself, rather than throwing the leftovers away, he stashed them in a Tupperware box on a shelf above the fridge and then collapsed out cold on the sofa.

The next morning, Saeed collected me at 7:30, and we drove straight to the office, leaving everyone left in the house to sleep off their hangovers. However, in my haste, I completely forgot to forewarn Amira, our housekeeper, who was due to arrive soon, that we'd had a bit of a party.

Amira came to the house every morning at 8 o'clock sharp. She could be rather jumpy and high strung at times, not the type to like surprises, and I cringed at the thought of the look on her face when she arrived.

She was a big, buxom Egyptian woman. Take it from me, you wouldn't want to mess with her. At close to 300 pounds, she would have made an intimidating opponent to most sumo wrestlers. She spoke very little English, and my Arabic was limited, so we didn't communicate easily. But she was a jovial, jolly lady and always went about her work humming a happy tune. After the party, there was a lot for her to do. When her initial shock wore off, she switched on her favorite radio station and got to work, singing as she went.

Clearly it was a more arduous workload than usual, so after a while, to catch her breath, Amira made herself a cup of tea and sat down at the kitchen table to take a break. That's when she spotted the Tupperware box. Amira wasn't afraid to admit that after she finished her work, she liked nothing more than to treat herself to a nice cup of sugary tea and a chocolate biscuit, or six.

Finding the cookies beyond moreish, Amira didn't limit herself to just one. Goodness knows how many she consumed, but when Gaz opened the kitchen door an hour later, in his underpants, Amira was sitting at the table, as high as a kite. "*Mish-mumkin* [not possible]," she babbled, her eyes on stalks as her chubby hands swatted away strange and extraordinary beings that she believed to be floating in front of her face.

Gaz put his arm around her. "Are you OK? Is everything all right?" he asked.

She was so delirious that she didn't even notice he was there. Then he saw the empty Tupperware tub and quickly put two and two together and realized it was his fault that Amira was utterly smashed.

He'd already got the majority of the neighborhood stoned the night before, and now getting Amira into this state was beyond the pale. Rather than coming clean to me, which would have been the sensible thing to do, Gaz made a call to the team of bouncers at Papa's Beach Club. He knew they would have just knocked off from their night shift and would most likely be winding down in a nearby café.

"I've got a bit of an emergency here, lad. I need your help at Paul's house," Gaz told one of the bouncers over the phone. "Please get here as soon as you can," he pleaded, as Amira's head rolled forward and slumped onto the table.

Now, the last time anyone had been called to my house in an emergency was the day that I was rushed to hospital, so the bouncers, who also didn't speak particularly good English, could be forgiven for assuming the worst when they heard the words "emergency, Paul's house, help."

Meanwhile, I was in my office, drinking a latte, happily counting my money, unaware at that moment that 10 bouncers had arrived at my house, and kicked the front door off its hinges. They had expected to find me in some state of distress, but instead they discovered a 300-pound lady on a chair in the kitchen and Gaz dancing around in a state of panic, in his Y-fronts, trying hopelessly to be helpful but unable to conceal his guilt.

"We need to get her home before Paul finds out," Gaz said to the bouncers, hoping that they knew where Amira lived.

"*Yalla*, pick her up," one of the bouncers said. They formed a scrum around Amira and carried her out of the house and into the back of a car waiting outside.

"We will take her home. She needs to sleep," one of the bouncers assured Gaz before they all sped off in a convoy and left Gaz standing in a plume of dust in the frame of the broken doorway.

Aware that he needed to fix the door and hide all the evidence, Gaz then called Saeed. "I need you to come over with your toolbox and help me with a few things around the house," he said. Saeed, always on hand to help, came within minutes, and together they re-attached the door.

"Thanks, brother!" Gaz said as he hugged Saeed after the door was safely back on its hinges. "Paul will never need to know. If he finds out, I'll know who told him."

"Don't worry, Mr. Gaz. I won't tell the boss," Saeed assured him, even though Gaz was joking.

Satisfied that he'd taken care of the problem, Gaz finished cleaning up the parts of the house where Amira had left off. Once no traces of evidence could be found, he lay back down on the sofa to nurse his hangover.

The next morning, I got up and went to work as usual. I was still oblivious to what had happened to Amira the previous morning. Gaz had remained tight-lipped, as had all the bouncers and Saeed. However, the problem came when Amira didn't show up at her usual 8 a.m. Still not willing to confess to what had happened, Gaz took it upon himself to cover for her and do the housework for the day, hoping that she would return to work the next day.

So, Gaz got started on cleaning the house. He ironed my shirts, cleaned my bathroom, and scrubbed my toilet and made everything in the house sparkle the same way that Amira would. All so that I wouldn't discover that Amira had gone AWOL.

Unfortunately for Gaz, Amira didn't come back for a whole month, and he had to keep up the pretense, while Lexi and I remained completely oblivious. Finally, poor Amira returned to work, but it wasn't long before Gaz was up to his usual antics and the next ridiculous thing happened. This would be the final straw for Amira.

There was a Hollywood-themed party at Papa's Bar and Gaz went dressed as Captain Jack Sparrow from *Pirates of the Caribbean*. True to form, he got fully into character and was the life and soul of the party for the whole night. However, while he was on the dance floor having had too many beers, he tripped, fell awkwardly and smacked his face on the ground, knocking out a tooth and giving himself a nasty cut above the eye. The fall wasn't enough to put an end to his night though, so he cleaned himself up using the first-aid box from behind the bar, secured a bandage over his eye with his pirate's eye patch, and carried on with the revelry until the wee hours of the morning.

As the sun was coming up, he staggered back along the beach to our house, still fully clothed in his pirate costume, which looked all the more authentic with the addition of a blood-stained bandage and broken tooth. He was so drunk that he had forgotten his wallet and keys at the bar, so when he arrived at the door, he wasn't able to let himself in. Rather than throwing a stone at my window to wake me up, he decided not to bother anyone and curled up on a deck chair on the terrace and went to sleep.

Six hours later he woke up blistered, burnt and completely parched. Aching to be let in and to down a glass of water, he peered through the kitchen window. Amira was busily sweeping the kitchen floor. He knocked on the windowpane to get her attention, and when she looked up, she got the fright of her life. She saw a sunburned, toothless madman covered in blood, wielding a sword, trying to break into the house. Amira screamed in horror at the sight of him, dropped her broom, grabbed her purse, and fled from the house in terror.

We never did see Amira again after that, and I always wondered what I'd done for her to leave so abruptly, until Gaz confessed on his last night in Hurghada that he had almost given that poor lady a heart attack on a couple of occasions. The first was when she ate the cookies, and the second was when she thought a sword-wielding maniac was breaking into the house. "And of course, there were all the other times that she had to vacuum around me while I lay on the sofa, scratching my bollocks," he chuckled. "I'm not sure how much more of me she could take."

"None evidently," I joked, "The woman is permanently traumatized! Probably just as well that you are going home soon."

I knew I'd be sad to see him go, and I was sad to lose Amira, too, for that matter. Since my illness, I hadn't had too many things to laugh about, and having Gaz and Amira around served as a reminder that laughter really can be the best medicine.

CHAPTER 24

THE MEANING OF LIFE

'll be the first to admit that I hadn't been the best boyfriend in the world. I'd made my fair share of mistakes. However, once Lexi and I decided to start afresh by moving to Egypt, I did my best to make it up to her. But that was before I got sick. After that, I really put her to the test. For a long time, she didn't know if I was going to live or die. She sat at my bedside day in and day out without knowing if we were ever going to return to the life we had made together. That kind of stress is often too much for a person, and Lexi was only 24 years old when, overnight, she went from being a happy-go-lucky free spirit to having to handle the horrors of the air ambulance, coma and the ICU. That changed everything.

Sometimes I look back and wonder what would have become of us if I hadn't got pancreatitis. I question what our lives would have been like and whether Lexi would have stayed with me if I'd never gotten ill and she didn't have to go through all of that.

When we returned to Egypt, something inside me had changed irreversibly, and I wanted to reject every part of me that was a reminder of the old Paul. I certainly didn't want to hurt her, but I could sense that we were both deeply affected in many ways by my illness. I honestly felt that if she had been given the opportunity, she would have seized the chance to get out and start all over again on her own.

The whole experience had taken its toll, and the cracks were showing. We became more and more distant and spent large amounts of time apart, despite often being in the same room. I just didn't have the heart to say, "It's over." Although, I thought about it many times, and it made me feel physically sick. Who could fall out of love with someone who had given so much of herself? What kind of person would that make me? I hated myself for it, but I knew the feeling wouldn't go away. Secretly I hoped she would make the first move, and being back at work full-time helped me take my mind off it.

Freek and I had begun working on an exciting new expansion plan for Papa's Beach Club, and we aimed to launch the new-look club and season of events with an impressive entertainment lineup, and to help make the improvements, I signed up a new dance and entertainment agency from the UK. The owner was an energetic, playful young woman called Aimee, and she quickly became the perfect distraction from the deepening rift at home.

I found myself emailing and calling Aimee at the slightest excuse. She was forward, funny and flirtatious. She was a refreshing change from what had been the norm of my life over the last six months, when I felt at times like I had completely lost my masculinity and dignity. She was a breath of fresh air, and very quickly our text messages and pictures turned from professional to playful to provocative. It became apparent that I was interested in more than simply making her business acquaintance.

By mid-February, Aimee was booked on a flight to come to Hurghada to spend six days with us to roll out the new show and club design. The night I collected her from the airport, I waited at the arrivals door, furtively hoping that all our flirting and teasing would lead to much more than a just a professional business relationship.

When she pranced through the sliding doors of arrivals, I recognized her instantly. Only a dancer could move like that. Her hair swung in a long, blond ponytail under a pink baseball cap, and she wore a loose, oversized T-shirt. She had hundreds of bangles stacked up on one wrist and a black glove on her other hand. She radiated energy, and as soon as she greeted me with a giggle and wide smile, I knew that we had the same thing in mind.

"Welcome to Hurghada!" I said, and gave her a peck on the cheek. Then, nudging her suggestively, I added, "The flight's taken the shine off your last photo."

"I'm still praying that this isn't some dodgy scam and I'm about to be stolen and sold for a camel," she playfully retorted.

She reached into her handbag and brought out an inch-long penknife and waved it at me in jest.

"What's that for?" I asked, sniggering.

"It's my defense in case you're going to mug me. My dad gave it to me so I could protect myself."

"I don't think you'll be needing that. Tell your dad you're safe with me," I replied.

"Ha! This is a business trip, remember. I didn't tell him I was actually just coming to meet you," she said with a flirtatious smile.

I dropped her off at the Zak hotel, just behind Papa's Bar, and promised to pick her up around nine-ish, leaving her to get a few hours' rest. My heart was pumping as we parted, and she suggestively winked and shook her hips with a saucy "See you later." I got back in the car to head home. Shit! I thought. I'm in trouble this time.

That night, having dinner at home with Lexi, I cleared my plate and mentioned cautiously, "I'm out again tonight, Lex. We've still got lots to do at the club ahead of the launch."

"Yeah," she replied, and took a sip of wine. "You already told me that this morning."

I was trying to read her tone, but I wasn't sure if she was irritated or just being matter-of-fact.

"I've already asked Becky to come over, so stay out as long as you like," she added.

"So you're not mad that I'm out all the time?" I asked.

"Me? Why would I be mad at you?"

I shrugged. "No reason. Just checking you're OK. That's all," I replied, as the guilt crept into my stomach. "OK. I'll see you later."

I grabbed my wallet, shoved it in my pocket, and hurried out the door before she could detect my nerves.

I raced back to the hotel to pick up Aimee. I blasted the car horn as she walked out of the hotel. She was wearing a daring black pinstriped suit that was cut almost to the waist. A black trilby hat was perched seductively at an angle on her head, and a sparkly bra top accentuated her full cleavage. Wow! I thought, as my eyes widened and I took a breath. How the hell am I going to take her out on the town without being noticed?

That was the start of a week-long secret love affair. Aimee made a great impression on us all. She added impact by introducing colorful dancers, dramatic choreography and some pretty raunchy stage and podium shows. By the end of the week, after spending the previous six days trying to find any private place we could to rip each other's clothes off, we knew what we had was more than just a fling. She left her mark on me in more ways than I can mention on these pages. When our steamy week was over, she returned to the UK, but I couldn't get her out of my mind.

It was time to be honest. Lexi could sense that something was amiss. It had been apparent for some time, but because of the obvious circumstances, neither one of us could admit that it was time for us to let go.

All of this was happening a month before by best friend, Tim, was due to get married. Before I went in for my operation, while in my hospital bed, he had read me a letter asking me to be the best man. The wedding was going to take place in April. So, 15 rowdy stags would arrive in Hurghada for a week of fun in the sun for Tim's stag do in March. The timing couldn't have been better.

"You won't want to be here while that rabble is here," I told Lexi slyly. "Why don't you go and take a week somewhere with the girls or go see your parents for a while."

Thinking of my ulterior motive, I figured that if Lexi went away for a few weeks, I could arrange for Aimee to join the party. No sooner had she agreed to book her flight than Aimee received a message on her phone: "Come back for a week. I miss you."

Aimee and some of her friends returned to Hurghada, and together with the lads, we enjoyed diving-boat trips, lazy days on the beach, loud nights at the club, and relaxing afternoons of laughter on the terrace at the house. Throughout the week I remained completely sober, of course, and I had never felt so alive and sure of where my new life was heading. By the end of the week, I was certain this was my new girl.

When Lexi returned from her week away, we took a long walk on the beach, as we had done so many times in the past. With tears in my eyes I told her that it was necessary for me to let her go in order to really change our lives for the better. It was the hardest conversation I'd ever had, and she agreed she felt the same way. She'd had enough and decided she wanted to return to life in England. We hugged and cried as we walked along the shore, and I hoped that I would never come to regret our decision after everything we'd been through.

The following month, Lexi packed up and moved back to UK. She was accepted into college to study nursing, something she was extremely excited about. I helped her settle into a lovely new flat close to her parents' house and bought her a little car as a parting gift, so that she had everything she needed to start over. I kissed her before saying goodbye and knew that it would probably be the last time I'd see her. "I love you, Paul," she said, showing confidence well beyond her years, "but I know this is best for both of us."

I attended Tim's big day as his best man before heading back to Hurghada as a single man. Of course, I didn't remain single for long. Aimee moved from England to Hurghada permanently in May, and 24 months later, she would return to the UK to deliver our son Cole. I was about to become a father.

CHAPTER 25

FIRE!

On a mild September day in 2005, as the sun dipped behind the palm trees, Freek and I took a moment on the deck at Papa's Bar to toast the future. We had just signed a momentous deal that would further ignite the region's nightlife and catapult Egypt's club scene onto the world stage. The 1990s brought the dawn of the megastar DJ era, and by the early 2000s, super-clubs were in full swing around the world. The most renowned name in the business was Ministry of Sound, and we had just signed them as our partners.

Earlier that day, Freek and I signed a contract to build two new venues on the beach in Hurghada under the Ministry of Sound name. We pledged to complete both projects by the end of the year, giving us only three months. One was to be named Ministry of Sound Beach. A loud, raucous, 3,000-capacity, open-air venue, it was destined to become the biggest night-club in the Middle East. The second club, positioned a few miles farther along the beachfront, to be named Ministry of Sound The Bar and would be the quieter sibling, offering a more relaxed lounge vibe.

We knew the timescale was ambitious and that there was a risk that we might have bitten off more than we could chew. However, after being in a coma, I believed that time was a perception to be experienced personally. It was obvious to me that the larger the opportunity, the greater the risk, but I also knew that by exerting massive action into every available second, we could maximize time and therefore make the seemingly impossible, possible.

Since recovering from such an acute illness, I wanted to think in bigger terms than I had before. I wanted to reject any limitations or boundaries. My drive to make my time on earth matter this time around was permanently at the forefront of my mind. Fortunately for me, Freek was on my wavelength, too. He was always as eager as I was to seize every opportunity, and he knew as well as I did how big the Ministry of Sound deal was for us.

"If we hammer it, we'll be ready to open for Christmas," Freek assured me, pondering the timeline for construction.

"Let's give it all we've got," I agreed. "To have both clubs open in December would be absolute gold."

Freek raised his eyebrows and puffed out his chest proudly. "We'd better get moving then," he joked. "If the Ministry of Sound guys are going to visit us on Boxing Day it means we've got only ten weeks to build two clubs."

"Then let's aim to open The Bar first, on December 19th, and then go large with an opening party for 3,000 people at MOS The Beach on New Year's Eve," I suggested excitedly. I patted him on the shoulder and smiled at him. "Mate, if it was anyone else, I'd think they were crazy! I know just how fucking crazy we are—so I know we can do it."

Freek placed his arm round my neck and stretched his other hand out in front of us, pointing his bottle across the sprawling landscape of Papa's Bar and down to the white-sand beach and crystal sea beyond. "Look," he said proudly, "a few years ago this place was a little bar on the beach, and now look at it. Hey, we've been through a lot in that time. But fuck it. It made us all stronger. We know what we need to do. We'll build it on time."

Then with a playful smirk, he added, "We just have to make sure absolutely nothing goes wrong."

"Love you, man," I said, clinking his bottle with my bottle of Diet Coke. "Cheers. Let's give them the best damn club they've ever seen."

The days of September, October and November were executed with near-military precision. Every minute of every day was meticulously planned. Our dedicated teams of architects, designers, entertainers and operational experts worked tirelessly to an organized plan of drawings, checklists and schedules, constantly monitoring and actioning every detail to the highest standard.

When December rolled around, both venues were ahead of schedule and near completion. We were immensely proud of our team's achievement; after all, it's not often that projects are ahead of schedule in the construction business, especially projects with such ambitious timescales.

On December 18, the night before the grand opening, as the finishing touches were being made, I walked around the bar and admired its cobalt blue, plush velvet seating and fresh white tables. From its high thatched ceilings, flowing material hung and billowed seductively in the breeze. A round DJ booth with enormous lighting rigs and an impressive sound system was positioned prominently on a raised platform in front of a feature waterfall, and on the opposite side of the room, a large cocktail bar backlit with a wall of blue lights was being stocked by the bar staff with colorful bottles and glassware. The massive room opened onto a vast beachfront deck of sun-loungers and hammocks stretching out into the twinkling blue sea. As I stood back and admired the place, I was sure that as soon as it opened its doors the next day, this bar would become the best place in town for sundowners and chilled-out nights under the stars.

But nothing ever runs so smoothly. Around eight hours later, at 2 a.m., I woke up to the sound of my phone ringing. Everything was about to change.

"Hi, boss. How are you?" Saeed asked.

"It's 2 a.m., Saeed. This had better be good. It's the big day today," I said, yawning.

"Well, boss," he said before pausing, "there's a small fire on the beach at MOS Bar."

On hearing the word *fire,* I sprang out of bed. "Fire? Saeed! Why the fuck are you still on the phone?" I yelled in surprise and panic. "Hang up and put the fucking fire out! I'll be there in a minute!"

I pulled my tracksuit pants on mid-run and fled the house, slamming the door behind me. I flung myself into my jeep and took off at speed along the Sheraton road. I had no idea what to expect.

From a distance, I could see the night sky was lit with an orange glow. I screeched around the corner to catch my first glimpse of what Saeed had described not 10 minutes earlier as "a small fire on the beach."

The entire building was engulfed in raging flames reaching as high as 20 feet in the air. As I got out of the car I could hear the thatched roof crackling and popping while the fire devoured it mercilessly. There was nothing that could be done to save it. I stood and watched helplessly as firefighters doused the flames. I couldn't believe my eyes.

Apparently, the fire started when sparks from a sign maker's welding torch flicked onto the thatched roof. The normally welcoming cool breeze that rose from the sea fanned the tiny embers, which soon spread across the dry tinder and developed into a furious blaze within minutes.

The fire ripped through the interior, destroying everything in its path; the beautiful blue velvet furniture, the cocktail bar and the DJ platform that I had admired only hours before were all reduced to piles of smoldering ash. A few locals gathered and threw buckets of seawater in a feeble attempt to stem the flames, but their efforts were hopeless. All that was salvageable was a portion of the toilet block; the rest was completely destroyed.

"It'll be a while before we solve this problem," I heard a slow, deep voice beside me say as I noted a strong smell of cigarette smoke among the fumes from the fire. I turned to see the city's fire chief standing beside me, dressed in full uniform. "The building is very badly damaged," he sighed as he puffed on his cigarette. "There will be a long investigation."

"Yes, I can see that!" I snapped sarcastically, as I lit a cigarette of my own and scoffed at the irony of a smoking fireman while I tried to process what his comments might imply.

The fire chief took another long draw on his cigarette as he paused to survey the damage. "We must discover how this fire started and make a case. That will take time," he said, then sucked his teeth to emphasize his disapproval.

I frowned. His patronizing attitude was beginning to rile me. He seemed to be reveling in the drama and showed little sympathy for the tragedy unfolding in front of us—on the final day after so much painstaking work.

"Time?" I gasped. "Time is something I don't have! We were supposed to open today! The whole city knows we're opening. Over a thousand people have an invitation to be here tonight. No, my friend, time is something we absolutely do not have."

He looked back at me blankly, as if nothing I had said made any impact on him. It was clear that his only interest was to investigate the case of the fire; he cared not a jot about the business, the opening event, or even the livelihoods that had just gone up in flames. I could sense that it was going to take more than a brief discussion over a cigarette to bring the fire chief around to my way of thinking. I needed a translator, so I called out to Saeed, who by that point was hopping through the piles of ash, covered head to toe in soot, making a pitiful attempt to be useful by shaking a half-liter bottle of water into the smoking debris.

"Tell him we need to be open on Christmas Day, Saeed," I said.

Saeed blinked in disbelief, revealing his eyelids as the only part of his face not black with soot. "What do you mean, boss?" he asked, unsure if he had heard me correctly. "Go on," I continued. "Ask him how long his investigation will take."

Saeed translated my question and said, "He says it will take months, boss. The whole building it burned down." Saeed pointed at the smoking building.

"Yes, Saeed, I can see it's burned down!" I scoffed. "The point is, we haven't got months, have we? We've got days! The Ministry of Sound people will be here in seven days, and all we've got is a burned building to show them."

"Boss, it's not possible," Saeed whispered from the side of his mouth, trying to prevent the fire chief from listening in on our conversation.

I put my arm around Saeed's shoulder and walked him a few steps away to give us some space. "Saeed, listen," I said. "I need you to talk to this guy and find out what he needs to close this case. He has the authority to let us get back to work, or he could sit on this for months. We need to get in and rebuild, and I need you to convince him to sign off in his record book that this was an accidental fire. Convince him there's nothing more to do here, let him go back to bed and grant us the permission to sort this shit out. OK?"

"OK, boss, I know what you mean," said Saeed. "I'll talk to him."

"Good man, Saeed. Now remember, don't come back until you have his approval. OK?" I said, shaking my finger to emphasize my point.

From the other side of the building, I saw that Freek and some of the team had huddled together on the beach. I could see they too were all covered in soot, holding buckets and empty bottles. They looked utterly exhausted, and they were visibly emotional. I joined them and offered some much-needed reassurance. "It's OK, guys. We're going to fix this. I promise," I said, giving them all a group hug. "Why don't you all go back to Papa's Bar, have something to eat and drink, and I'll come to you in an hour with more news. OK?"

As the team members consoled each other, Saeed returned with a skip in his step. He was eager to tell me that the fire chief had agreed to close the case and grant us permission to get back on site as soon as the building was declared safe to re-enter. The fire brigade had obtained statements from onlookers and the signage company. They corroborated the information that sparks from a welding torch caused the fire, so the fire chief agreed to forgo a lengthy investigation.

"Great news! Well done, Saeed," I said, wiping smoky sweat from my face with the sleeve of my T-shirt. I turned to Rami, one of our bar managers, who had been the first on the scene of the fire. "Rami, take Saeed and the rest of the team back to Papa's Bar, give them towels and whatever else they need to get cleaned up, and ask the chef to rustle up some food.

"Sure thing, boss. It's been a long night," Rami replied. "Everyone could do with some rest and something to eat."

"I'll come over in an hour or so, and then we'll all re-group and figure out what we are going to do to get this show back on the road," I said, as Rami and the rest of the team began to make their way along the beach to Papa's Bar.

I stood on the beach with my back to the smoldering rubble and watched my team walk away. How the hell am I going to fix this? I wondered. It would take a while to figure it out, but with permission to get back on site, I had a glimmer of hope that we could salvage something from the ruins.

I climbed back into my jeep and drove home to take a shower and change my clothes. As I drove back along the seafront road with the fresh air blowing in my face, flashbacks of the engulfed building and images of my Ministry of Sound contract going up in flames flashed through my mind. Damn it! I thought. Why is everything so fucking hard? I looked at my blackened, soot-covered hands gripping the steering wheel and felt my heart pounding hard in my chest. The pain and frustration stung my eyes. I pressed the accelerator and let out a roar from the depths of my lungs.

Two hours later, a team of my 20 best managers and supervisors gathered in Papa's Bar, nursing what looked like seriously bad hangovers. If only that were the case! I had to find the right words to motivate them and bring them out of their state of shock. They had worked tirelessly over the last three months, and I was sure they felt like all their efforts had amounted to nothing. It was pure emotional robbery, and now I was about to ask them to pick themselves up, dust themselves off, and to do it all over again, but this time in supersonic time.

I cleared my throat and began. "OK," I said. "There's no easy way to say this, guys. What has happened tonight was the stuff of nightmares. None of you deserve to have your hard work go up in flames, but reality is sometimes a bitch ,and there's nothing you can do about it. What I will say is that I know we have the best team in this town, and it'll take more than a fire to destroy our spirit."

I watched their faces for signs that my words were having a positive effect. I could see the sadness in their eyes as I continued. "This actually isn't the worst thing that could have happened, though. Yes, it's bad. But hey, it's just bricks and mortar! No one died. No one even suffered a scratch. We can rebuild all of it!"

I could see a flicker of hope behind their eyes, and I could feel their confidence resurfacing, so I continued. "So, here's the challenge: We need to be open on the twenty-sixth, and yes, I realize that's only seven days away."

Any signs of enthusiasm in their faces disappeared instantly. Twenty pairs of eyes stared back at me with a mixture of horror and surprise. "Seven days?" I heard someone gasp, followed by an echo of doubting sighs. "It's impossible! How can we build a whole new club in seven days?" said someone else, from the other side of the group. Skeptical chatter swept around the room as all of team agreed that it couldn't be done.

"Guys, we can't give up," I insisted. "We have to pull together and give it our best shot. Yes, we're tired. Yes, we feel defeated, but if we think differently, then we can make the difference. We can do this!"

"So, if you think we really can do it, Paul, we're going to need a bigger team," Rami said. "A huge team, working in shifts, nonstop, twenty-four hours a day."

Everyone took a breath.

"OK, Rami. Now we're getting somewhere," Freek said, jumping in to lend his support. "Yes, we can arrange as many people as we need."

Slowly but surely, they began to get behind the idea that to rebuild from scratch in seven days was possible. "Are we in?" I asked. "Fuck it; let's do it!"

We started the project-management plan all over again, documenting a detailed plan of what was needed, and within the hour we had established that the rebuild could be achieved if we pulled together multiple teams of bricklayers, cement and metal workers, carpenters, and painters and decorators. Each team would work systematically through the venue, from the front to the back, in consecutive waves, nonstop, 24 hours a day until the job was completed.

The first team would rebuild the walls. The next team would dry them off with heat guns. Behind the heat gun team would be a team of plasterers, and behind them the final team would sand down all the walls to ensure we had a flat surface primed for the painters and decorators to begin.

Then we'd start on the floors, compacting, cementing and laying tiles. As soon as each section dried, the next team would follow behind, rebuilding and upholstering the furniture, the cocktail bar and the DJ booth, and installing the waterfall feature. Meanwhile outside, a team of ironmongers would build a new set of frames for the thatched roof, which would be completed in the final stage of the rebuild.

Of course, before the work could begin, we had the monumental task of cleaning up the debris from the fire. I told the team to circulate a message around town that we were willing to pay three times the daily rate to any general laborer who was willing to help immediately until the job was done. As soon as the sun came up, men arrived with shovels and buckets, keen to earn a triple-day's wage. By 9 a.m. we were well underway, with 10 trucks and more than 100 men excavating the burned remnants of what had been MOS Bar 1. And so, the countdown began.

Thirty-six hours later, 70 truckloads of burned debris, black rubble, charred plaster, broken couches, melted plastic and scorched sand had been cleared. The site was finally ready for us to begin the process of re-building, and that's when the conveyor belt system we had planned kicked into gear.

Teams of tradesmen operating simultaneously, wave after wave, completed each task on the checklist. We worked around the clock, stealing only a few moments from time to time to rest on a sun-lounger or nip home for a quick shower and a change of clothes.

Exactly seven days later, on December 25, an excited crowd gathered outside for the opening of the doors at 8 p.m. Inside, where the paint was barely dry, there was a flurry of activity right down to the final seconds. The bar team busily polished glasses and prepared the bar. The DJ tested his equipment, and the dancers practiced their routines. The waiters polished their tables and straightened chairs, while the hostesses were poised and ready for the onslaught of guests as soon as the doors opened.

As the seconds counted down, the only thing left to do was to loop the last length of flowing fabric from the rooftop. Six sewing-machinists worked frantically to stitch and hang the 130-foot-long fabric and, as soon as it was in place, the signal was given to prepare the team for the doors to open.

Because the front door was blocked by 500 people waiting outside on the red carpet to get in, the only way to get the six tailors, their machines and all the leftover material out of the club was to have them wade into the sea and swim around the barrier fence.

And so, as the first guests walked into the glittering venue, the last of the decorators and six seamstresses carrying their sewing machines slipped unnoticed into the sea and onto the neighboring stretch of beach. Seven days after the fire, with zero seconds to spare, we opened.

With the party underway, I found myself a comfy little chair in the corner and quietly passed out.

CHAPTER 26

MIND OVER MATTER

imee blew kisses from the other side of the passport-control barrier, while I waved to her until she finally disappeared from view. It was April 2005, almost exactly one year since she had moved to Hurghada to be with me. In that time, we had lived in what I can only describe as wedded bliss—although we hadn't officially tied the knot.

She was on her way back to England 15 weeks ahead of the much-anticipated arrival of our baby boy. I planned to commute back and forth from Egypt to be with her whenever I could. We both wanted our son to be born in England and thought it was best for Aimee to be around her family for the remainder of the pregnancy and to be in the safest hands when the big day finally came.

Unbeknown to Aimee, during my trips to England to visit her, I also stole time to see Dr. Stevens. I didn't want to worry her during her pregnancy, but shortly after the fire, I had begun experiencing abdominal pain. At the time, I put it down to stress and exhaustion, but I knew that something wasn't right. I got it checked out and to my horror, I discovered that I had developed a pancreatic cyst the size of a grapefruit. The news hit me like a truck. Just as everything in my life was falling into order, now this. It seemed so unfair.

Since my last fateful vodka and Red Bull had plunged me into a coma I had done everything I could to turn my life around. I wanted nothing more than to fix the damage that I had done to myself. I had been determined to overcome my diagnosis as a diabetic. Because Dr. Stevens had left a tiny fragment of my pancreas behind, I believed it was still possible to condition my body to produce enough of its own insulin by following a thorough regime of diet, exercise and careful monitoring of my blood. Despite my efforts to maintain the healthiest lifestyle, my beleaguered pancreas had other plans.

While I should have been overjoyed at the thought of becoming a father for the first time, instead I was afraid that I could become ill all over again. I had no idea how to tell Aimee, so until I knew more, I decided not to tell her a thing.

Dr. Stevens told me that I needed to have the cyst removed immediately. If it popped, almost certainly I'd land back in the ICU. But I was terrified that I would miss the birth of my son, and that wasn't an option.

"Isn't there any other way to get rid of the cyst rather than operating on it?" I asked Dr. Stevens, hoping he might be able to give me some kind of medicine.

"It's like removing a leg, Paul," he replied in his familiar flat tone. "The only way to remove it is to operate."

With each visit to England, I went to see Dr. Stevens on the sly. On the third visit, he booked me in to have the cyst removed in the very same week that our son, Cole, was due to be born.

While I was in Egypt and Aimee was in England, getting rid of the cyst was all I could think about. With each day that passed, I fervently stuck to my health program. It might sound silly, but I actually began meditating and visualizing the cyst being diced, sliced and obliterated by an imaginary army of tiny little warriors inside my body. Every night I lay alone in bed and pictured them attacking the cyst, shredding and chopping it up into miniscule pieces until it was gone.

By the time Aimee called me on July 15, a Friday, to say her first contractions had started, I had convinced myself that my body had destroyed the cyst. Perhaps it was crazy to think that way, but on the upside, it stopped me from feeling so anxious about the alternative outcome, that I could end up back in hospital.

Flights from Hurghada left for England only once a week, on Friday, so I was already booked on a flight for later that day. The excitement of knowing my son was on the way couldn't make the plane fly fast enough. As soon as I touched down in the evening, I fled at breakneck speed to the hospital. Aimee had just been admitted, and her mum and dad were waiting for me in the reception of the maternity ward as I burst through the doors.

"She's fine, Paul. She's having regular contractions now every five minutes or so," Aimee's mum told me happily. "You've made it on time. The midwife just told us that they'll keep her in now. We'll just have to wait for the little man to come."

I was overcome with joy that everything was OK. I had been paranoid that something would happen, and Cole would come early, and I would miss his birth. Or worse, that my pancreas would ruin the whole happy event. I went to the bathroom to wash my face and take a moment to compose myself.

The night passed, as did the next day. It seemed that the waiting would go on forever. After Aimee had spent 36 hours in labor, finally the moment came. I held her hand until the sound of our baby's cry filled the room. All was well. Our son had arrived. The nurses brought him over and placed him in Aimee's arms. No words were spoken. We both just held him, kissed him and together, admired our little son for the first time.

Nothing prepares you for that feeling, for the intensity of the love that courses through your body the first time you hold your new-born child. I felt a seismic shift in my heart. At that moment, nothing in the whole world was more important to me than our son.

Soon afterward, when Aimee and Cole were taken to their new room to rest, I sent a message to all the family back in Egypt: "As the sun rises over the Red Sea, Cole Evans was born, 17th July, 2005."

As much as I wanted to stay with them and watch my little family sleep, I knew there was the business of the cyst to take care of while they rested. I kissed Aimee on the forehead and told her that I'd be back later to visit. Neither of us had slept for nearly 48 hours, so she was completely away with the fairies anyway. I thought it best not to tell her that I was booked for an operation of my own later the next day. The joy of Cole's arrival and the happiness of being a mum was the only thing I wanted her to think about.

Leaving the maternity ward, I dialed Dr. Stevens' number. I confirmed that I'd be there first thing in the morning. I drove back to Aimee's parents' house, battling to stay awake and concentrate on the road. Thoughts raced through my mind. I'd just become a father, but the worry of relapsing and becoming ill again made me feel sick. An intense jumble of relief, worry, joy, fear, doubt, pride, protectiveness and pain gripped me. Raw, inexpressible emotions raged through my body as I pulled up outside the house.

I clasped my hands over my mouth as I felt my stomach lurch. I turned the key in the lock and ran to the bathroom without a second to spare. My body felt like it was going to explode. I threw myself to my knees in front of the toilet bowl and spewed up my guts. The sickness continued until I couldn't produce anything more. As if that wasn't enough, my bowels groaned and twisted painfully, and let's just say I thundered through an extremely unpleasant attack of diarrhea for the next few hours, similar to my E. coli experience.

I lay down on my bed, completely shattered. What the heck had caused that violent reaction? I thought. I couldn't remember eating anything at the hospital. It was a complete mystery. My eyes grew heavy as I my thoughts turned to my son, and I descended into a deep sleep.

The next morning, as I drove into the car park at the hospital, the skies turned gray and the heavens opened. After finding the open parking spot closest to front of the hospital, I ran from the car through the puddles. I greeted the receptionist at the check-in counter and shook the rain water from my hair and shoulders. "Hi. I'm Paul Evans. I'm here for my operation with Dr. Stevens."

The nurses showed me into a room on the ward. They gave me a surgical gown and invited me to make myself comfortable on the bed. "Been there, done that," I said with shrug.

They wheeled me onto a surgical ward and pulled a curtain around the bed. Once they'd performed a few standard tests, Dr. Stevens arrived. He hadn't changed. He was every bit as stern and emotionless as he was the first time I met him. But now, I found his manner reassuring. I think that if I ever saw him in a flap, I'd be seriously worried.

He peered at me over his clipboard and said, "We'll be ready for you in the operating room in a few hours. The nurses will prepare you for an endoscopy now, so I can have a look at you with a camera first before we proceed. OK?"

"Yeah, sure," I replied. I wasn't really sure what else to say. To Dr. Stevens, shoving a camera down my throat was as normal as brushing his teeth in the morning. I wasn't about to remind him that his bedside manner needed a bit of work. I just wanted to get it over and done with as soon as possible so I could get back to Aimee and Cole.

I lay on the operating table and looked up at the sterile ceiling as they administered the anesthetic. I remember counting backward from 10 as I felt the needle scratch the back of my hand. I don't remember counting past five.

A few hours later, I woke up in the recovery ward. I was alone and anxious. I recalled when I woke up after my last surgery and felt like I was a human Christmas cracker that had been pulled apart at the middle. I was petrified to look down under the blankets and see how they had stitched me up this time. What if they'd connected me to hideous drainage pipes like before? I thought. Strangely, though, I didn't feel anything. I didn't feel any numbness or tightness anywhere. I felt totally normal. This is some kick-ass morphine you've got, Dr. Stevens! I joked to myself.

As I came around more, I discovered that super-strength morphine had nothing to do with the way I felt. I wasn't wearing any bandages! I examined my stomach and touched my chest and sides suspiciously in total shock and surprise. Where are all the stitches? Have I had the operation yet? Then I panicked. Oh God, am I too ill to be operated on?

I buzzed for the nurse.

"Why haven't you operated on me?" I asked as the nurse entered the room.

"Ah, you're awake, Mr. Evans," she replied warmly. "I'll go and fetch Dr. Stevens."

I was so confused. I didn't know if this was good or bad. Maybe I should have told my family where I was after all. I wondered what Dr. Stevens was about to tell me and prayed for it to be good news.

A few minutes later the doctor arrived. "Well, Paul," he said, "you'll be glad to hear that we didn't find any cyst to remove. It appears your body has taken care of it all by itself."

I stared at him in disbelief. "But it was there before. How has it just gone? Are you sure?" I asked.

Instead of answering me, Dr. Stevens continued. "And further good news, Paul, is that your readings are showing no signs of insulin dependence, which means you are clinically free of diabetes."

I couldn't believe what I was hearing. It was a miracle! I closed my eyes and took a long breath.

"So I'm clear, doctor? No more hospitals, no more diabetes, no more operations?" I asked.

"As far as I'm concerned, Paul, you are free to go and enjoy your life."

I lay in silence and processed how the hell I had made a cyst disappear from my body. Was that what the sickness was all about? Had the excitement of Cole's arrival triggered some kind of chemical reaction, or had the imaginary army really killed the cyst and cured me through mind over matter?

An hour or so later, I walked out of the of the lobby and strode across the car park and inhaled the fresh air. I felt like a new man. I went straight back to the maternity hospital, where Aimee and Cole were preparing to go home. As soon as I saw Aimee I threw my arms around her and kissed her passionately.

"Where have you been, mister?" she asked. "We were about to send out a search party."

"Well, the last time I saw you, you were sound asleep, so I didn't want to wake you and tell you that I had a check-up appointment with Dr. Stevens," I replied. "And the good news is, this daddy isn't diabetic anymore."

WAKE-UP CALL 8
FATHERHOOD

It took seven wake-up calls for me to understand my purpose in life.

It took an eighth to give my life meaning.

Becoming a father upturned my outlook on life in a second. In the same vein, an even deeper understanding, love and respect for my parents blossomed.

I hope my sons don't ever put me through the type of drama that I put my poor parents through. (Just seeing them at the dentist was enough.) One thing is for sure, both my sons will always be the absolute light of my life. All that I do today is for them.

I believe I was always searching for the holy grail of happiness. I can say I found it in fatherhood.

CHAPTER 27

TERRORIST ATTACK

Five days after Cole was born, I headed back to Hurghada with an even more changed outlook on life. I had always been ambitious, and I don't mean to sound boastful, but I had done pretty well for myself. I owned the largest condo on the beach, and I had a range of expensive cars parked in my driveway and a seven-figure sum in my bank account. I was friends with all the movers and shakers in Egypt; my phone stored the personal numbers of the country's most powerful people.

Yet, nothing that I owned and no one who I knew came close to making me feel as good as I did about being a father.

The title came with a whole new set of responsibilities, and this little person who I had known for just over 100 hours had totally changed my world.

After the birth, Aimee stayed behind in England with Cole for a while. I was itching to get back to Egypt. I needed to prepare the house for their return. Besides, I wanted to throw myself into my business even more than I had in the past to ensure that I did everything I could to give my little boy and Aimee all they could ever dream of.

In the earlier part of 2005, before Cole was born, we had turned our ambitions to Sharm El Sheik. Sharm was the tourist capital of Egypt. My company, Solutions Leisure, already had the lion's share of the hospitality and entertainment sector in Hurghada. If there was a bar, restaurant or club in town that was worth going to, it was likely that we owned it. It was the natural progression to expand our Ministry of Sound franchise and our beloved Papa's Bar brand across the water.

The expansion meant long road trips and ferry crossings every weekend. I would get up on Saturday morning and leave on the 6 o'clock ferry from Hurghada to Sharm El Sheikh. I'd spend the whole weekend there, and then, because there was no return ferry late at night, I'd drive 550 miles up along the Gulf of Suez, around the tip of the gulf, and back down the other side, following the coastal road back to the Red Sea town of Hurghada.

Our first bar in Sharm El Sheik was Papa's Tavern. Soon after we opened it, we signed a contract to partner with the world-famous Pacha nightclub in Naama Bay. That was a deal to bring our Ministry of Sound franchise to Pacha every Friday and Saturday night. It was a very exciting time.

The weekend that I arrived back in Egypt after Cole was born was the first weekend we were scheduled to run Ministry of Sound at Pacha. I flew in the day before, and after a rough sleep, I boarded the ferry the next morning and crossed the Red Sea to meet the team in Sharm and run through the final details for the event.

I remember it well; it was Friday, July 22, 2005.

The team was well organized. They ran me through the event plan and informed me that ticket sales were going well. The DJ had arrived from Ibiza and was already relaxing in his hotel ahead of the gig. The decorations were being installed, and flyers and ads were being distributed at the airport and in key tourist locations across the city. The word on the street was that people were buzzing with excitement about the event.

Later that afternoon, I did a walk-around at Pacha with the PR team and satisfied myself that everything was ready. Still feeling tired from the crazy week I'd had, I went back to my hotel room to relax and have a shower and something to eat. I would head out again for the big event just after midnight.

I left the hotel feeling refreshed. It was a lovely, bustling summer night in Naama Bay in Sharm's central tourist area. The enticing aroma of grilled food and baked bread filled the air under brightly lit streets and flickering neon signs. The sound of music and laughter spilled out onto the streets from the Naama Bay's hundreds of bustling bars and restaurants. I parked my car, tucked a box of flyers under my arm, and crossed the busy street.

I was just two blocks away from Pacha when I heard the loudest bang. It was like nothing I'd ever heard or felt before. The concrete shook beneath my feet, and I felt vibrations in my chest. Absolute mayhem ensued. Thousands of people were running everywhere. Screams and cries came from every direction. I smelled smoke and detected the acrid taste at the back of my throat. I looked behind me and saw a ball of fire and smoke bellowing from the Ghazala Gardens Hotel.

I stood frozen for a second, not knowing what to do. Amid the hysteria, I wasn't sure if I should go back to my car and try to get away as quickly as possible or run like hell to Pacha. I didn't know which way was the route to safety. I decided to run to Pacha to be with my team and make sure everyone was OK. Perhaps they needed me.

A second blast thundered nearby, followed by another immediately afterward. The scene was apocalyptic as I put my head down and ran for my life. I arrived at the doors of the club and threw myself into the building.

I'd later learn that two of the explosions were car bombs, and the third was a suicide bomber. They detonated with devastating effect near a taxi stand and busy market. Eighty or more people were killed and hundreds more injured in what many now consider the darkest day in Egypt's modern history.

The police and the army locked down the entire street. I stayed at Pacha with the team until the early hours of the morning. We were stuck there until around 6 or 7 o'clock. When the army eventually permitted us to leave, we walked back through Naama Bay. It was like a war zone. The cordoned-off area where one bomb had gone off, near the taxi stand, was about 500 feet in front of me. I felt a lump in my throat and wiped away tears as I witnessed the devastation. Cars were strewn everywhere. Rubble and debris hung dangerously from broken buildings. Body bags and white tents were all over the place. It was a grim and desperate scene.

News of the bombs made headlines back in England. Because the phone lines were down, I hadn't been able to call Aimee. Understandably, she was panicking all night. She tried to call me, but with the lines dead, she feared the worst. Finally, I arrived back at my hotel and was able to make contact and reassure everyone that I was OK, and thankfully everyone in my team was accounted for. It goes without saying that it was a very emotional phone call.

Only tourists were permitted to leave the city—by way of police-escorted bus convoys. They were whisked directly from their hotels to the airport, where they were evacuated home on emergency flights. I had to say in Sharm for a few days, until the road blocks were lifted and I was able to drive the 10 hours back to Hurghada. Alone in the car on that that ride home, I had a very long time to reflect on the meaning of life. How many more times would I elude death? Is it possible that someone or something really is watching over me? I remembered the voice that had called to me through the darkness, that told me to wake up from my coma. Could it be that this was another sign that a more powerful being was directing my fate, or are my second chances and narrow escapes simply to be put down to luck?

CHAPTER 28

LICENSED AND ON THE RUN

After the Sharm bombings, the Egyptian authorities clamped down hard on security and did all they could to boost the economy. To stabilize the tourist industry, endless amounts of money was spent on marketing the country as a prime holiday destination, and the efforts paid off. From 2005 to 2008, the number of tourists visiting Egypt was at the highest level since such records were kept, with more than 2 million people checking into hotels in Hurghada in each of those years.

By then, I owned eight venues. Each one was mobbed every night, and Hurghada itself was buzzing. It seemed we had found a business sweet spot, and all of us were keen to let it continue and move on from the terrible day in Sharm and the dark shadow that it had cast on the region.

Along the beautiful coastline of Hurghada was a derelict marina that had been neglected for years. In March of 2008, I heard through the grapevine that a proposal for its renovation along with a boulevard of shops, restaurants and bars had been approved. The excavation work to flatten and prepare the area for construction had already started. The rumor was that the city council was looking for a developer to propose a concept. Curious to know more about the opportunity, I made calls to a few of my influential business contacts to get the inside scoop.

I discovered that there were funds for the development, but so far, no company had won the bid or been awarded the contract. I was confident that Solutions Leisure had a good chance.

Licensed and on the Run   213

I was in my office in Papa's Beach Club one morning when a call came in from the general of the office of Hurghada City Council. He heard that I had been making inquiries about the project and wanted to see how serious my interest was.

"Yes, Mr. Paul, how are you today, my friend?" he asked before introducing himself. "This is General Mohammed of Hurghada City Council."

I vaguely knew the general through various business interactions. However, his addressing me as "my friend" was a little overly familiar.

"How is the family?" he continued. "Your son, he is growing fast, isn't he?"

In the Arab world, it is often customary to engage in small talk and compliment the other person's family first before doing business. The fact that he was doing this satisfied my assumption that his call was an invitation to pitch.

Then he got straight to the point. "I know that you have made inquiries about the site along the coast, near to your Papa's Beach Club," the general said. "We intend to develop this area into a beautiful marina. I think that it will be a very exciting opportunity for you."

"My friend," he continued, "I will very much like for you to be part of the project; we want only the best quality to be involved."

He waited for me to respond.

"Well thank you, General Mohammed," I replied. "Thank you. Yes, you are right. I can see that there is a lot of potential to develop the area. We have been watching the construction for a while. Perhaps you could run me through the plans and what you are looking for?"

By the time he finished explaining the project to me, General Mohammed had attempted to whet my appetite by offering to include another Papa's Bar within the development. He tried to entice my interest further by discounting the lease price for multiple outlets. I had bigger ideas.

I knew that there weren't many people in Hurghada confident enough to get involved in a project of that scale. The region didn't have enough people who possessed the skills, ability or industry expertise to pull it off. But this was the project I had been waiting for.

The following morning, I sat around the table at our regular team meeting and presented my idea. "Guys, this is our opportunity to raise the bar," I said. "I want to propose that the Solutions Leisure team manage the entire marina. They aren't going to expect us to propose anything of that scale. I really want to give them something to think about. Let's not play small with this. Let's go all in! Let's take over the whole city!"

My team didn't disappoint. They were as excited about my vision as I was. For the rest of the day and into the wee hours of the following morning we sat around the table, chain-smoking cigarettes and drinking bottomless cups of coffee until we had conjured up every conceivable idea from the ludicrous to the luxurious to include in our plan. By 9 o'clock the next morning, I had a glossy prospectus in my hand ready to take to General Mohammed.

Our proposal for Hurghada Marina included a glorious seaside promenade along the banks of the Red Sea. A jetty of beautiful yachts would provide a stunning backdrop to a lively network of streets with an Egyptian souk theme. The streets would be lined with fabulous bars, restaurants and shops. The world-class entertainment would include an arcade, an open-air cinema, a live-music arena and an open-air nightclub. Our version of Hurghada Marina promised to be the tourist hub of the city. It would be alive with colorful street parades, vendors, artists, dancers and performers—enough to amaze every visitor from sunrise to sunset.

The plans for the development included more than 100 bars, restaurants and shops. We predicted a minimum of 20,000 tourists per day. To reach that number, all venues would need to operate at full capacity throughout the peak tourism seasons. We proposed that Solutions Leisure manage all of the site's leasing and control all of the marketing activity.

After the prospectus was hand-delivered by courier to General Mohammed, I waited for him to respond. Two hours later my phone rang.

"Yes, Mr. Paul, *habibi*. "We received your very nice brochure. Thank you!" General Mohammed said. "We would like to talk to you about your ideas some more."

I could tell the general was enthralled.

"Sure, General Mohammed," I said. "I'm delighted you like our plan."

I continued, "General Mohammed, my friend, while I have you on the line, let me just get an understanding of what the current situation is. If I'm right, presently you've got one salesman to rent each unit to individual operators. Am I correct?"

"Yes, that's right," he replied.

"And there are over one hundred units that you need to rent?" I asked.

"That's correct," he affirmed.

"I reckon it'll be impossible for him to do it all single-handedly," I said. "It could take him a year."

I paused to allow him to think about what I was saying. I could almost hear his brain ticking.

"Here's my solution," I said. "I propose that you give the whole lot to me and let us take that headache away. We can work on a management fee, and for that you can rent six or seven venues to me at half price. I'll take a commission off all the rentals. That way, I shoulder all the risk, and you retain the majority of the gross profit. How does that sound?'

General Mohammed went quiet. He knew it made sense.

"Indeed, this idea is a very good one, Paul," he said. "Let's meet to discuss the details, and I'm sure by next week we will have a deal on the table."

He ended the call. I didn't expect a deal to be on the table quite so fast; nothing in Egypt ever moved that quickly, but I was confident it would happen. To my surprise, four weeks later the deal was done and was worth a whopping 25 million dollars.

Now the fun would start.

With the ink on the contract barely dry, I rallied the team and together we rang absolutely every person we knew, starting with the fat cats. These were the retailers, landlords, shopkeepers, tour agents, hotel concierge, land owners and boat buyers. Everyone received a sales call, not just the millionaires. Eight weeks later, we'd rented the whole lot, and what's more, we'd signed contracts with every tour company and hotel in the city to bring us a minimum of two tourist buses per day seven days a week.

We had four months to be ready. Endless days of around-the-clock work ensued. Freek and I managed the construction of 127 venues across the whole site. Freek brought his endlessly creative talent to the project, and I took on the role of fiercely focused developer. (Our relationship is still like that today.) Surviving on only one or two hours of sleep per night, we each had three phones and a walkie-talkie to coordinate a vast team of site workers, architects, engineers and servicemen. Day by day the site took shape, and minute by minute we were on everyone's backs to deliver every tiny detail to perfection.

The administration of the project came with a lot of paperwork and permissions. It was no small undertaking. To build anything in Egypt requires careful navigation through a painfully complicated and outdated fee-paying system. Every stage of the arduous rubber-stamping process carries a fee: fees to get sign-offs from military generals, fees for permissions from police officials, and fees for licenses from government departments, and of course, there are fines for not paying the fees.

Given the project's short schedule, it would have been logical to consolidate all the approvals and licenses for the entire site into one neat license-and-payment bundle. But logic doesn't always apply, so we had to apply for 127 individual business licenses, one for each unit in the complex.

It was a ludicrously lengthy process, and we knew that by the time the doors opened, much of the paperwork could still be in process. But I didn't let documentation delays pose too much of a concern. After all, almost every well-heeled businessman in the city had invested in the project, and having the right people in the right places ensured that the show would go on, paperwork or no paperwork.

The opening ceremony was a triumph. Freek and I stood back proudly as the new Hurghada Marina lit up the night's sky in a spectacular show of lights, fireworks, dancing and live music. Throughout the night, 50,000 people enjoyed themselves along the glittering new boulevard of bars, restaurants, open market stalls, exclusive shops and expensive yachts.

Hurghada Marina quickly became a regional tourist destination. General Mohammed, the investors and the Solutions Leisure Group were the toasts of the town and, for a while, we were all happy.

One Tuesday morning, as I was walking along the boulevard at sunrise, just as the shops were preparing to open, I received a call from Rami, the general manager of the new Papa's Bar. "Boss, I've got to go to Cairo today, to the Ministry of Tourism office," he said. "I need to collect the original license for the bar, so that we can display it in the bar and avoid a fine."

"OK, Rami. Is there anything you need from me?" I asked.

"The guy from the Ministry of Tourism says that he needs 3,000 Egyptian pounds to release the license."

"Ah, OK," I said. I wasn't at all surprised. A fee for releasing a document that I'd already paid for wasn't uncommon.

"Take the money from the safe and bring me the receipt when you get back," I said. "OK, mate?"

"Yes, boss. Thank you. I'll go now and be back by evening," Rami said.

"Drive safe, Rami. See you later." I smiled before hanging up.

I sat down outside one of the coffee shops that looked out to sea and ordered a latte from the waiter and didn't think anything more of the bar license or the fee. I had no idea that our call had been recorded, or that it would be the last time I'd hear from Rami.

Twenty-four hours later, on Wednesday morning, Rami still hadn't returned from Cairo. He hadn't turned up for duty at Papa's Bar the previous evening, as he said he would, and we had been trying to locate him ever since. We hoped that he'd simply had a heavy night in Cairo and that he'd show up eventually, but I knew that would be out of character for him. I was beginning to fear the worst.

At about 8 a.m., I was in the kitchen, making myself some breakfast, when I heard the phone ring. I hoped it was Rami, or someone from the team to tell me that he had turned up with a lame excuse and an apology.

"Paul, it's Ali." Ali was my lawyer, and his tone was even more serious than usual. "I've just heard that Rami is in jail in Cairo."

"What the hell? Why?" I stopped buttering my toast to listen to every word he was about to say.

"It seems he's got himself involved in a bribery case with the Ministry of Tourism," Ali explained in a matter-of-fact way. "Something to do with a payment he made for the Papa's Bar license. Evidently the guy at the MOT is dodgy and has been taking money for issuing permits and any other kind of document that he can charge for. I think this could just be the tip of the iceberg."

My heart sank. This didn't sound good at all. "So the guy that Rami paid, is he in prison too then?" I asked.

"Well yes, he is," Ali said. "And from what I can make out, it is alleged that he has been scamming the system for a long time. Rami's payment is the final one of a long string of similar corruption charges being brought against him. But the reason why Rami was arrested is because it looks like this payment was rigged by the police to catch him."

"But, Ali, it surely hasn't got anything to do with Rami. We already have a license," I said, trying to correct Ali in case he wasn't aware of all the facts.

"I bought and paid for it myself and have a copy of it in Papa's Bar. It was just the original document that Rami was told by the MOT to collect and pay a fee for its release. So surely they'll know that he has done nothing wrong and they'll just let him go, right?"

"Let's hope so, my friend," said Ali doubtfully. "But because Rami met the MOT guy in a hotel, things have become a little complicated for him."

"Hotel? What hotel?" I asked, sounding confused. "Rami didn't mention anything about a hotel. He said he was going to the MOT office."

"It seems that Rami paid the guy in a hotel room, not in the MOT office," Ali explained cynically.

I knew from my own experience that it was quite common for government officials to use hotel lobbies to do business over coffee. That was nothing out of the ordinary, but the exchange of money in a hotel room did seem rather strange. Ali explained that Rami met someone in the hotel lobby and was lured to the hotel room. The person he met was actually an undercover police officer posing as an MOT official. The room he had been taken to was rigged with microphones and cameras, and as soon as Rami made the payment, he was arrested by a team of officers who had been waiting to pounce.

"So what happens now, Ali?" I sighed.

"Now, Paul, we will need you to come to Cairo," Ali instructed.

I put down my coffee cup. "Me? Why? What do they need me for?" I asked, feeling perturbed.

"Rami was recorded making a phone call to you, and he used your money to pay for the bribe," said Ali, as if he was stating the obvious.

The whole dynamic of the conversation quickly shifted.

"Bribe? No one has bribed anyone, Ali!" I was shocked at my sudden involvement.

"Are you saying that the police think Rami and I are somehow involved in this?" I said as my voice rose.

"No, I'm sure they will be aware of all the facts. Don't worry," Ali reassured me. "You just need to come to Cairo to clear everything up. It will all blow over in a few days. Just make sure you bring your passport and an overnight bag."

"Wait! An overnight bag? What the fuck do you mean Ali?" I began to sense that this situation was more serious than Ali wanted me to know.

"Well," he said and then paused. "They will arrest you. You will go in front of the judge to register your name, then you will stay four days in jail until the hearing, where you will be named as a state witness. Then you'll be released. It's simple really."

Ali made it sound like I was a kid going to a sleepover at a friend's house.

"You make that sound really easy, Ali," I said. "But here's the problem: I'm not fucking going to Cairo, and I'm not fucking going to prison!"

Ali tried to talk me round by explaining that in Egypt, the police will arrest all three parties involved in bribery cases: the person who benefitted from the bribe (apparently that was me), the person who made the payment (that was Rami), and the person who took the payment (that was the dodgy MOT officer). Ali said that the court would require me to state on the record that I authorized the payment, for Rami to state that he made the payment, and for us both to stand as state witnesses for the Egyptian government so that it could prosecute the government official.

I sat silently at the kitchen table, shaking my head as I listened to Ali rattle off the likely sequence of events. When he finished, I gave my final reply calmly but firmly. "That's all well and good, Ali, but I'm a husband and a father, and I am not going to Cairo to spend four days in jail for anyone." I ended the call and slammed the handset down on the kitchen table.

Fuck! I thought.

Aimee appeared in the doorway. "Is everything OK?" she asked sleepily. "What was all that about? What's happened to Rami?"

"He's in a bit of trouble, babes. But we'll deal with it. Everything will be fine. Just a silly misunderstanding over a bit of paper. Nothing that a few phone calls won't fix." I was sure that Ali would ring back in a few hours to say he'd sorted it.

But the phone call never came.

Twenty-four hours later, Thursday morning, I still hadn't heard from Ali. So, I headed over to the office at about 10 a.m., as usual, to meet Saeed for the delivery of the cash takings from all our bars. With coffee in hand, I sat down at my desk and began counting and bagging the cash for Saeed to take to the bank. My desk was piled high with thick wedges of notes and coins under a cloud of cigarette smoke, when a call came from an unknown number.

"Paul Evans?" a deep voice asked in a strong Arab accent.

"Yes," I replied cautiously. "This is Colonel Khadir of the Internal Affairs Department."

"Good morning, Colonel Khadir, how can I help you?" I replied, crushing out my cigarette.

"You are aware that your employee, he is arrested and is in Cairo now in bribery case, yes?" he asked in broken English.

"Yes, sir, I was told this yesterday," I said as I lit another cigarette.

"Well, Mr. Paul, you are required to come to Cairo now for state witness purpose and serve for prosecution. Please, you come now."

Colonel Khadir didn't sound like the kind of man who was going to negotiate.

As I tied a bundle of cash with an elastic band, I answered him. "I understand you need me to come to Cairo to help with your inquiries, sir, and of course I will come, but I will not be put in jail for four days. I will come only if I will stay in a hotel with my lawyer. I have done nothing wrong and see no reason why I should be arrested. I have a family and a business that rely on me, and I also have a medical condition."

I waited for his response as I shoveled the bundles of cash into cloth bags.

Nothing we can do, Mr. Paul," said the colonel. "It's a policy in Egypt. You will be arrested, four days later you go in front of a judge, and then you'll be released."

He was the second person who made it sound like being kept in an Egyptian prison for four days was like a walk in the park.

"Yeah? Well I'm not going," I replied bluntly.

"What you mean? You not come?" Colonel Khadir sounded surprised.

"No! I not come!" I shot back at him.

Khadir burst into an indignant tirade in Arabic. I couldn't understand, but his displeasure at my refusal to cooperate was obvious. Spitting with fury, he ended with a threat: "I will come and get you!"

"Speak to my lawyer!" I sneered back. "You can't get me."

The call abruptly ended with that standoff.

I screwed the cigarette butt into the overflowing ashtray, and still in a rage, I rang Ali. The whole situation seemed so absurd. The events of the last 48 hours seemed to be spinning out of control.

Aware that arguing with a high-ranking official probably wasn't the best move, as these guys had a habit of holding grudges, I told Ali, "I've just had some colonel on the phone threatening to come and get me. I don't think he knows quite who he's dealing with here. There's no way on God's earth that anyone in this town is putting me in jail over a silly piece of paper and 3,000 Egyptian pounds! No one will see any sense in it at all. I'm a good guy. I employ thousands of people, and any respected businessmen in Egypt that know me will vouch for me. This is utter bollocks, and this colonel guy needs to calm down. You need to do your job now, Ali, and make this thing go away. The whole thing is pointless."

"Yes, Paul, leave it to me," Ali reassured. "But listen, Paul, I've given this some thought, and I think in the meantime maybe you should go for a little trip to England until this all blows over. When they realize you're not around, they'll proceed with the case. Rami will be the sole state witness, and the case will be closed. The government guy will be prosecuted, and then you can come back."

"You know what, Ali, that's probably not a bad idea," I said. "I think you're probably right: If I'm not here, they can't do much."

I bagged the last bundle of cash, opened the safe, and placed the money inside. I ended the call and took a small metal box from the back of the safe and opened it. Inside were my family's passports. I stuffed them into my pocket and kept one of the cloth bags of cash for myself and left the office.

I got home and met Aimee in the kitchen. I laid out the passports and the cloth money bag on the table. "Babes, listen," I said, "there's something going on."

I pulled up a chair next to me. "Come sit down," I said.

She gave a me a nervous look as she sat down cautiously and looked at the items in front of her. "This is to do with Rami, right?" she asked.

"Yes, babes, but my lawyer, Ali, and I are going to sort it out."

Aimee blinked sharply and looked at me. "Yes, you'd better sort it!" she said. "The whole thing is ridiculous! You said it was nothing and now you're leaving the country? You haven't done anything wrong! C'mon, you're Paul Evans. You fix everything for everyone. Surely you can fix this?"

Babes, the best thing for me to do right now is go to England," I explained, trying to calm her nerves. "Just until Rami is out, and everything gets back to normal."

I took her hand. "It'll all get sorted. Nothing's going to happen to me. It'll maybe just take a few weeks for the court case to close. So, Ali has recommended I go and stay with Tim for a bit and get out of the way."

"Ok," she said. "That seems the best idea, but it'll be just for a few weeks, right? Then you'll be able to come back?"

Her big, brown eyes were searching my face for an answer.

"Aimee, if there is the slightest suggestion that things aren't going to plan, then I will want you to round everyone up and get on a plane back to England, too." I pointed at the passports. "That's why you need to keep these here and not in my safe at work. If I'm not here, you will need to look after everyone, OK?" I picked up the passports and placed them in her hand. "Keep these here in the house. Take this money and keep all of it somewhere safe, just in case I can't come back any sooner." She took the passports and peeked inside the bag of money. "So when are you going to go?" she asked.

"There's a flight tomorrow," I replied.

She giggled flirtatiously and clutched the bag of money close to her chest. "Well, get going, would you. I have some shopping to do."

I checked in at the Thomas Cook counter at Hurghada International Airport the following morning. There was only one regular flight direct to Manchester each week, and as I nodded my way through the usual security questions, I couldn't help but wonder if I had done the right thing by encouraging Aimee and the rest of the family not to come with me.

I put the thought to one side by remembering Ali's assurance that the problem would all go away naturally, if I was outside the country.

"Flying to?" the attendant interrupted my chain of thought with her dull, monotone voice.

"Err, Manchester," I answered.

"Gate 2, boarding at 12:45," she said while haphazardly circling the number and the time in blue pen without looking at the ticket.

"Thank you," I said, offering a smile that was immediately lost on her blank face as she turned to the next customer.

I picked up my hand luggage and briskly walked through a set of sliding double doors toward a line of people at the passport-control desk. When it was my turn to step forward, I handed the immigration officer my passport for him to stamp. He was a slim man in his fifties wearing a uniform of white trousers and white shirt with black military-style details on the shoulders. His hair was dark and thick and combed into place with so much hairspray I thought it might be a toupee. I stared at his hair, looking for signs of balding underneath as he flicked through the pages of my passport. He stopped on the photograph page, took a closer look, and then typed into his computer.

He made a quick radio call to a colleague, who arrived within seconds. They both examined information on the computer screen, and then after agreeing on the point of their discussion, the hair-sprayed man looked up and said, "Ah, no. You no fly. Not possible."

I looked at both men in disbelief, "What do you mean *no fly?*" I noticed four police officers advancing at pace through the sliding doors.

"You have police case. You no fly!" the other man explained as he waved his hands at the police.

"Whoa! Whoa! Whoa! Hang on a minute. What's going on?" I panicked as the four police officers arrived behind me and began grabbing at my wrists to handcuff me.

"You have prosecution case," one of the police officers said flatly. "No fly. You come now to police station."

"Wait!" I ordered, trying to shake my hands free before they cuffed me. "Just wait! There is a mistake! I'll call General Hindawi. He is your boss here in the airport.'

Hearing his name, they relented. "You know General Hindawi?" the police officer who had tried to handcuff me asked.

"Yes, I know him," I said. "He is good friend of mine. We have many businesses together. You let me talk to him."

I hoped that dropping the general's name would be enough to grant me a get-out-of-jail-free card.

General Hindawi arrived a few minutes later, fully dressed in Egyptian military police attire. He stretched out his arms and hugged my shoulders. "Paul, what is happening here my friend?" he asked, as the four police guards stood at attention in a row.

"General, there seems to be some kind of mistake. Your officers are telling me I can't leave the country, that I have to go with them to the police station," I said, trying to make the whole thing sound absurd.

He ordered the officer wearing the toupee out of his chair with a quick flick of his finger and read through the notes that were logged on the computer.

"True, Paul, you are on a no-fly list," said General Hindawi. "You are required by the Ministry of Internal Affairs. The notes here say you are to report to Colonel Khadir in Cairo."

It all made sense. I knew I'd pissed off Colonel Khadir on the phone, but it didn't occur to me that he'd blacklist my name within the immigration department.

"Paul, you have to go to the police station," General Hindawi explained.

"Yes, I know," I agreed. "But if I go to Cairo, they have already told me that they'll put me in jail for four days, and, my friend, you know my medical condition all too well."

General Hindawi smiled at me fondly.

"I'll find another way of ensuring this crazy colonel in Cairo gets the paperwork he needs. I promise," I said. "But please, just let me go and don't handcuff me in the middle of this airport like a criminal. You know I am no criminal."

"OK, let me do one thing, Paul," he said firmly. "I will sanction this release, but you cannot fly. You must go to Cairo and report there yourself. It's up to you, OK? That's the best I can do for you, my friend."

"That's more than enough," I said. "Thank you, my friend, for being so understanding. I will go to Cairo to sort this mess out. I promise."

The general turned to the officers and gave them all instructions in Arabic. They nodded, and the coiffured man handed me back my passport.

"Come, Paul," said General Hindawi. "I'll walk you back to the check-in area."

We walked back through the sliding doors together, through the security baggage check and back into the public area of the airport.

"There is nothing more you can do, Paul," the general said. "You must go to Cairo. The police will put a warrant out for your arrest if you don't. Please don't make things more difficult for yourself in the long run. That is all I can say." He held out his hand. "Take care, my friend."

We shook hands and parted company.

As soon as he left, I turned on my heels and headed back outside into the midday heat. I hailed a taxi and pulled my mobile phone from my pocket and called Aimee.

"Babe, there's been a change of plan," I said. "They wouldn't let me leave the country. They nearly fucking arrested me, so I had to pull favor from General Hindawi to get them to release me. Listen, I need to you to pack me a bag of clothes, and I'll call you back to tell you where to drop it once I've figured all this out. OK? Do not tell anyone you have spoken to me. If anyone asks, tell them that I have gone to England. OK?"

I ended the call without giving her the chance to ask me any questions; it was possible that my call was being recorded.

As the taxi wound through the streets of Hurghada, my mind raced. I needed to figure out where I was going to stay until all of this drama blew over. It wouldn't be long before the police came looking for me at my house, so going home wasn't an option. I called Samir, a friend who owned a property-rental company. I told him I needed to use one of his apartments for a few nights. I didn't want to alarm him that I was in any kind of trouble, so I made up a story that Aimee and I had just had a huge row and I needed somewhere to stay.

"Yeah sure, Paul, no problem," he said. "But be careful. You might like my apartments a bit too much and not want to make up with her."

"That's great, mate. Thanks," said. "And hey, just keep this quiet between us. I don't want the whole town knowing my personal stuff."

"I understand, Paul. No problem," he happily replied.

I called Aimee back. She said that the police had already knocked at the door to ask where I was. "They're parked in a car outside the house, Paul!" I could hear panic in her voice.

"Throw your phone away right now, Aimee, and get rid of the SIM card," I told her.

I hung up, pulled the battery and SIM card out of my phone, and threw them out of the window. I was certain that if the police were outside of my house, they had bugged my phone. So I didn't dare tell Aimee my location. I needed more time to think things through. There was no way I was going to hand myself in and no way I was going to make it easy for them to find me. That way they'd be forced to close the case without me.

I arrived at the apartment that Samir had arranged for me and scoped the area for any police. To my relief, I couldn't see any signs of police anywhere. Just to be sure, I told the taxi driver to loop around and drop me off a few blocks from the door. I made my way back, dipping and ducking amid the chaos of the busy street. I slipped unnoticed into the alleyway that led to the apartment. Samir had left the key in the door, so I let myself in quietly and drew the curtains in each room before I collapsed on the sofa and buried my head in the cushions.

I was on the run.

CHAPTER 29

FRIENDS IN LOW PLACES

I woke up at sunrise with the familiar sound of the call to prayer echoing throughout the city. The streets below were coming alive with the hustle and bustle of shopkeepers and the beeping of car horns and ring of bicycle bells. Although for me, it was strangely quiet in the apartment. All alone, I felt the absence of my wife and son and their usual morning giggles. I walked around the apartment in silence. I hadn't noticed much of my surroundings when I arrived the night before in the dark, but in the morning light, as I peeked out from behind the curtain, I noticed that I was familiar with this neighborhood, as my wife's friend Susie lived in the block directly opposite.

I was very pleasantly surprised by Samir's generosity. The place was tastefully decorated with fresh white walls and colorful Arab-style fabric and furniture. It had all the mod-cons, a large TV with video games, a modern kitchen and a large master bedroom with a bathroom finished in plush marble. "I reckon I can I handle a week or two of this," I said to myself as I turned the taps on full to have a steaming-hot shower. I closed my eyes and let my mind wander as I stood under the gushing water.

I didn't have any experience at how to evade arrest, and I didn't know how long I was going to have to remain hidden. A fortnight maybe, and then the whole charade would be over, I thought. I called upon all the James Bond movies I'd seen and made mental notes of how they did it in the spy movies: untraceable mobile phones, traffic diversions, coded messages, disguises, hiding in shadows and movements in the dead of night. Perhaps some of those ideas might come in handy.

I counted the cash I had in my wallet. It was about 3,000 Egyptian pounds, which was enough for 10 pay-as-you-go mobile phones, or "burners," as we called them. Being ultra-careful not to be seen, I closed the door quietly behind me and headed downstairs.

In Egypt, every shopkeeper has a useful "brother," who can source just about anything. So, it didn't take long to find the kind of phones I was looking for from a local man with a fruit-and-veg shop. "Ten mobiles?" I asked in basic Arabic.

"Yes, yes!" the shopkeeper happily replied, nodding his head. "You wait. My brother he brings!"

He blurted instructions in Arabic to a scruffy kid at the back of the shop. "Aiwa!" the boy replied and then quickly disappeared into the bustling street.

No less than five minutes later, the boy returned with a plastic bag full of burners, handed them to the shopkeeper, grinned at me, and turned on his heels and scurried out of the shop.

"I'll give you 2,000 pounds," I haggled, keeping my wallet in my pocket.

"Twenty-five hundred!" he replied.

I raised an eyebrow and said, "Twenty-two fifty. Done. Final offer."

The shopkeeper held out his hand, opened the cash register without saying a word, and accepted my money. With 10 mobile phones in one bag and some essential groceries in another, I tip-toed back up to the apartment to fix myself some breakfast and plan my next move.

I had no doubt that the phone I had thrown away was being recorded. After all, Rami's calls had been monitored. Because of that, I was pretty sure that Aimee's phone would be tapped, too. There was a possibility that even my parents and business colleagues were under surveillance, so I wasn't going to leave anything to chance. I emptied the bag of phones onto the sofa, I put a few aside for myself and allocated one each to Aimee; Dad; Ali, my lawyer; and Saeed, my trusty assistant.

I dialed Aimee's number first.

"Babes, I need you to come over to the street where Susie lives," I told her. "Drive along the coast road, circle back on yourself, get onto the main highway, circle back again, and come back along the coast road. Be sure no one is following you. Come as soon as you can. And only you. Don't bring Cole. I don't want them to stop you with him in the car. OK? Come alone. Bring some money and some clothes. Tell everyone I'm safe, I'm fine and I'll be in touch soon. Stay outside Susie's door, and I'll find you. And babe, throw away your phone now."

"Ok, baby," Aimee whispered and then hung up.

I saw her from the window a few hours later, her blond hair hidden under a bright pink baseball cap. Bless her, I thought, she's trying not to be noticed. I watched her park her car across the street and make her way up the small lane to Susie's door. I let her stand there for a few minutes while I looked around for anyone loitering suspiciously. There was no one other than a few kids kicking a ball around in the parking lot. I ran halfway down the stairs and opened the window that overlooked Susie's door.

"Psst, Aimee."

She looked up and saw me pointing to the entrance to my apartment below. I ran down to meet her, and when I closed the door behind us, we threw our arms around each other. I could feel she was shaking.

"C'mon, babes," I said, "let's get inside."

We sat on the sofa and talked and hugged for hours. I didn't know when I was going to see her next, so I had to make sure she and Cole had everything they needed and that she could relay as much information as I could give her to Dad, Ali and Saeed. I gave her the phones to distribute.

"Make sure you buy a new burner every few days and throw the old one away," I said. "Never keep the same phone to call me for anything more than a week."

"Ok, got it," she agreed. "What else?"

"When you come to see me here, always circle back a few times. Stop off at a shop or at one of our venues to shake any potential followers off the scent," I said. "Tell everyone else the same. They are definitely going to follow you if you leave directly from home."

"Yes, I know." Her eyes widened, and she lit a cigarette as she spoke. "They are sitting in a car outside the house all the time. It bloody freaks me out."

"Yeah, well, they're not the brightest lot, so I'm pretty sure you'll manage to shake them off," I said, nudging her playfully and then kissing her.

"But what if it all goes wrong? Shouldn't I just take Cole now and get on a plane?" Aimee asked. "What if by their following me everywhere gets you in trouble?"

"Babes, just remember, I didn't do anything wrong," I said. "This is all going to blow over. It's not me they want. It's the fuck-wit who stole 10 million pounds. They'll give up asking me soon enough, and I'll be able to come home." I hugged her. "I promise."

She slipped back though the door after we said our final goodbyes. I felt a lump in my throat as she drove away. Fuck, Paul, you'd better be right! I thought.

A few hours later, my burner rang.

"All right, son, thanks for the new phone. You could've got me a nicer one, though," Dad joked.

"All right, Dad, you OK?"

"Yeah, we're all fine," he said. "We just saw Aimee, and she told us all your plans. How's about I come tomorrow, and I'll bring you a few things? Is there anything you want particularly?"

"Can you bring me some books and a laptop with a week's worth of movies on it, please, Dad?"

"Yes," said Dad "I'll bring some of those chick flicks your mum's been watching, shall I? You like them."

"Very funny," I said as we both giggled.

"See you tomorrow, son."

Dad's voice made me feel normal again. Hearing his silly jokes put me at ease, and I lay back on the sofa and let out a deep breath. I felt my shoulders relax. Fuck 'em! I thought, they aren't going to find me!

In the movies, they don't show James Bond sitting around, waiting for hours with nothing to do in the time between episodes of nail-biting action. Now here I was with so much time on my hands I didn't know what to do with it. I was so fed up. Less than 24 hours ago I was a busy businessman, wired on espresso, with a phone that never stopped ringing and an agenda that would take most men a year to complete. Each night I'd literally get into bed, roll over, kiss the wife, get out, jump in the shower, and do it all over again. Now, I found myself pacing around a strange apartment in silence with nothing to do, no one to talk to, no ringing phone and nowhere to go. I don't remember James Bond ever being this bored.

Following the same directions as I had given to Aimee the day before, Dad dropped by the next day and brought his laptop and food from Mum. So after he left, I settled into a week-long movie binge and waited for Ali's call. But no news came.

One week turned into two, and I was beginning to go crazy. I'd see Dad or Aimee in secret for a few hours every three or four days, but for the most part, I was on my own and becoming increasingly frustrated. I lost my patience regularly with Ali when he'd call to tell me that progress was slow and that the issue of the case still had not been resolved. Meanwhile in Cairo, Colonel Khadir at the Ministry of Internal Affairs remained adamant that I was to report to the police station for arrest. It seemed that the two of us were becoming increasingly entrenched. Neither of us was going to budge, and it seemed my lack of respect was becoming a serious irritant to the colonel.

Two weeks turned into four, and by then the consequences of my actions were bearing down on me, and I began preparing myself to go to jail again. The apartment I was hiding in had become a prison in itself. During the long days on my own, I watched the entire *Banged up Abroad* series about hapless Europeans who found themselves incarcerated in Mexican prisons or Bolivian sweat boxes and asked myself, What's an Egyptian jail going to be like compared with this? I watched every video I could find about the conditions inside foreign prisons, to get an understanding of what I could be faced with if I didn't manage to resolve the situation, so that if the worst did happen, I'd be ready for it.

Then one night after Dad returned home from visiting me, he rang to say he thought that someone had followed him home.

"Are you sure you're not just being paranoid, Dad?" I asked.

"Maybe, Paul, but I'm quite sure that the same car followed me back along the coast road and drove past the house," he said. "You need to be careful."

My phone woke me at around 2:30 a.m. It was Tariq, my accountant. Like all of us, he had friends with a "brother" in the police force. In fact, most of the police were our friends. They ate and drank most days in our venues. His friend's "brother" had given him inside information.

"Boss," he said, "they know where you are, and they are coming for you now! You have to go now, quick! My brother, he just called me now from the station!"

I hung up and called Saeed immediately.

"Come now!" I told him. "They're coming! Don't come to the apartment. I'll find you farther up the highway road!"

I threw some things into a bag, ran downstairs, and fled across the street, down a narrow lane, across a fence, and into the scrubland. I headed in the direction of a long row of palm trees lit up in front of me in the distance, until I scrambled up a sandy verge at the side of the highway road. Saeed's car screeched to a halt beside me minutes later, and we sped off.

"Keep driving! Keep driving!" I said as the panic in my voice rose.

Saeed's little Nissan Sunny's engine revved faster than it ever had as the car roared along the dusty roads and into the night.

It was the middle of the night, so no one apart from my family (and I couldn't contact them) would be able to help me until the morning. Saeed and I drove until the sun came up. At about 7 a.m., we stopped for breakfast and water at a deserted roadside café. Fuck, I thought, that was close!

Soon afterward, I was off the streets and hidden away again, safe in a tiny bedroom in someone's house nearby. I have no idea where I was or whose house I was in, likely one of Saeed's friend's, but I was surely grateful to them for opening their home to me until the dust settled. Later, Samir called and informed me of the next hiding place he could give me.

"I'm sorry, Paul" he said, "this one isn't very fancy, but it's all I have at the moment. As soon as something else comes up, I'll let you know."

But still the nightmare continued, and two months on, I had moved under the cover of darkness to various apartments owned or rented by Samir and other friends spanning a 50-mile radius. I'd lay low in a place only for as long as seven days before disappearing again into the shadows at the slightest suspicion that I was being watched, or when it was possible that a visitor had been tailed. I hadn't seen my son or had any contact with my business, and my tolerance of the situation had all but evaporated. I was paranoid and restless, and the uncertainty of how this was all going to end was eating away at my nerves.

While I was in hiding, Dad had done his best to reason with the colonel and to try to put an end to this standoff, but nothing worked. Khadir dug his heels in and during one heated telephone argument with my father, he asserted that unless I handed myself in, he would even move every Egyptian satellite in the country to find me.

What an asshole, I thought.

There was no way I was going surrender to the colonel and be flung into some filthy Egyptian prison. Despite my innocence, this was still Egypt, and it was impossible to know who to trust. I sure as hell didn't trust the colonel. I wasn't going to compromise and put my faith in the Egyptian judicial system. No way! With tempers reaching boiling point, it was time to up the stakes.

Yet, the political situation in Egypt at the time was heightening. People were understandably being incredibly cautious. The last thing anyone wanted was to get themselves involved in a court case that had already stirred up a hornet's nest with high-ranking government officials. But that was exactly what I was about to ask someone to do. I had to leverage the *wasta*, or influence, of one of my well-connected contacts, someone who could influence the colonel's boss or better still, a high-court judge, to listen to my plea. I had a little black book full of the names of the great and the good, and I thought that surely one of them would vouch for me. But there was one person who was bigger than all the rest.

Without naming names, let's just say "My Big Friend" was about as big as big gets. He was one of the wealthiest and most powerful people in the entire country, and his family and mine had become close over the years. MBF was the only person I thought would pull out the big guns on my behalf. But saying that, I'd never called on a favor of this magnitude before.

I decided to go for it. The phone call lasted all of five seconds.

"I need your help," I said. "I need you to get my case in front of the chief prosecutor. Can you do that?"

"Leave it with me, Paul," MBF said. "I will call you back."

I believe he called the chief prosecutor and suggested that they consider confiscating my passport, my father's passport and my son's passport and then allow me to come to the police station. They'd be able to conduct their interviews and once finished, let me go home or stay in a hotel in Cairo. He made a point of emphasizing my medical condition, so that they would not put me in a cell.

I waited nervously for MBF to call back. When he did, I knew by the tone of his voice that the result wasn't good.

"I'm really sorry, Paul, but I am afraid you have to go to Cairo," he said. "They will hold you there for four days. There is nothing more I can do. They are not in the mood to negotiate."

After three months in hiding I felt beaten. If MBF couldn't help me, then it seemed unlikely that there was any way out of this mess. Perhaps by going on the run I'd actually made it 10 times worse for myself. Because I had pissed off the colonel so much, I feared that the four days I was originally marked down for might be extended. I had turned things over in my head so many times that I couldn't think rationally anymore. There was no logic to it anyway. Fuck it! I thought. It was a gamble, and I was the key to all of it. I finally decided to just let them grab me. At least then it would be over and done with.

But just as I thought I had run out of options, my phone rang. It was Ali, my lawyer, saying he heard they were going to begin court proceedings without me. My knees went weak. Should I believe it? Was this the result I was waiting for? Could this be the work of MBF and he just didn't want to give me false hope? I had no idea, but I was so tired of waiting, I was desperate for it to be true.

The courts and the colonel had insisted that they needed me to be present in order for them to prosecute the government official who had embezzled close to 10 million Egyptian pounds. Were they were going to begin without me?

Later that day, I received call from my friend Omar, the general manager of the Europa Hotel in Hurghada. Omar and I went back years. His hotel had been one of the first to support us with the opening of Ministry of

Sound and Papa's Bar. He was a very smart man, well-educated and from a good family in Cairo. He even had a bit of a legal background, so hearing from him was a reassuring sign, and he sounded very upbeat.

"Paul, I think I've solved this mess for you," He proclaimed proudly. "The judge who is going to try your case is willing to meet you confirm your statement. He has told me personally that he will act as your guarantor. He will take your passport, and you'll have to stay in a hotel in Cairo for the duration of the case, but don't worry, my friend, you'll be OK. Come to the hotel tomorrow at 10 a.m., and the judge and I will talk it all through with you."

It sounded exactly like the proposal that MBF had made to the chief prosecutor. I put two and two together and decided that this was the sign I had been waiting for. And if it wasn't, well, I was fucked anyway.

CHAPTER 30

CHICKENS AND OTHER PRISONERS

It was a sunny morning in Hurghada. At 9:30, Saeed picked me up on the street outside what would be my final hiding place. We drove in silence toward the Europa Hotel to meet Omar, and as we dodged in and out of the traffic, I watched people going about their business and wondered why everything seemed different since the last time I was able to move around the city with such freedom. I figured that maybe nothing had changed at all. Perhaps it was me that was different. After all, I hadn't ventured outside much in the last three months, so that was probably why everything seemed so unfamiliar.

I knew that trusting Omar was my only option to end the standoff between Colonel Khadir and me. I hadn't seen my son or had any direct contact with anyone in my business since I'd gone on the run, so I decided that even if things didn't go my way, by that point a few days in prison was an option worth considering, if it meant that I could be with my family at the end of it all.

The double doors of the hotel's entrance opened directly onto the street. I told Saeed to circle around the block a few times before we stopped, to make sure we weren't being followed. Even though there were no signs of the police, I remained super cautious. We parked outside a small restaurant a little farther down the street and waited in the car until 10:15 a.m. That way I was sure to be the last person to arrive for the meeting with Omar and the judge.

I stepped out of the car and crossed the street. In broad daylight for the first time in ages, I felt as though everyone was looking at me while I briskly made my way toward the brightly lit doors of the Europa. The doorman welcomed me and nodded his head politely as I entered the hotel. I passed the concierge desk and traversed the vast lobby. My eyes searched constantly for signs to trigger an alarm to run, but to my relief, nothing happened. I continued down the corridor to Omar's office with the mounting sense that my ordeal would soon be over.

I walked along a series of long corridors and arrived at the door to Omar's office. Taking a deep breath, I knocked twice before pushing down on the handle and letting myself in. His office was spacious, furnished with the same style furniture and plush carpets as the rest of the hotel. Omar sat behind a large and imposing mahogany desk facing an enormous panoramic window that looked out across the beautiful Red Sea.

When I saw that the judge wasn't in the office with Omar, I knew instantly it was a set up. Omar didn't say a word. He just looked at me, bit his bottom lip, and looked away. I heard the door close behind me and a side-door to my right fling open. Dozens of armed police pointing M14 rifles and handguns burst into the room.

"You fucker!" I shouted at Omar, as the police officers pushed me forward against his desk, and wrestled me to the floor, at gunpoint.

The officers pushed my face into the carpet, clamped handcuffs around my wrists, and bound my ankles so that I couldn't move. I lay trussed up, flat on my chest. The policemen stepped aside, and Omar stood up respectfully as Colonel Khadir entered the room. He was shorter and rounder than I had imagined him to be. He appeared to be around 45 and for all the world looked more like a geeky accountant than a police chief. He had a pale and sinister, balloon-shaped face, little round glasses, and a shiny bald head with short gray hair on the sides. He wore what looked like an expensive dark blue suit that gave him an air of importance. As he slowly paced around me and I could sense his loathing.

"I told you," he sneered at me before turning to his officers and, in Arabic, ordering, "Take him!"

They grabbed my arms and ankles and carried me from Omar's office back along the corridors and though the hotel lobby. Shocked guests and onlookers stood by and gasped. If must have looked like the Egyptian special forces were taking down a terrorist.

That was the last time I ever saw Omar. Perhaps Khadir had found some dirt on him that he could use as leverage. Maybe he had been offered a deal he couldn't refuse to help Khadir catch me. Who knows. But his betrayal felt needlessly cruel.

I was manhandled out of the hotel and pushed carelessly, with my nose sliding along the steel floor, into a police van parked on the pavement in front of the Hotel. A crowd had gathered to witness the drama unfold. Sirens wailed, and blue lights flashed. Six or so police officers jumped into and the van and kicked me heedlessly with their heavy-duty boots. The doors slammed closed, and the van jerked forward.

I was taken to the Ministry of Interior Affairs building, where I was left abandoned, handcuffed, face-down, for about an hour and a half in a cell lit by a dim, flickering strip light. Colonel Khadir was in no hurry to hand me over for new-inmate processing. Instead, he took his time to taunt me. I blocked out his voice and refused to react to his insults. I wasn't going to let that asshole break me, so I fixed my eyes on the light creeping in from below the cell door. I thought of how ironic it was that the only way he had been able to catch me was by resorting to bribery himself. Then I turned my attention to Omar and what I would do to that wanker if I ever saw him again.

Khadir continued to try to intimidate me, prowling around me as I lay bound on the dusty floor. He stopped next to my head, his feet so close that his leather shoes pressed against my nose.

"I told you I'd get you, *kosomak agnabi!*" he growled. I knew that meant "fucking foreigner." Then he sucked the entire contents of his nasal cavity to the back of his throat and spat the disgusting clot into my eye.

"Enjoy the peace of this cell. It won't be like this in Cairo." He laughed malevolently and stamped out a cigarette in front of my face before leaving my cell.

Four hours later, my body was numb from lying on the hard floor with my hands tied behind my back. I lost the feeling in my arms completely, and the strain on my neck sent pain shooting up and down my spine. When the cell door finally opened, a pack of burly officers entered and wrestled me to my feet, giving me a rush of blood to the head that made the room spin. I could feel my muscles tingle with pins and needles from my shoulders all the way down to my fingertips. As the officers pulled me toward the door, I felt heavy and dizzy from being on the stone floor for so long, and my legs buckled with cramps.

"Woah, what the fuck?" I said drowsily, but they paid no attention and dragged me, with my ankles trailing behind, out of the cell and into the lobby, where Colonel Khadir stood waiting for me.

"Now we go to Cairo," he said with a sarcastic smile. "Put him in the van."

The guards carried me outside and without opening the tailgate, threw me into the back of a blue police pickup truck as though they were throwing a garbage bag into a dumpster. Two officers on either side of me jumped in and put their boots on me, using me like I was a human foot stool. Colonel Khadir climbed into the front seat with the driver.

I was certain that by then the news of my arrest was circulating around my friends and sending ripples across the city. I knew help would be on its way, but would it be fast enough to get me out of this?

"Get your fucking feet off me!" I told them, just before feeling a kick to my ribs as the van bounced along the dusty highway. "Untie me!" I demanded, but they ignored me. "Let me sit up for fuck's sake!"

Each time the van hit a bump, my head smacked against the floor, but the police officers' only response was to use their feet to hold me down.

Halfway into the journey, my anger reached the breaking point. I had been in the same position with the handcuffs on for what seemed like an eternity, and I'd had enough. I figured they couldn't beat the crap out of me, shoot me or kill me, so I wriggled and kicked as much as I could until I caused enough of a commotion to make one of the officers bang his hand on the window to signal the driver to pull over.

When the van stopped, I heard Khadir's phone ringing. I understood enough Arabic to know that whoever was on the other end of the telephone was giving him shit in a big way. He got out of the van and paced up and down the side of the road. I screamed, hoping that whoever it was on the phone could hear I was in distress. Colonel Khadir stopped, turned and looked into the back of the van, where I was still lying at the officers' feet.

It was the first time I had seen Colonel Khadir flustered. "Shush," he demanded, pressing his fat fingers to his lips. "Shhhh, shhhh, shhhhhh." He held the mobile phone away from his face and put his other hand over the handset in an attempt to mute the call.

"No, you fucking shush!" I yelled back at him. "Tell your men to get their fucking feet off me now!"

To my amazement, he reached into the van and held the phone to my ear.

"Hello, Paul?" It was MBF. His voice was strong and authoritative. "Are you OK, Paul?"

I glared at the colonel, who was looking sheepish. "No, I'm not OK!" I said. "I've been handcuffed and lying on my face for hours. I'm now pinned on the floor of a truck with police officers' boots on me, and the second they untie me I'm going to go fucking ballistic!"

"Relax, Paul," MBF said. "Trust me, you need to stay as calm as you can. I will handle this. Now give the phone back to the colonel. I will talk to him again. Don't worry."

Colonel Khadir continued to talk to MBF politely. Then he turned and opened the van's tailgate and ordered his officers to let me out.

It was the first time I stood upright since being arrested. My muscles ached, and my body felt bruised all over. I could feel deep cuts around my wrists where the handcuffs dug into my skin. In Arabic, Colonel Khadir instructed the officers to take the cuffs off. Without hesitation, they unlocked the steel from around my wrists. As soon as the metal slipped away, I felt immediate, gratifying relief as the pressure on my shoulders released and my hands were freed.

"*Yalla!*" Colonel Khadir said to me, "take the phone!"

I composed myself as he handed me the handset. I expected to talk to MBF again, but the voice I heard was Aimee's. Her soft tone was so comforting. I could feel tears building in my eyes.

"Paul, are you OK?" Aimee asked.

"Yes, babe, I will be now that I know you and MBF are there," I sniffed, holding back tears.

I turned my back to Colonel Khadir for some privacy. How I wished I could be in the console in Singapore at that moment and teleport myself through the telephone to be with Aimee.

"We know where they are taking you," she said. "Your dad is on his way now with Saeed. Don't worry. MBF knows the senior policeman in Cairo.

He knows this Colonel Khadir guy, and you're going to be treated differently now. We are all over this, Paul. We will sort this shit out."

MBF came back on the line. "Don't worry, Paul," he said. "Everything's under control now, and my lawyer, Lassad, is on the way over. He will meet you in Cairo, OK?"

"Yeah, OK, and thank you." I drew in a huge sigh of relief and ended the call.

Over the previous eight hours or so, I had experienced every emotion possible. After the call, I felt my confidence returning. Things were going to be resolved. I got back in the truck, but this time when the police officers tried to make me sit on the floor, I refused. "Fuck you! I'm sitting here!" I yelled, and sat myself down on the bench.

Colonel Khadir butted in. "No, you can't sit there."

I hurled back at him. "I am sitting on this bench all the way to Cairo, and if you don't like it, you're going to have to drag me off and handcuff me again. I've been on my face all fucking day, and I'm not sitting on the fucking floor!"

"*Yalla*!" one police officer said, urging his colleague to get into the truck.

"*Mash'allah*!" the other officer replied hastily in prayer as he pulled himself into the van and plonked himself on the floor.

I sniggered at how quickly the call from MBF had changed the situation. Only five minutes ago his boots were in my back. Now our roles were reversed.

We arrived in Cairo at 10 p.m. The officers escorted me into the police station, where I was surprised to be greeted by an extremely friendly senior officer, who made an exaggerated point of shaking my hand, offering me the kind of welcome that I'd expect upon arrival as a guest in an upmarket hotel, not the central police station in Cairo.

"Hello, Mr. Paul, I'm Captain Amir," he said, smiling broadly. "Would you like me to arrange for you a drink? Some cigarettes? Some food? Please, sit down."

He was an older man, perhaps in his late 60s, with wiry gray hair. His darkly tanned skin was creased and leathered, which indicated a tough life. Unlike Colonel Khadir, he didn't appear to have any reason to dislike me. He seemed genuine. Assessing my condition, he snapped his fingers and called for me to have a chair, a blanket and a bottle of water immediately.

I sat down and watched him talk to Colonel Khadir behind the glass screen of his office in what appeared to be a very animated and heated exchange. Soon afterward, the colonel left briskly, looking very pissed off. Without even glancing in my direction, he slammed the door behind him. I wondered what they had argued about. Perhaps they were arguing about me?

Was Captain Amir a friend of Colonel Khadir's? I pondered. Or perhaps he was a friend of MBF? I couldn't tell yet. Previous experience taught me that having useful connections is priceless when you're in prison. If Captain Amir was a friend of MBF's, then perhaps my stay would be better than I'd anticipated.

I must have dozed off under the blanket in the waiting room, because about two hours later, a commotion woke me with a start. Captain Amir was finishing his duties for the evening and was bidding farewell to the next officer who had arrived to replace him on the reception desk. Then, as soon as Captain Amir had left the building, in marched Colonel Khadir again, with all guns blazing. His timing was no coincidence and I sussed out pretty quickly that this must have been what the earlier argument was about. Colonel Khadir ordered for me to be put back into the van, and without Captain Amir there to object, I was taken in the middle of the night to the Ministry of Internal Affairs.

I was escorted along a long corridor of iron-doored cells. Near the end of the corridor, in an unoccupied cell was a wooden table and three plastic chairs. "Sit," Colonel Khadir commanded as he pulled out a chair.

The interrogation lasted six exhausting hours. The same questions about the case were asked, in different ways, over and over again. As time went on, sleep deprivation made my speech loose, and I fought to keep my eyes open. Each time my mind became fuzzy and my eyelids heavy, I'd be slapped on the side of the head by the officer in the chair beside me. I suspect Captain Amir had refused to allow Khadir to interrogate me under those conditions.

Although I didn't like him, I could see that Khadir was a clever man. His sharp cross-examination skills were impressive, although despite trying almost every trick in the book, he didn't find what he was looking for. I had nothing to hide regarding the bribery case, and although I had been on the run and caused him much embarrassment, I had nothing to be guilty of. So, finally he conceded and returned me to the police station.

Dad was waiting for me when I arrived, with a tall man who looked like an Arab version of Penn from the duo Penn and Teller. It was obvious to me, given his appearance, that he was Lassad, MBF's lawyer.

This was the man who I had been waiting to meet. He was by far the most powerful lawyer in Egypt, a man used to dealing with high-profile cases for some of the richest people in the world. I felt so humbled that he was standing in front of me and grateful to MBF for sending him to help me. Dad introduced Lassad proudly.

"Hi, Paul," he said as he shook my hand.

"Thank you so much for taking the time to come," I replied. "I can't tell you how much I appreciate your help, although you'll have to excuse my appearance. I've had a rough 24 hours."

"This won't take long," Lassad said as he nodded. "I just need to take down a few details."

We sat in the waiting area, and Lassad scribbled notes in a leather-bound notebook as I recounted as much information about the case as I could and the details of my recent interview with Colonel Khadir in the cell. I wanted to relay as many tiny details as I could remember, but I was physically and mentally exhausted.

"It's OK. I have all I need," Lassad said.

He stood up, looked at me and nodded to Dad. "I'll go to the courthouse now and get things moving. Leave this to me. In the meantime, I suggest you get some sleep."

I thanked him again as he left. Dad and I hugged, then the officer on duty separated us and escorted me downstairs to a filthy, claustrophobic, cockroach-infested cell that would be my home for the coming days. I didn't know what was in store, but I pleaded for this horrendous ordeal to be over. I lay down on the piss-infested mattress as tears rolled down my face. How the fuck had I ended up in prison again? I wondered. I must have cried myself to sleep.

I woke up on the floor of the cell. As I returned to consciousness, I studied the Arabic graffiti on the chalky walls above me. I looked at the scribbles and tried to imagine who had been in this hellish place before me. I wondered what they had done to be put in here, what had happened to them, and where they were now. Maybe they were murderers and rapists? Or maybe they were just guys like me who got caught up in similarly ludicrous situations.

Lassad appeared behind the barred door window. My heart beat anxiously. I knew he had news for me. Dad stood a few paces behind him. Was he going to tell me I was going home, or was the case going court? What had the judge said?

Lassad had presented a plea to the judge highlighting my medical condition. He had asked for it to be noted that I was a high-risk prisoner and that I was only serving as a witness to a crime that had allegedly been committed. Based on that, he had recommended that my case be reviewed and my release granted, immediately.

Considering all that, plus multiple statements providing compelling evidence to exonerate me from any deliberate wrongdoing, we were all sure the judge would rule that the best course of action would be to let me go, or at the very worst, permit me to be held in a hospital rather than a jail cell.

We were wrong.

I saw the stony expression on Lassad's face as he stood in front of me. "The judge has rejected our plea," he said disappointedly. "You will go in front of the court, today."

My heart sank. Dad entered my cell with a bag of clothes that Aimee had packed for me. "Best get dressed, son," he said, and passed me the bag reluctantly. I got dressed and was then handcuffed to a sleepy-looking officer and escorted upstairs into the back of a waiting taxi and taken to the Cairo courthouse.

It seemed odd to me, but according to Saeed it wasn't uncommon, for prisoners to be taken by taxi to the courthouse. So, I climbed into the backseat of the taxi followed by the yawning policeman I was handcuffed to. I sat in the middle. Saeed joined me on my left in case I needed a translator, and Dad sat in the front. We began the 30-minute journey to the courthouse as thoughts of what was going to happen when we got there buzzed through my mind. I was nervous and could feel my heart beating increasingly faster as we bumped along in the back of the car.

When we pulled up outside, the policeman, who still hadn't said very much, opened the door, pulling at my handcuffed wrist. I followed him out of the taxi and joined Dad and Saeed on the pavement in front of the entrance as the taxi drove away. Then, just as we were about to walk up the steps to the courthouse, the policeman froze. Then he began tapping frantically at his hips and pockets with his free hand. He had obviously lost something. He turned to me with a look of shock on his face and asked in broken English, "You have gun?"

I stared back at him in surprise.

He asked again, this time pointing at me impatiently, "You? You take my gun?"

"No, I didn't take your gun," I replied, scoffing at the absurdity of the question.

He turned to Saeed in a state of growing panic. "You! You take my gun?"

"No," Saeed said, shrugging nonchalantly.

The policeman's face lost all its color. It dawned on him that he must have left the firearm somewhere.

He turned to Dad. "You! You take my gun?"

Dad, elegantly replied with an ever-so-calm demeanor, "Firstly, my friend, why would Paul take your gun? After all, he is handcuffed to you. And secondly, why would I take your gun? I'm an old man on my way to a courthouse surrounded by police officers. I think it's likely you've left it in the taxi."

"Oh, gun in taxi. Quick, call taxi. Call taxi," he muttered to himself nervously as he redialed the taxi driver's number and directed him to turn back through the heavy traffic as quickly as possible.

"Is this actually a happening?" I giggled to Dad out of the corner of my mouth. "This guy is fucking useless."

Finally, after we had been standing in a huddle on a street corner for what seemed like ages, with me handcuffed to the agitated officer, the taxi rolled up. The officer threw himself at the door, pulling me with him as he searched the back seat for his gun.

"Ah, I have it!" he said, retrieving it triumphantly from the floor of the cab and returning it to its holster. He turned to us and, with a big smile, said, "Now, we go." Dad and I rolled our eyes in disbelief and followed him into the courthouse.

Lassad met us at the entrance to the courthouse. He, Dad and Saeed went ahead while I was led by my dozy police officer through a side door that opened into a huge iron-barred cage that stretched the entire length of the courtroom. The cage was already full, with about 40 detainees all chained together in one long line. Most of them wore the standard prison-issue white overalls. A sinister-faced police officer cuffed my other wrist to the chain and freed me from my careless supervisor. Then he nudged me forward, threading me along the line.

Inside the cage, was noisy and chaotic. All the prisoners jostled and pushed each other, rattling the bars, shouting and tugging at the chain that bound us together. It was utterly terrifying. These guys were the meanest-looking lineup of Cairo's worst criminals. A line of police officers wearing full riot gear stood in front of the cage, suggesting that absolute mayhem could break out at any time.

I looked out from the cage into the courtroom. The pews were packed with families and legal teams, all waiting nervously amid the noise for their case names to be called. I could see Dad, Lassad and Saeed looking conspicuous as they sat on a wooden pew near the front of the judge's panel. The judge began calling out names and case numbers like he was auctioning cattle. One after the other, prisoners shuffled to the front of the cage to make themselves visible to the judge.

The cage kept filling up as prisoners were added to the chain. The court process was painfully slow. The atmosphere was becoming unbearable. With everyone crammed in like battery chickens, the heat from the sweaty bodies made it stiflingly hot. Finally, "Paul Evans!" I pushed my way to the front of the cage and could see the judge quickly skim-reading my file. Without looking up from his notes or any change of expression, he leaned forward and spoke into his microphone. "*Arbet ayam!*" he called and then placed my papers to one side and moved on to the next case file.

"What? What did he just say?" I was confused and stunned at how quickly he had issued his verdict. My fingers gripped the bars of the cage as I searched for Dad and Lassad to see their reactions. "Saeed! What did he say?" I shouted in a panic.

Saeed turned around and slid along to the end of his pew so I could hear him. "Four days, boss," he said. "He gives you four days in jail."

"And then what?" I asked.

"And then we come back again," said Saeed.

"Fuck!"

My fingers let go of the bars as the other prisoners pushed me to the back of the cage. It was over so quickly, without any explanation or opportunity for appeal. I had to stand and wait in the cage, attached to the chain, until the final case file was heard. Then the riot officers opened the cage door and herded all of us out of the courtroom and into large police trucks, which, in a convoy, took us back to the police station.

"Ok, can someone please explain to me what the fuck's going to happen now?" I asked Lassad when we all congregated back at the station. "Because I really don't fancy getting into that cage with all those stinking bastards again!"

Lassad waved his hands, motioning for us all to remain calm. "We mustn't lose our heads," he said, taking a sip of tea from a polystyrene cup. "We have four days."

"Lose our heads? Too late for that! I think I lost my mind when they arrested me and drove me here at gun point," I scoffed.

"I will get to work and present all the facts of the case to the court and try to get a private meeting with the judge," Lassad said. "Then in four days' time, I'm sorry, Paul, you will have to go back into the cage. But, when the judge reviews your case, because you have done the required four days, you will be released immediately, or he will decide to detain you for a further eight days. But I don't think that is likely."

Dad interrupted. "Whoa! Hang on! What are you talking about? Another eight days? I thought you'd said this was only going to take four days. There has never been any mention that it would be longer than that. We have always been told that Paul would be a state witness and released after four days! What's changed?"

"Yes, four days for the bribery case. That part is true," Lassad agreed. Then he paused. "But as Paul has angered Colonel Khadir so much, he has made things a little more complicated for us."

"Yeah?" I said. "Even if I have pissed him off, I haven't done anything wrong, so I shouldn't be locked up at all. So they can go fuck themselves. Especially Khadir."

"Yes," Lassad said, "there is no question of that, Paul. But let's face it, fairness does not apply. How we play the game will be what gets you out, not what's fair or what's right."

"This is so fucked up," I huffed. "Ok, so why would the judge decide to keep me for longer? And if he does, then what happens?"

Lassad paused to think of how to answer without freaking us all out. "After four days, the judge can decide, for any reason, to prolong a prisoner's detention for another eight days, making that a total of 12 days" he said frankly. "Then on or around the 12th day, another court session happens. At that hearing, he has powers to release, convict or detain for another 31 days."

"Jesus!" I gasped. "So you're telling me if they don't let me go in four days' time, I'll be here for another eight days, and then after that they could keep me for another month?"

"Yes, that's exactly what I'm saying. But I really don't want you guys to worry about it coming to that. It's only the real bad guys that get 31 days, and it's not likely that they're ever getting out, no matter who their lawyer is." Lassad tried to laugh, but his joke landed flat. He adjusted the cuffs of his jacket and coughed awkwardly. "Anyway, we are just looking at four days. So please, let's not upset ourselves with today's result."

For the next four days, while I waited for my upcoming court appearance, Captain Amir kindly opened my cell in the daytime and allowed me to sit upstairs in the waiting area with Dad and any friends who came to see me, on the condition that I didn't try to leave the police station, of course. To pass the time, we'd drink coffee, play cards, and tell stories and jokes. Occasionally, if the door was open, we were able to watch sports on the small TV in the guard's office without him noticing. But at night, I had to return to my grim, graffiti-covered cell with the disgusting pillow and stinking mattress.

On the second day, as I sat with Dad and Saeed, playing cards, the doors of the police station flung open. A group of flustered police officers scurried in from the street, carrying yellow plastic crates. We were hit immediately by the smell, dust and feathers that blew through the doors with them. The policemen began stacking the stinking crates on the floor next to us, coughing and gagging as they set them down one upon the other. We couldn't believe what we were seeing as the waiting area filled up with squawking yellow boxes. "Holy fuck," I yelped, "those crates are full of live chickens!"

Trying to make sense of what was going on, we presumed that the police had arrested someone outside with a lorry full of chickens that they didn't know what to do with. Eventually the last of the crates were carried in, leaving us surrounded by yellow towers of flapping birds.

"Saeed, you have to find out what's going on here," I giggled, swatting away tufts of feathers that floated in the air. "Go and ask that officer over there what the fuck is going on." I noticed he was the same officer who had lost his gun the day we went to court, so I was expecting his response to be comical.

Saeed stood up and covered his nose and mouth with his shirt sleeve. He weaved his way carefully around the columns of chirping crates to make his inquiry, as Dad and I sat back chuckling with amusement. The police officer looked serious as he explained the reason for the chicken stockpile. Saeed's body language turned from conveying curiosity to confusion, and when he returned to us, we held our bellies with laughter.

"All the chickens have been arrested," Saeed explained. "Bird flu." He shrugged, looking puzzled. Dad and I roared with laughter.

"Oh my God, Colonel Khadir has lost the plot," I laughed. "This place is mad. First they arrest me for absolutely nothing, and now they're arresting innocent chickens."

We looked at the dopey police officer, who nodded enthusiastically as he pointed at the crates. "Birds. Very dangerous," he warned flatly.

Still laughing, we picked up our chairs and coffee cups, and I made my way down to my dingy cell, joking to the officer as I passed. "Guard, we're going to keep out of the way of those dangerous chickens. We'd rather hang out with the murderers."

"Yes, boss," he replied, unaware of what I found so funny.

On the night before my court appearance, Dad, Saeed and Gary sat with me in the waiting room. There was a different buzz of excitement in the police station that night. I didn't know what was causing the banter, but it was obvious that something on the outside was happening. I could hear car horns blasting and people cheering on the streets. Captain Amir came over to us, with a big smile on his face. We were all surprised to see him so animated.

"You like football?" he asked us excitedly.

"Like it? We love it!" I replied.

"Tonight we watch football together. Come," he said, waving his hands for us to follow him to his office, where we and all of the guards crammed around a small TV.

It soon became clear that Egypt's biggest football game of the year, between Zamalek and Al-Masri, was about to start. The captain opened a bottle of non-alcoholic beer and handed it to me. "*Insha'*Allah we win!" he beamed.

I took the beer and nodded my thanks to him as the game started. The guards roared with excitement and the car horns continued to blast in the streets. Just like football fans the world over, we sat back with packets of crisps and cold beer and got into the game. It was all extremely surreal. Only three days ago, I was handcuffed and face down in the back of a police truck, having the shit kicked out of me. Now here I was, sitting in jail, watching the biggest football game of the year with Dad, my friends, some prison guards and the captain himself.

But then I fucked up. I made the error of not asking the captain which team he supported. Twenty minutes into the game, Zumalek scored. I presumed that was his team and yelled with excitement. It was instantly evident that I'd picked the wrong team. The captain was so offended at my celebration that he stood up, grabbed the telephone and in Arabic, summoned two officers to come to his office and kick us out of his room. He ordered Dad and my friends to leave immediately and had me taken back to my cell and the door locked.

I lay on my mattress and tried to comprehend the utter madness of the place. Over the din of car horns and cheering from beyond the bars of my cell, I imagined what was going to happen the next day. Lassad had already told me to expect the same sequence of events in court as the last time. I would be cuffed and taken to the courthouse by the police in a cab. I'd have to go back into the cage, but this time he was confident that the judge would release me. Tomorrow was going be a better day. I was sure of it.

The next morning, I stood nervously chained to the other prisoners in the cage in the courtroom and waited for my case number to be called. To my surprise, Lassad appeared at the end of the pew nearest to the cage and curled his finger to call me forward. He looked serious and didn't offer a smile when our eyes met. I leaned forward so I could hear him.

"The prosecution has not presented their evidence yet," said, looking disappointed.

"So what does that mean?' I asked.

"Don't get your hopes up, Paul. It means they have deliberately delayed, and it's likely the judge will have to rule for you to stay for another eight days."

"Those bastards!" I sneered. "Khadir! He did that on purpose!"

My number was called, and just as Lassad predicted, my case couldn't be heard, so the judge ordered that I serve another eight days in detention. I was devastated. This ruling put me into very dangerous waters. The next time we would come to court would be my final chance, and the stakes would be as high as they could be.

I knew four days in this shithole was do-able. Eight days was almost bearable. But if I didn't get out next time, I'd be sentenced to another 31 days and be transferred to the central jail. And that would be a whole new ball game.

The days that followed were a roller coaster, and not just for me. We threw everything we could at the case. Lassad submitted every medical report and financial statement that I was able to produce. And Dad received a letter from the British embassy stating there was "nothing they could do to help," which was a huge blow to our support. Dad responded by resigning from his position as Honorary British Consul in Hurghada. Aimee had contacted three or four tabloid newspapers in the UK that were keen to run my story. But at the last minute we decided that thrusting Egypt into a negative-media spotlight could backfire on us, so we dropped that idea, too. As the days ticked by, it seemed that our resources were drying up.

Stress began to show. I hadn't seen my son since I had gone on the run more than three months ago. The inconsistencies of the judicial system were almost impossible to predict. Colonel Khadir's personal vendetta toward me was unrelenting, and I was beginning to doubt Lassad's influence. I feared there was a real possibility that the next time I went in front of the judge, my life would change forever.

Despite my football faux pas, was that Captain Amir continued to allow me upstairs during the day, and that saved my sanity. Nighttime in the cells was a horrifying experience.

My cell was the last one on the row; the female prisoners' cells were on the other side of my wall. Many of the women were pregnant, and I could hear the guards taunting and beating them throughout the night. I could hear their screams as they were dragged by their hair from their cells and kicked and punched just outside my door.

The prison guards were never held accountable for their actions. They could beat whoever they wanted, whenever they wanted, and were never reprimanded. Most of the prisoners were desperate and very frightened. They would often harm themselves as a way of getting out of their cells. Petrified of the possibility they may end up in the notorious central jail forever, some were willing to do anything.

One night, a guy in the cell opposite mine ripped apart a soda can and slashed his throat with it. I was lying on my mattress when I heard the commotion. I got up and peered out of the window on my tiptoes and saw the blood spurting from his neck, which he had split wide open. I found out later he had died in the cell. Faced with a lifetime in central jail, he decided that slicing his throat was a better option.

To be honest, I toyed with the idea of making myself ill in an attempt to be taken to hospital. I didn't eat for three or four days. However, if I did pass out, there was no guarantee that I'd receive the proper treatment or even be taken to hospital. That was a very risky gamble. I didn't want my case to end up being the one in which an Egyptian judge had to explain why a British national died in one of his prisons.

I had to trust that Lassad knew how to play the game and get me out. There was one constant topic of conversation between Aimee, Dad, Lassad and me in the days before my final appearance in front of the judge. I would lie on my mattress and text them about it incessantly. How should I present myself in court? Should I go into the courtroom looking scruffy or looking smart and clean-shaven? I hadn't shaved since being detained, and on the night before my final court date, I looked like I'd been sleeping rough for months. I just couldn't decide. I was losing my mind with the thought that such a simple thing could cost me my freedom. I had to get it right. Should I go in front of the judge looking like I was on death's door and hope to win his sympathy, or should I go in looking like a well-heeled British businessman obviously in the wrong place at the wrong time?

The debate continued; the messages pinged back and forth, over and over again between us. Smart or scruffy? Shaven or rough? We had to decide which was the best approach. Should I shave and look smart? Yes! Or should I go for sympathy? Yes! Oh God, which decision would be the right one? Round and round, for hours and hours. Finally, we all voted to go with the sympathy plea, so I made the decision not to shave and to present myself in the morning as unkempt and frail.

At 3:30 a.m., I was woken by my phone ringing. It was Aimee in a panic. "MBF just called," she said. "He thinks you need to go smart!"

Sitting up in the dark, I tried to see what time it was. "Babe, you're hysterical," I huffed. "It's 3:30 in the morning. How am I going to shave now? They won't even allow me out of my cell. What am I going to do? They'll be taking me to court at 7 o'clock."

"No, you've got to shave!" she ordered. "MBF has a plan, and you have to look business-like!"

I had to take Aimee's word for it that MBF knew something I didn't. I searched around my cell in the dark and found the blunt Bic razor that I had hidden earlier. I had only a small drop of water left in a plastic bottle, which was of no use at all. I turned to a corner of the cell. It was the second time in my life that I stooped to my knees to behold the water at the bottom of an Egyptian toilet. I tried my best to shave without cutting myself as I leaned over the toilet bowl and hacked away at my beard in the dark and hoped to God that it would be worth it.

At 6 a.m., Dad was allowed into my cell. Seeing what I had done to my face, he had tears in his eyes as he helped to trim and tidy the bits that I'd missed. He hugged me before I was handcuffed once more and loaded into the police van to set off for the courthouse for the last time.

Inside the van I was handcuffed and linked by a chain to 20 other prisoners, some wearing prison-issue whites; some, like me, were permitted to wear civilian clothes. In one long chain gang, we arrived at the courthouse. Our van joined the line of other police vans full of detainees waiting to be processed batch by batch. We waited for what seemed like hours, chained together in the stifling heat. The smell of body odor and raw nerves made me want to retch. Every one of the men I was chained to looked rabid, dangerous and completely unpredictable.

I was unaware that while I was being driven to the courthouse, MBF had arrived in Cairo by private jet from Switzerland to meet with the district attorney. I was due to go in front of the judge at noon. MBF planned to meet with the D.A. at 9 a.m. and offer himself as a guarantor if I was released. Because my phone had been bagged up when I left the police station, there was no way of getting that information to me, and so I was unaware of this huge power move.

A bang on the van door signaled it was our turn to get moving. It was 11:30 a.m. when we all stepped out of the van into the blistering midday sun and headed straight to the courthouse cage. We stood handcuffed together inside the cage, jostling nervously for the court proceedings to begin at noon. When the clock struck 12, the most bizarre thing happened. The judge's mobile phone started ringing. He looked up, turned and looked straight at me. It was the first time I had seen his face. The courtroom fell silent. He answered the call. "*Aiwa,*" he said and continued to talk in Arabic to the caller for about 10 seconds. He ended the call, placed his phone back on the table, and reached for a file in front of him.

"Two, seven, two, six, nine!" he announced.

The guards uncuffed me from the chain and led me from the cage to a step in front of the judge. I stood quivering, while everything around me fell silent. He looked down at me over the rim of his reading glasses and said four words: "You have been released."

I burst into tears.

The relief was unlike anything I have ever felt. I thought I was going to collapse with the sheer emotional release. MBF had made a deal with the district attorney and arranged to have me released under his guardianship. I dread to think what could have happened if that phone call hadn't come through. It doesn't bear thinking about.

The feeling of relief was short-lived. Seconds later, a guard pulled me to one side by the wrists. I didn't understand. I thought I was free to go home. "Didn't the judge just say released?" I asked.

The guard continued to tug at my wrists while the judge ignored me and moved on to the next case number. Another guard appeared on my other side, and I was led away, still handcuffed and completely confused.

Trying to catch eyes with Dad, I saw Lassad making a beeline for me. At a small table at the side of the courtroom, he explained to me that although I was technically released from the court, I was now required to complete an exit procedure and be officially cleared by all other government departments. He explained that over the next 24 hours I'd have to visit the Drugs Enforcement Agency, the Counterterrorism Agency, the Fraud Department and any other prosecution agency and obtain their stamps of approval before I'd be granted full release. But in the meantime, I'd have to go downstairs to the holding cell and wait to be taken back to the police station.

"But I'm free to go!" I protested. "I'm not being put in a cell with all those nutters again!"

But the guard tugged at my wrists as the judge called out yet another number. "You must go down right now," the guard said. "The judge will change his mind if you don't."

As I was led away, I tried to catch sight of Dad, but I couldn't see him anywhere. My heart raced as I was led through a set of double doors and out of the courtroom. I stood at the top of a wide set of stairs and peered down. I could hear the noise of hundreds of men coming from below. I was in a daze as the guards led me down the stairs. The sounds grew louder and louder. At the foot of the stairs we turned a corner to face a large iron door with a small window. Two guards stood at either side. I was now aware that I was to be put into a cell full of the day's convicts.

The guard unlocked the door as we approached. I stepped into the doorway and witnessed the shocking scene of more than 100 men crammed into a room that was about 30 feet by 60 feet. It was so overcrowded that there was only room to stand. I noticed some men huddled in the corners and just about lying on top of each other. It was the most frightening place on earth. The noise was deafening—men shouting and arguing. As I entered, my handcuffs were removed. I felt the shift in the atmosphere. I now wished I had remained scruffy and dirty; I would not have been so obviously the only white guy in that dreadful room.

CHAPTER 31

VIOLENT ATTACK

I tried to stay as close to the door as possible. A cloud of sweat and stale urine hung in the air, making the walls wet and my skin itch. The stares of 100 pairs of convicts' eyes, all fixated in my direction, intensified the already claustrophobic atmosphere. The chaotic noise vibrated around the room and got louder and louder as men in sweat-drenched prison uniforms pushed and jostled all around me. I was trying to avoid any eye contact, when I felt a hand grab at my wrist and pull at my watch. I swatted it away. Then I felt fingers scratching at the back of my neck, pulling on my silver chain. I tugged myself free and felt the chain snap and fall away.

Before I knew it, there were hands everywhere. Frantically, I batted and elbowed them off as I tried to defend my personal space. I could sense I was being pushed through the crowd into a corner, where I was sure I was going to be robbed. I reassured myself that it wasn't me they were interested in. More likely they just wanted my belongings, not that I had any. Then it dawned in me that I'd been separated from the main group of men and pushed around a corner, behind a wall, and into a foul-smelling space with three filthy toilet holes in the ground.

My feet were kicked out from under me, and I landed on my back in a pool of cold piss. The piss stung my eyes. I gasped to catch my breath through the acidic stench. Then five sweaty-faced, sinister-eyed men pinned me to the floor, one on each arm, one on each leg, and one straddled across my chest.

Fuck, I thought, these guys don't want to rob me; they're going to fucking rape me!

The man who was sitting on top of me leaned forward and slowly licked my face from my chin up to my forehead. His heavy breath stank like dog shit. Holy fuck! This was about to go very wrong. I could feel two of the men pulling at my trousers—rough hands with long nails grabbing and scratching at me, squeezing my dick as I tried to kick my legs and force them off me. Everything seemed to be happening in slow motion.

"Let's fuck the foreigner!" I heard the man who was bearing down on my stomach say in Arabic. Then time stood still.

As he said those words, I turned my face to draw a breath and yell in terror. As I did so, a large bead of sweat trickled down his hooked nose and dropped straight into my open mouth and onto my tongue. The salty droplet set off what felt like an atom bomb of anger and repulsion. As my brain registered the taste and made the connection with what it was, I became like a wild animal.

I decided to take these bastards one at a time. I was going to go fast, be hard, be horrific, and do whatever it took. I didn't have a choice. I was going to have to fight with every cell of my being to stop those fuckers from getting my trousers off. If I didn't, something appalling was sure to happen to me. I hadn't survived all the shit in my life just to be violated in this hell hole by these barbaric, evil, raping bastards.

I wrestled my head free and pulled my right arm toward me while one of the men spat in my face. He struggled to keep his grip on my forearm. With his hand close enough to my mouth, I jolted forward and sank my teeth into the fleshy part of his hand between his thumb and first finger. I bit down as hard as I could, locking my jaw and shaking my head until he let go of my arm and pulled away from me, screaming in agony.

With my right arm free, I hammer-fisted the guy on top of me across the jaw, grabbed his ear, and pulled his head down, forcing him off my chest. I pushed my hand into his face as he tried to hold me down. Finding his eye socket, I plunged my thumb into the corner of his eye. Adrenalin-fueled anger pumped through my body as he slumped to the floor, holding his face.

I turned and locked eyes with the guy who was holding my left arm. I roared in his face as I punched him in the eye and grabbed him by the ear. As his head rolled, I pulled his face toward me and bit down on his nose. When I let go, he threw himself backward, stumbling into the stinking toilet hole.

With my arms free, I pushed and twisted myself until I was sitting upright. Two of the men still held on to my legs and were pulling at my trousers. I elbowed the man on my left in the face, while the guy on my right, who was the smallest of them all, surrendered and let go of me. I got to my feet and tackled the guy who I'd just elbowed to the floor. I grabbed him by his hair and smashed his face into the floor.

The next thing I knew, someone from the crowd was pulling at my waist and steering me away from the fight.

I stood up and looked around. There was blood everywhere—on the walls, on the floor, in my mouth. My hands were cut to bits, and my knuckles burst. My clothes were ripped to shreds, blood-stained and covered in the foul contents of the toilet floor. The sun beamed from the barred window on the shit-caked wall on the other side of the room, casting its light in the direction of the cell door.

Between me and the way out of this hellhole stood a wall of Egyptian criminals. I was either going to make it to the door, or they were going to kill me. I took my chances and yelled at the top of my voice as I charged through the crowd, pushing men aside like bowling balls, and hurled myself at the iron door. I humped on it furiously with my bruised fists, stamping bloody handprints all over it.

"Get me out of here!" I screamed through the tiny glass window in the door.

A sleepy-looking policeman peered through the glass and saw the terror in my eyes. His nonchalant expression quickly turned to panic as he hurried to open the lock. I flung myself out and onto the floor as he slammed the door behind me.

He helped me to my knees as I tried to straighten my torn clothes and do my trousers up. Finding me a chair in the corridor, he kept asking me in Arabic what had happened, but I couldn't say a word. I slumped down on the chair and shooed him away. I leaned forward and hung my head to catch my breath and calm myself.

As the adrenalin wore off and my heart slowed, I took a deep breath. I looked at my trembling, bleeding hands and saw my chest and arms covered in blood and God knows what else. I knew I needed to clean myself up as much as I could and get the hell out of there before they discovered the carnage in the cell. The policeman thought that I had been beaten, and I wasn't going to let him think anything different. He hadn't seen what had happened to me. All he had seen was the only white guy in the cell with his shirt ripped to pieces, screaming like a crazy person at the door. He didn't even look inside the cell. He sat back down on his chair at the side of the cell door and continued reading his newspaper.

I pulled my shirt off and used it to wipe my face and body. I spat the mess from my lips, dried my mouth, and then threw away my shirt. I sat bare-chested, ignored the background noise, and listened to my own breath. Concentrating on my innermost thoughts, I processed what had just happened and justified how I felt. I sensed a deep feeling of relief and mercy that the horror of what could have been hadn't happened. I took comfort knowing I had been able to save myself from that. I acknowledged that I had just survived the fight for my life.

I considered what would have become of me had those men overpowered me. Would I be dead? Or worse still, would I have spent the rest of my life suffering from mind-bending mental torture? A deep strength had saved me from a rape that would have most certainly traumatized me forever. That shit you never get over. I thought not about how lucky I was to be alive, but about how grateful I was that I had kept my integrity and forever protected my sanity.

"Boss!" Saeed said as he shook my shoulders, bringing me out of my trance. "What happen? What happen?"

I looked up and saw the concern on his face, but there was no way any living soul was ever going to know what had happened in there. After all, no good would come of it.

"Just been in a bit of a fight. Nothing to worry about," I replied coolly. "Have they told you when we are getting the fuck out of here?"

"Yes, boss. First we go back to the police station. Then from there we will process all that needs to be done to finish the case," he explained. "Then they will release you tomorrow morning. *Yalla!* Let's go. The truck it's waiting."

"Wait, Saeed. I need you to get me a new shirt," I said, still feeling a bit dizzy.

"Shirt? Boss, really, we need to go. The van it's waiting."

"Saeed, I said get me a fucking shirt!" I shouted, giving him no other option.

Looking surprised, he nodded and scurried up the stairs.

I was aware that as soon as I got to the top of the stairs I'd need to have my head back in the game. I needed to look as strong and composed as I could, and although I couldn't stop trembling, I didn't want Dad or any of my friends who may be have been waiting for me back at the police station to have any idea of what had just gone on. While I waited for Saeed to return, I tried to control my sobbing. I'm safe, I thought. I'm OK. It was just a scuffle. I'm getting out of here.

Saeed returned within minutes with a T-shirt and two prison officers who tried to handcuff me. I froze, looked at them, and turned to Saeed. "I don't need cuffs!" I said.

Said pulled out his wallet and slapped some money into each of their hands. They immediately stepped aside and gestured for me to make my way up the stairs as they slipped the money into their pockets.

The top of the stairs opened into the courtroom. This time it was empty, apart from a small huddle of police officers and Dad. He turned and threw his arms around me as I broke down in tears. He hugged me until he felt my shoulders relax and then stood back to take a good look at me. He inspected my cuts and bruises.

"Don't ask," I said. "I'm all right."

We were escorted in single file through the narrow corridor to the waiting police van. Dad helped me up, stepped in, and sat on the bench next to me. Saeed sat opposite as the doors were closed behind us. The engine started, and the van jolted into gear.

The cabin smelled of the same stale sweat and piss as the cell, and I gasped to get some fresh air. I could feel my face turn pale and the bile sting the back of my throat. My head started spinning. I looked at my feet and saw the shitty, bloody gunge from the cell floor stuck to my soles. A memory of the drop of sweat that landed on my tongue flashed in front of my eyes, and I lurched forward and vomited on the floor.

Dad wrapped his arm around my shoulders and pulled me close to him. I leaned into him and buried my head into his chest and howled in relief as the van drove us away.

"It's OK, son. I've got you now."

CHAPTER 32

FREE MAN

Egypt had no centralized criminal data base. So, despite being freed by the judge, I still had to be cleared at each crime agency before I could be released from custody. The Mogamma is a colossal imperial building on Tahir Square in the center of Cairo. This hugely intimidating place served as the headquarters for all of Egypt's government departments. This is where I had to go to have my paperwork processed and obtain permission to go home to my family.

After leaving the courtroom, we were supposed to return to the police station, have one final set of photographs and fingerprints taken, and bring them with us to the Mogamma to be stamped. The traffic was thick and chaotic. I sat in the police van with Dad's arm around me. Visions of the events of the last 18 hours came back to me. I looked away to stem the flood of images in my mind, and I noticed Saeed nervously glancing at his watch as the van bounced and jolted, stopping and starting every few seconds. Saeed leaned over and whispered, "Boss, we will take too long if we go to the station first and then to the Mogamma. I am worried you will not make it in time because of this traffic. If it closes, you will have to come again tomorrow. If that happens, maybe they won't release you until the day after. We have to do something to get there quicker."

Dad and I knew he was right; time was ticking, and if we arrived at the Mogamma in the late afternoon, there was no guarantee we'd collect all the necessary stamps before it closed. That meant another night on the pissy mattress in my cell.

"My friend!" Saeed shouted through the hatch window to the policeman in the front seat. After an animated conversation in Arabic, they appeared to have reached a compromise. Saeed reached into his wallet and pulled out a fistful of notes and passed them through the hatch to him. The policeman counted the cash and put it in his pocket. Then he tapped the driver on the elbow and directed him to take the next exit.

"What's happening, Saeed?" Dad asked. My head still rested comfortably on his shoulder while I thought of how I had shaved from the filthy toilet bowl in my cell that morning.

"We will not go to the police station to collect your papers," Saeed replied with a smile. "To save time, we will make what we need on the way."

No sooner had he finished explaining the change of plan than the van stopped in a lay-by. With the engine still running, the police officer jumped out and jogged across the street. He returned a few minutes later with some white notepaper and a blue inkpad. He handed them both to Dad through the hatch. "We will go fast," he said. "You make fingerprint on the way." The policeman took his seat quickly, lit a cigarette, and instructed the driver to move off.

"You're joking," Dad said, laughing as he placed the ink pad and paper on the bench between us. "This is going to get messy. Give me your thumb, Paul."

Waking me from another vivid flashback, Dad took my hand and opened the lid of the inkpad. The van jerked forward and then stopped abruptly, making the palm of my hand slide across the ink and turning blue.

"Oops," I said, "one down, nine to go." I giggled at Dad as the van rocked, and my fingerprint smudged onto the paper. I felt relieved that the absurdity of what we were being asked to do interrupted, momentarily, my memories of the courtroom and the jail cell.

Trying our best to concentrate and hold steady, we couldn't help but laugh as we were thrown about in the back of the speeding van. "Two," I said, plunging my finger on the paper just as the van leapt over a speed bump.

"Three." My finger skidded across the inkpad as the van sharply turned a corner. By the time I had pressed all 10 fingers on the page, we had managed to get ink on our faces, noses, ears, trousers and all over the seats. It reminded me of a video I once saw of people trying to drink milkshakes on a roller coaster.

Minutes later, the van stopped the van outside the public library. "Photo here!" the policeman shouted over his shoulder. "*Yalla!*" Hurriedly, we piled out of the van and into the library, where groups of mothers were reading to their young children and students sat with their noses in literature. I was led through the vast room, past the high columns of books. I watched the children's innocent eyes look up in confusion to see a prisoner—beaten, bruised and covered in blue ink—pass by them.

In a small room at the end of the library hall, a shy lady who looked completely lost for words took my mugshot. She blinded me with the flash of her camera. For fuck's sake, when is this day ever going to end! I thought as I shielded my eyes, my spirit feeling truly broken.

"I'm sorry," she whispered, offering some consolation as she quickly printed multiple copies of my photograph before trimming them down to passport-sized pictures.

"'My sister,'" the policeman proudly explained.

She put the photographs in a small envelope and politely gave it to Dad.

"Thank you," Dad said, smiling. "You are very kind."

"*Yalla!* Let's go!" the policeman commanded, and we turned to make our way back past the children who were no longer interested in what they were reading but instead looked wide-eyed at the policeman, pointing in excitement at his gun.

For a moment, I forgot how I appeared—beaten, bruised and covered in blue ink—and caught the eye of one little boy and smiled at him. His mother turned him toward her and covered his face. I don't suppose I can blame her. She just added to the absurdity of the day as we climbed back into the van to head for the Mogamma.

To me, the Mogamma, a dark, concrete superstructure, looked like it was straight out of a sci-fi movie. As we passed through the security gate, the van driver was directed by the guard to drive us to an enormous underground car park that was heavily lined with armed police officers in bulletproof uniforms.

Aside from the prison, the Mogamma was the most intimidating place I'd ever been. Escorted from the van, we shuffled into a tiny and rickety old elevator. It was barely big enough to fit five grown men. Given the size of the building, the logic was lost on me. But in Egypt, nothing ever fully makes sense.

The elevator car moved at such a painfully slow pace that we wished we had taken the stairs. We were crammed in so tightly that Dad's hair tickled my nostrils every time he turned his head. I felt sorry that everyone had to stand so close to me, given that in the past 18 hours I had hadn't slept, I'd shaved in a prison cell toilet, been caged with Egypt's worst criminals, and been severely beaten on the floor of the most squalid shithole imaginable. I had fought to save myself from being raped, been sick on myself, and then to top it off, I had managed to cover myself in blue ink. And my day still wasn't over.

The lift continued to rumble upward until it stopped at a floor that we had not selected. Whoever was waiting for the lift to arrive wasn't in luck; we were already sandwiched in. Until that moment, I had been consumed by my dreams of freedom, but as the door slid open, it revealed an image of what could have been me. A tall white man, with blond hair and about my age, stood on the other side of the door. He was wearing prison-issue white overalls, and he was shackled and flanked by armed police guards.

In the split second that our eyes locked, it was as if each of us could see inside the other man's soul. I could so easily be him, I thought.

Of course, I had no idea who he was or what he had done. I didn't know where he had come from or where he was going, but as I stood there, I felt like I was on the ropes. By the look in his eyes, I knew that he was totally finished. He wasn't going to see his family again; he wasn't going to appreciate the wonders of the world. He was going to disappear.

Maybe he had done something terrible. Or maybe was a business owner just like me and had pissed off the wrong person on the wrong day and was not fortunate enough to know people like MBF. The relief hit me like a steam train through my subconscious when the door slowly slid shut and he was gone.

That poor bastard. I'll never forget him.

The lift stopped on the tenth floor, and the policeman nudged us to move out. The hallways and corridors were wood-paneled and had an air of grandeur from days gone by. Although like most things in Egypt, the building's interior had been unloved and was now in a sorry state of disrepair. We walked to the end of a long corridor of administration offices in which the desks were covered with piles of paper, cups of tea and overflowing ashtrays. There were numerous people about, and I assumed they were employees, but they didn't appear to be doing much of anything. We entered an office in which portraits of Egyptian military figures hung proudly on the walls. I felt the policeman nudge me in the back, signaling me to stand up straight.

"Name?" a middle-aged man in a beige military uniform huffed.

"Paul Evans," I replied.

"Why are you here?" he asked curtly.

"Because I have just been released from a bribery case…"

"What do you know about Israel?" he said, interrupting me before I answered the previous question.

"Err, I don't know anything about Israel."

I was unprepared for his question and hoped that I had given him the correct answer, assuming that he wasn't giving me a general-knowledge test.

"When were you last in Israel?" he asked, looking at me suspiciously.

"I have never been to Israel."

"Do you know anything about the situation in Palestine and the Israelis?" he continued. expressionless.

"No sir, I don't know anything about that."

"OK. You may go," he said, shooing me with the back of his hand.

We backed out of his office gently.

"What the hell was that?" I whispered in Saeed's ear as soon as we were back in the corridor and out of sight.

"Counter Terrorism Department, boss." he replied.

I shook my head in disbelief. Just when I thought things couldn't get any more surreal.

We continued along more corridors that also were occupied by employees who were drinking tea and busy doing nothing.

We entered the next office and were introduced to another official-looking man. He was wearing a beige uniform like the one the guy in the other office wore. I stood at attention without being prompted by the policeman and wondered what ridiculous question he was going to ask me.

"Are you a spy?" he asked in a strong Arab accent

I tried to keep a straight face. This is getting silly, I thought.

"No, sir, I am not a spy. I own a business in Egypt; that is all."

"Have you been approached by anyone from any embassy while you have been here in Egypt?"

"No, I have not," I replied. I thought it was best to keep my answers short and to the point. I didn't want to give any sort of witty answer and risk ending up like the guy I saw outside the lift.

"OK, you are free to go."

I sighed with relief as we left his office. I looked at Saeed. "Internal Affairs, Home Security," he said, nodding.

"*Yalla!* We need to keep going," the policeman said. It was getting close to closing time, and everyone, not just me, was exhausted and wanted to get out of there. "We must finish!"

I was pushed into another office to give the same set of answers: "no," "no," "no." And then another office: "no," "no," "no." At last, we reached the final agency, Narcotics.

"Have you ever done any drugs?"

"No," I said, trying not to snigger.

"Do you know anyone who sells drugs?"

"Absolutely not, sir."

"Do you sell drugs yourself?"

"No, I do not."

"You may go," the officer said, as he stamped the final inky department badge onto my paper.

I was finished!

As we were leaving the office, I stopped, turned, popped my head back around the door, and asked, "Does anyone ever answer yes to any of your questions?" I asked.

I could feel Dad and Saeed tugging at my arms. The officer looked up and smiled. "No," I heard him say as they pulled me away.

"We're done. Let's get the fuck out of here," I said, sighing with delight and waving my fingerprinted notepaper, complete with all the stamps we needed. We finally made our escape from the Mogamma and back to the van.

Awake on pure adrenaline, we drove back to the police station as the sun was setting. We felt like a band of brothers, including the police officers. The day was soon to be over, and although I never learned his name, the police-man who was with us all the way from the courtroom to the Mogamma was one of the genuinely good guys. He put the radio on and shared his cigarettes. It felt like we had all worked together to pull off a heist. We had conquered the Mogamma, and that felt like something to celebrate.

Captain Amir was at the station when we arrived. It was past dark, so I was surprised to see him still there. He said he was waiting for our return.

"Congratulations, Paul!" he grinned. "Everything is good. You got the clearance from the Mogamma, so tomorrow, you will be free to go back to your family."

He shook my shaking, inky hand and added, "I hope you understand that it was not our will to keep you here, but I hope we made everything as easy for you as we could."

I paused to think before I answered. "Well, perhaps you don't actually need to keep me here tonight," I said flatly. "We know that the paperwork is all done, so if you really mean that, you'll have no objection to letting me go ."

The captain let go of my hand and gave my proposal some thought.

"I mean, really, can't I just stay in a hotel tonight?" I asked. "You have my passport. You have my father's passport. You have all the documents you will ever need. So really, why do I need to stay in the cell again tonight?"

I was pleading with every fiber I had.

"Dad, maybe the captain would like some tea while he decides to let us stay in a hotel tonight," I said, nudging Dad with my elbow. He quickly found some coins in his pocket for the vending machine.

"But where will you stay?" Captain Amir asked. "I will need to know which hotel."

Bingo! I thought, and asked Saeed to give me his phone. I scrolled though Saeed's contacts until I saw the number for Bashir—alphabetically, the first name in a long list of names of my friends who were hotel owners in Egypt. I dialed the number and waited impatiently for him to pick up before the captain changed his mind.

"Hello, Bashir. It's Paul. I can't stay on the line for long. I need an urgent favor, mate. Can you give my dad and me a room in your hotel in Cairo tonight? I'm due for release tomorrow and…"

"Of course, Paul. Whatever you need," Bashir said. His voice was like music to my ears.

I handed the handset to the captain, and he and Bashir exchanged details of the hotel's location and the name of the manager in charge. The Captain Amir ended the call and handed the phone back to me.

"You must be back here at 8:30 a.m. so I can release you officially," he said. "Please, you must promise me you will not tell anyone about this."

I looked into his eyes and said, "I promise I won't tell a fucking soul."

I was actually grateful that the day had been so hectic. I hadn't been able to reflect upon the events. My mind was doing cartwheels as Saeed drove us to the hotel. As I sat in the back seat of the car, I could feel the exhaustion and adrenaline coursing through my body. I descended into a trance, recalling the gruesome fight in the holding cell, the bloodshed, my thumb in an eye, the taste of flesh in my mouth, the smell of sweaty skin, the screams of anger and fear. The car door opened, interrupting my thoughts, and for the first time in over three months, I walked into a building as a free man.

I could feel my chest tighten with emotion. Bashir had arranged for two rooms, but as we checked in, I corrected the receptionist politely and asked her to change the booking to only one room. There was no way I was going to be on my own. I needed to be with Dad. I was nervous, twitchy and exhausted, and I couldn't wait to get up to the room, where I could have a shower and lie on a soft, clean bed.

The elevator pinged as the door closed, reminding me of the man in white overalls and handcuffs. The door reopened into a lovely, brightly decorated corridor, with art and expensive mirrors hanging from the walls. I avoided any glimpse of my reflection as we walked down the corridor to the room. Dad fussed around, trying to ensure everything was to my liking. The coffee machine worked, and the shower water was hot, and the bubble bath gel smelled nice. Still, my head was spinning.

Dad's phone rang. "It's Bashir," he said, looking at the caller ID. "It'll be for you. You take the call while I'll run you a nice bath."

I smiled sleepily and took the phone. "I can't thank you enough, Bashir. I'm telling you, this is fucking amazing."

"I'm so glad I can help you, Paul," Bashir said. "What they did to you was so unfair. Everybody knows it. How are you now? What was it like in there?"

"I can't lie, mate. I've been through hell. It was fucking horrendous. I can't even describe it. But you know, I survived. I just kept my head down and got on with it."

"Yes, I can only imagine what that must have been like," he said. "At least now you're back where you belong. You can rest. Please, try to feel at home. And of course, if you need me to send someone in to shit in the corner of your room to help you feel more comfortable, I can arrange it."

We both burst out laughing as he hung up the phone. Standing in the middle of the room, I continued laughing hysterically.

"Your bath's ready," Dad called from the bathroom.

But I couldn't move.

As my emotions spilled over, I stood frozen by hysterics and exhaustion—a heady mixture. Months of built-up anxiety, terror, dread, guilt, anger, determination, pressure, spent energy and hope all flooded out.

Dad threw his arms around me and consoled me as I howled.

"Come on now," he said, "it's all going to be OK now. It's all over."

In the bath I washed off my day from hell. I studied my knuckles and fingernails as I scrubbed at them feverishly. I examined my whole body inch by inch, to erase any traces of my vicious attackers. I washed away my tears, the blood, the shit and the realization of how close I'd come to a lifetime of hell in a Cairo jail.

Eventually, after wrapping myself in a fresh, clean dressing gown, I fell asleep next to Dad on his single bed.

CHAPTER 33

THE SPRING HAS SPRUNG

I woke up a free man. Today was the day I'd get to hug my son, Aimee, Mum and my friends. I was free to walk on the beach, and perhaps I'd even stop to have coffee in the shop on the marina, where I sat to admire the sea just before the whole nightmare began. I awoke a different man. I felt a feeling that I had experienced many times before. I had grown to recognize it as one of the best feelings a man can ever have—the freedom and gratitude to really be alive.

We checked out of the hotel and brought Captain Amir coffee to thank him for his kindness in allowing me to stay in the hotel rather than a jail cell for my final night in Cairo. After signing a bail check for 20,000 Egyptian pounds (10,000 for me and the same for Rami), he signed my release papers, and we shook hands firmly. While I had grown to like him, I sincerely hoped I'd never see him or that police station again. Saeed was waiting for us when Dad and I walked out into the sunny street, with wide smiles and our arms across each other's shoulders. We punched the air in triumph to be going home at last.

Had I been able to put all of my family and friends on a plane there and then and fly them out of Egypt never to return, I would have done so. But we all knew that wasn't possible; a court battle was still to take place to settle the fate of the dodgy government official, the man who was the source of the bribe, the asshole who landed me and Rami in custody in the first place. Until the case was closed, and he was behind bars, I remained on the no-fly list and wouldn't be boarding any plane to anywhere.

So, we began our six-hour drive from Cairo back to Hurghada. Saeed drove, and Dad and I reflected on the case. We talked about Lassad, the judge, and the kindness of Captain Amir, and between moments of deeper rumination, we found ourselves laughing at all the farcical events. We giggled about the imprisoned chickens, about watching football and cheering for the wrong team, the lost police gun, inking ourselves in the back of the police van, and the best part of all, the disbelief on the faces of the people in the courtroom when MBF made the call to the judge.

We left Cairo at midday and stopped only once on the way for a quick roadside pit stop. I was so desperate to be home that I couldn't sit still. "Put your foot down, Saeed," I kept teasing him, playfully slapping his ear from the seat behind.

While we drove, my phone pinged and beeped constantly with "Welcome home! Can't wait to see you!" messages from Aimee, Andy and Lindy, Gary, Freek, Mum, and everyone else who had heard that I had been released and was on my way home. I was overwhelmed with the number of text messages I received. While I'd been in hiding, I'd only seen or heard from one person every few days. Aimee was able to visit only twice in those early days, and I hadn't seen Mum at all. I could barely contain myself at the thought of being reunited with everyone after so long.

Finally, when we pulled into Kalagia, our idyllic cluster of villas by the beach, Saeed beeped the car horn crazily. My heart was beating so hard, I could see it pumping through my shirt as the car turned the corner and pulled up at the door of my home. Twenty-five of my nearest and dearest people in the world spilled out onto the driveway, whooping and hollering, holding huge bunches of helium balloons and popping streamers.

I couldn't get out of the car fast enough to hug and kiss them all, as my little son, Cole, pushed his way through the crowd and grabbed me around my shins. I dropped to my knees and threw my arms around him and burst into tears of joy.

Aimee and the team from Papa's Bar had decorated the house for my homecoming. The chefs had laid out a huge spread in the garden, with a barbecue and a fridge packed with drinks. The celebration went on into the night. The drinks flowed, and the music played. I went from chair to chair, mingling with everyone, with Cole never leaving my knee.

By then it was late in 2010. After a few days to slow down and enjoy time with Aimee and Cole, I was keen to put everything behind me. The long, boring days I had spent in hiding and the lonely times in my cell made me crave being busy. I missed my team and the daily hustle and bustle of our venues. Aimee would sometimes ask me about my time in prison, especially when she noticed me disappearing into my own thoughts, but I could never answer her. I told myself that no good would ever come of talking about it, and it was better to lock those thoughts away in the deepest, darkest recesses of my mind forever.

Christmas was just around the corner, so it was the busiest time of the year. Bands and DJs had to be arranged, parties and tourist bookings confirmed, decorations and entertainment organized, staff, advertising, deals and promotions—it was all systems go. Better to be busy than dwell on the past, I thought.

But I couldn't deny I had changed. A niggling feeling was slowly eating away at me. It left me feeling empty despite it being the fullest time of the year. It was a feeling of insecurity, betrayal and fear that at any moment my fortunes could change, and the carpet could be ripped out from under me. I wasn't prepared to let that happen to me ever again. Always one to trust my gut, I knew it was time to begin thinking about our exit plan. The fact was, I'd fallen out of love with Egypt. We enjoyed an especially warm and celebratory festive season together as family at home, although I knew it would be our last Christmas in Egypt. I just hadn't told anyone yet.

If I needed any more reason to put my house on the market and make plans to move my family out of Egypt, it came one night just after I had put Cole to bed. The phone rang, and it was Ali, my lawyer in Hurghada.

"Ali, how are you?" I said. "Hope you're calling me with good news. Last time we spoke you were telling me I was under arrest."

"Hi, Paul. It's good to hear your voice, I hope you and the family are all well, *Insh'Allah*."

"Yes, Ali, we are all very good, thanks. So what's your news?" I asked.

"Paul, we have news from Cairo."

"Oh?" I said suspiciously.

"The district attorney of Southern Cairo has decided to drop the case against the government official involved in your case."

"Sorry, what?" I asked.

"For you, this is good news," Ali continued. "It means that neither you or Rami are required to stand as state witness anymore, and so all requirements by the state are now lifted."

"Yes, Ali, I get that. But it also means all of this was fucking meaningless!" I said. "Everything Rami and I went through was for nothing! How can that be possible?"

"I don't know, Paul. Like I said, the case is dropped. There is nothing more I can say."

I was furious.

"And my money? The 20,000 Egyptian pounds that I paid as bail for Rami and me, which is more than the damn bribe in the first place, am I going to get that back?"

"I don't have any record of this money, Paul," Ali said. "I think it will be difficult to trace it. You know the situation right now. It's really very bad. It is difficult to know who to trust…" His voice trailed away.

"And what does that mean exactly, Ali?"

"If you really want my advice, Paul, take your family and leave Egypt. That is all I can say."

He hung up.

My blood was boiling. To think that everything I had been through was for nothing and that the case had just disappeared into thin air was more than I could take. There had to be more to it. Ali sounded like he knew more but wouldn't or couldn't discuss it over the phone. I was determined to do some digging and find out what was really going on. That night I rung around my friends and some business contacts to ask them to sniff out some information. It didn't take long to get some feedback. Along with the usual stories of lies, backstabbing, backhanders and hush money, I received the golden nugget, the information that made everything make sense: the dirt on Colonel Khadir.

I can't say I was surprised. After all, why would someone of his seniority have made my case so personal? When I heard it was Colonel Khadir's own brother who was the dodgy official who had set off the whole chain of events, everything clicked into place. Why hadn't I seen it before? It was so obvious. In the beginning, Colonel Khadir wanted me to come to Cairo as soon as possible, make a statement, spend four days in custody, and get the process over and done with quickly. I had no idea that after he got me to testify, his only intention was to bury his brother's case deep within the corridors of the Mogamma. That way it was likely that his case would never see the light of day. But the colonel hadn't bargained on my putting a fly in the ointment.

As long as I evaded captivity, his brother was locked up, too. There was nothing Colonel Khadir could do to get him out. His brother needed me to stand as state witness to be able to present his own case and convince the judge that there wasn't evidence to convict him. But I had gone on the run, and that fucked with the colonel's plan. By the time he caught up with me three months later in the Europa Hotel, his brother had probably been buggered so many times in prison for having a high-ranking policeman as a brother that any further punishment couldn't be justified. In the end, I suppose, justice was served—the Egyptian way.

So, I decided to make peace with it all. I had my health, my family, a good business, the sunshine on my back, and freedom. Or so I thought.

News was spreading on social media about unrest in Tunisia. Every day, the TV and radio stations reported stories about protests and gangs of youths that were intent on stirring up trouble with the authorities. No one was really taking it seriously, as it was common in the region to have pockets of social unrest. The pop of a gun in the street or the beating of a political prisoner was a common reality. But I remembered Ali's warning. He had told me to pack up and leave. At the time, I thought he was being dramatic, so I hadn't taken particular notice.

It was a Saturday in early January 2011. I went with Dad to a charity football game in Hurghada. Unlike the usual banter that went on in the stands of the stadium, the subject on everyone's lips that day was Tunisia and how bad the situation was there. As the players kicked the ball around on the pitch, in the stands rumors circulated that Tunisia was in total chaos, that President Ben Ali was going to resign and flee the country. We heard a group next to us joke about how it would be Egypt and Mubarak next. Everyone in our section of the stadium erupted with laughter, and we continued to eat and drink and cheer on the game. It seemed a ludicrous notion. After all, the president of Egypt had been in power for 30 years. There was no way he was going anywhere.

We were wrong, of course. Within seven days, the internet signal across the country was constantly being shut off. TV and radio stations were broadcasting endless reels of presidential propaganda, and a heavy presence of armed guards was visible on the streets. The center of all the action seemed to be in and around Cairo. All the news channels were churning out footage of protesters being blasted with water cannons outside the Mogamma. Meanwhile in Hurghada, we still believed it was nothing to worry about, and that it would blow over in a day or two. But two days turned into thee and then four, and the protests only intensified, until there was a definite change in the air throughout our beautiful Red Sea town. The dive boats remained moored. As the sun went down at the end of each day, an eerie emptiness swept across the beaches. We began to worry that this wasn't just a scuffle in Cairo.

By early February, nearly all flights in and out of Egypt were grounded. With the airport closed, there was no way for anyone to get in, and worse, there was no way for anyone to get out. The TVs showed images of major riots, looting and violence in the streets of Cairo, with tanks, burning tires, tear gas and gunfire. From my office, after watching one too many news journalists' eye-witness accounts of the mayhem, I decided to make a call to MBF.

"I think we've reached the point where it's time to go," I told him. "I don't think this situation is going to pass anytime soon. And if it gets any worse, it won't be safe for my family to be here anymore. I'll stay and protect the business, but I need to call in one last favor, as I've just heard the last flights went out yesterday. So if it's here, what are the possibilities of using your plane?"

That now sounds like something Bruce Willis would say in an action movie: "I'm gonna have to use your plane." But that's exactly how it happened.

I called Dad immediately after speaking with MBF and told him, "Dad, it's time to go. This is all going to kick off, and it's too dangerous. They have taken the police off the streets because they've lost control, and they've opened the doors of all the prisons. I'm afraid you're going to have to leave *My Rosetta*. You and Mum have to pack your things tonight. This place isn't safe anymore, so I'm getting you out of here tomorrow with Aimee and Cole, Marcus, Holly and their little baby, Alfie."

"But, Paul," Dad said, "the airport is closed. There aren't any planes going."

"There's MBF's Learjet, Dad, and you and Mum are getting on it."

"Right then," Dad said, sounding surprised but in no mood to muck around. "I'll tell your mother."

I emptied the office safe, taking all the money and important documents, and locked the office door. I walked through the bar and instructed everyone, "Take some beer. Go home and stay indoors. Keep your phones on until I have more information for you."

Turning to Saeed, who was sitting in the corner watching a news broadcast, I said, "Saeed, turn that off and send a message out to anyone left in the business to go home. Then have all our businesses locked down." '

"Yes, boss. On it," he said, jumping to his feet and turning the TV off quickly.

I drove home and told Aimee that it was time for her to pack up and that at first light the following morning she would be heading home. "But what about you?" she asked, looking worried.

"I need to stay and look after everyone here, so that there's something for you all to come back to," I said. "Don't worry. I've survived worse."

The next morning, we drove to the airfield, where MBF's pilot was waiting for us. "Nee-naw truck!" Cole yelled with innocent delight as he pointed at the army vehicles speeding past us in the opposite direction. Under other circumstances, this would have been noted as one of life's special memories: the time when you borrow your friend's private jet for a family trip. But this trip was bittersweet. I wasn't going with my family, and I had no idea when I would see them again.

Marcus and Holly, with their new-born Alfie, pulled up in in a taxi near the airport hangar just as Mum and Dad arrived in another taxi. "Great, you all made it," I smiled as everyone exchanged hugs.

"Are you all ready for your first trip on a private jet then?" Dad beamed everyone walked across the tarmac to MBF's jet.

The pilot greeted us at the foot of the aircraft's steps, and I heard my family's oohs and aahs as they entered the cabin. We goofed around for a while, taking photographs and taking turns pretending to be the captain in the cockpit, until the pilot announced it was time to leave. I shook his hand sternly and said, "Fly safe, mate. And thank you."

I leaned over and kissed Aimee, Cole and Mum and hugged Dad. "I'm the one airlifting you all home now!" I laughed before I stepped off the plane and the door was shut behind me. I stood on the tarmac and waved, blew kisses and shouted love to them until the plane taxied down the runaway and finally took off. I felt such enormous relief that they were going and would be safely back in England within a few hours.

The streets descended into chaos very soon afterward. The police were overwhelmed. The army and plain-clothed military were trying to restore order but failing, it seemed. People in cities and towns all over the country were rioting. Prisons had been overrun, and the streets were lawless places with sporadic violence erupting everywhere. Hundreds, if not thousands of people were being injured in fighting in Cairo, and many were butchered in the streets live on TV.

The last flights from Hurghada had evacuated thousands of people. There were no police anywhere, and with the prisons open, the wealthy tourist town became a ghost town overnight. Looters and robbers were everywhere. Our Red Sea paradise had become a very dangerous place, indeed.

Everything stopped. Every shop, restaurant, office, public building and service was closed, and a sunset curfew was put in place. I called all my team and neighbors and told them to come to my house. I felt we would be safe there, as the walls and gates were too high to jump over, and the property was accessible from only one side. If absolutely necessary, we could escape into the sea. By that evening, I had 25 people in my house, with more on the way.

We barricaded ourselves in, with knives and baseball bats on hand. We made more weapons from sticks and broken glass. As the word got out, more people arrived, and by the next day there were more than 70 in my house, all working in shifts on a round-the-clock watch to protect our little community. We ate fish straight from the sea, made huge pots of rice, and baked bread. We kept my boats moored on the beach, with their fuel topped up, so that we could escape if things got out of hand. Fortunately, it never came to that. We would hear the rioters at night in the street, smashing windows and trying to steal cars. They'd bang on the doors and try to rattle the windows, but my guess was that they could sense our compound was full of people armed and ready to fight, which wasn't what they were looking for. They were looking for free and easy takings.

We emerged from our barricade on February 11, when the news came that President Mubarak had resigned, and the civil war was over. I walked along the beach to the marina, where I saw that my beloved businesses had been looted and ransacked. It was heartbreaking. As I looked at the devastation in front of me with tears in my eyes, I knew that my days of running a business in Egypt were over. The business that I had rebuilt three times after illness, fire and prison was long gone. Egypt had been a great country for me and my family. We had enjoyed a fantastic life there, but it took away what it had given us. The heartache of losing my business in the revolution and the physical and mental scars I was left with after prison were just too much to bear. Perhaps, by toppling the regime, Egypt had changed, but the damage done in the process would take years to repair.

In the aftermath of the revolution, once law and order were restored, Aimee and the rest of my family returned to Hurghada. It was close to the end of March, and the business was in tatters. My workdays were spent with the team, repairing the damage caused to the venues. We tried every way we could to pay the bills and the staff, but without tourists, Hurghada was dead.

To make matters worse, with a breakdown in the law, many landlords exploited the situation and became greedy and ruthless. Business agreements were no longer worth even the paper that they were written on. We lost more than 50 percent of the assets that Solutions Leisure Group managed. Disregarding ethics, loyalty or history, and regardless of how much money we had spent on fit-out and décor, property owners, one by one, reclaimed the venues that they had rented to us, without allowing us the opportunity to negotiate or recoup any of our investment. The writing was on the wall. It was only a matter of time before anyone left would pack up and move on. And there was no escaping the fact that it was time for us to move on, too.

I always dreamed of living in Dubai. I had been there on holiday many times. It would be a secure and safe place for the family, and a place I could relocate Solutions Leisure. I studied the market in Dubai and decided that the city needed something else apart from its reputation of being all glitz, glamor and seven-star hotels. I thought the Dubai would benefit from the friendly, everyone's-welcome, customer-first approach that Solutions Leisure had become famous for across the Red Sea.

However, it was crucial that nobody knew I was planning to leave, not even my work colleagues. I decided to let them think I was scoping Dubai out for future opportunities. Given what I had been through, I was plagued with insecurity. I was petrified that if the local authorities caught wind that I might be leaving, and that more businesses would therefore close, or they would do something to stop me from going. So, Aimee and I kept our plans completely under wraps.

By mid-March, we had set the wheels in motion, selling off our personal belonging—the boats, the cars and furniture—under the guise, to anyone who asked, that we were simply trying to claw back any money we could after the revolution.

The last, and most important, thing on my to-do list before moving to Dubai was to marry Aimee. We had been engaged for eight years, but we never got around to planning the big day. We agreed that the last big hurrah to mark our lives in Egypt would be our wedding, and I promised her that we'd pull out all the stops. We set the date for July 5, and Aimee, true to form, went all in with the preparations for our day, arranging a marquee on the beach at one of our beach clubs called 360 in El Gouna. Aimee wanted the fairy tale, and although I had no idea how I was going to pay for it, I also wanted to make it a wedding to remember. After all, with the way things were, a good party would keep us and our minds busy.

One hundred and fifty of our family and closest friends joined us for the magical day; aunties, uncles, cousins and friends from near and far flew to Hurghada to celebrate with us. Aimee stopped at nothing to put on a show for them. We had a glass dancefloor over a swimming pool, fireworks, a live band, DJs, our names in the sky, and an obscene amount of champagne.

Of course, I had to find a way to pay for it. Unbeknown to Aimee, we had little left in Egypt. I had to sell my beloved Porsche 911 that I had kept in England for years. It was my pride and joy and had been my dream car since Dad bought me the toy version of it as a kid. I used to keep the toy beside my bed. But I thought, What the hell, I'll buy another Porsche when I make it in Dubai anyway. So, Aimee got her perfect day.

A week after the last of the guests had left Hurghada, I bought our tickets to Dubai. I had one final asset to sell: the house. I had almost resigned myself to never being able to sell it. What were the chances of selling a five-bedroom luxury property when the Muslim Brotherhood was running the country, and any scent of business or tourism had all but vanished. The sale of the house was going to be our only means of getting off to a good start in Dubai. If a sale didn't happen, things would work out in quite a different way.

But on the morning of August 10, the day before we were due to fly to Dubai, we got an offer on the house. It was less than half of what the house was worth, but the buyer said he had the means to complete the sale quickly.

"Like how quickly?" I asked.

The banks barred anyone from transferring more than 10,000 dollars in or out of Egypt at any one time. So, when the gentleman replied, "This afternoon," I thought I hadn't heard him correctly. But I agreed to his price before he could re-think it.

As soon as the ink was dry on the sale agreement, we raced to the bank to spend the next for four hours tediously transferring tiny batches of money from his account to mine until the sale was complete. Parting ways that evening, I promised him the keys would be in his hands at 5 o'clock the next morning.

I hurried home to tell Aimee the good news. I sat at the kitchen table and proudly produced the bank statement, which gave the balance of our account following the sale of the house. She burst into tears of relief. We had enough money to start our life in Dubai. "Woohoo! Let's order pizza and finish packing!" She shouted while jumping around the kitchen and doing a little dance.

I arranged for a minibus to pick us up in the wee hours of the following morning. The only cash I had left was the 7,000 dollars in my suitcase. I had to figure out how I was going to get the rest of our money out of Egypt, but it would do for now. We still hadn't told anyone that we were leaving for good, and we wanted to keep it that way until we were safely in the air and on our way to Dubai. As the final sunrise that I'd see in Egypt appeared over the roof of my house, I handed the keys to the new owner and jumped into the minibus with Aimee, Cole and my parents, all nervous, strapped in and ready to go.

"*Yalla!*" we all shouted.

"Airport please, driver," I said.

The first flight was a short one from Hurghada to Cairo. I was so used to that flight that it was like jumping on a bus. We were through the airport and on the aircraft within minutes. But looming on the horizon was the next flight, the one that had my stomach in knots. It would be the first time I'd be asked to hand over my passport since the day I went on the run. I was petrified something would go wrong. Despite being told that I wasn't on the no-fly list anymore, I wasn't sure if I could trust the immigration authorities. But I thought, There is only one way to find out.

I was a bag of nerves. Aimee checked in the bags while I cradled Cole. "Bingo!" she said, grinning as we got our boarding passes and made our way to the passport control. My whole body shook as I approached the counter. Aimee and Cole breezed through confidently, while I waited anxiously to be called forward.

The officer looked up and nodded for me to approach. Taking my passport, he studied my face and then flicked through the pages. He seemed to take forever. He checked his screen, looked at me, looked back at his screen, then looked at my passport repeatedly. My heart was racing. I wondered if he was the same guy who stopped me the first time, the guy with the toupee. Then I heard the reassuring *clunk*, as he stamped the exit badge on the page and handed the passport back to me.

"*Ma'salama,*" he said and waived Mum forward. She stood behind me, looking equally as nervous. I walked through the gate and heaved a breath into my lungs. "Oh, thank God," I sighed as I hugged Aimee.

We boarded the aircraft. I was speechless with anticipation. I sat in a row with Aimee and Cole on one side and Mum and Dad on the other. I didn't dare say a word until we were in the air. I hoped and prayed over and over for the plane to move. "Is it going to go? Is it going to go?" I said to myself while adrenaline pumped through my body. "Please don't give up on me. Please let me go. Please let this plane get me out of here. Please!"

The plane pushed back and taxied down the runway, and as I felt it accelerate, my heart raced, and my throat tightened. "Please let me go. Please let me go! Come on! Come on!"

Then I felt the weightlessness of takeoff as the wheels left Egyptian soil, and my eyes filled with tears of relief.

We were safe, and I was free!

I vowed I would never return to Egypt. I gazed out the window in contemplation at what I was leaving behind and with high hopes of what we were yet to find in our new life in Dubai. We flew through the most beautiful sunrise. It appeared to be the same scene that I had encountered in my dream on the beach in Singapore with my grandfather. I gazed at it in wonder and squeezed Cole's hand gently. Isn't life a fucking crazy thing, I thought, as I put my hand in my pocket and pulled out the black 911 Porsche toy model that my father had given to me as a boy. I handed it to Cole and watched his eyes light up. It was obvious to me there and then, that he was the reason for all my second chances. Leaving Egypt safely and starting again in Dubai with my family would be the last second chance I would ever need.

Or would it?

THE STORY CONTINUES...

Landing in Dubai with his money and worldly belongings in a suitcase on August 11, 2011, Paul Evans began all over again.

After relocating his wife, four-year-old son and parents to a city where he knew no one, he made ends meet at first by selling denim jeans from the trunk of his car and by buying and selling secondhand cars on the local community website.

Within five years, he had become one of the most celebrated entrepreneurs in Dubai, creating many of the city's most popular independent bars and restaurants, rebuilding his beloved Solutions Leisure Group from scratch into a multi-award-winning business.

The Solutions Leisure Group went on to win more than 100 industry awards, and in that time, Paul was named as Restaurateur of the Year 2015, Dubai's F&B Heavyweight in both 2016 and 2017, number one on the Caterer Power 50 list for 2017, and Entrepreneur of the Year 2018, and he received the prestigious award for Outstanding Contribution in 2018.

Yet there is some truth in the saying that the higher they climb the harder they fall. Just as things were on the up in business, Paul's marriage fell apart. He and Aimee divorced. His two sons, Cole and Ethan, relocated back to England. Losing the daily interaction with his two boys has been the hardest and most heartbreaking obstacle he has ever had to overcome.

An advocate for personal development and positive mental health, Paul found the support he needed to tackle depression through the help of a professional coach. Her name is Carolyn Coe. Today, Paul and Carolyn work together daily, and he believes that having a coach and engaging in regular management psychology sessions to share his innermost thoughts and feelings on a regular basis is essential for his well-being and happiness. Carolyn is the one person he trusted to coauthor this book.

Paul hopes that his story serves as inspiration to anyone with a desire to turn their life around, to defy the odds and become the best version of themselves.

ABOUT THE AUTHORS

Paul Evans currently resides in Dubai as Founder and CEO of Solutions Leisure Group, the United Arab Emirates' fastest-growing food and beverage group. Along with his beloved Solutions Leisure Group, he has a passion for the ocean and scuba diving, but most of all, his proudest accomplishment is being a father to his two boys.

Previously based in Britain, and once GE Capital's "Golden Boy" of sales, Paul left the financial services sector in 2000, moved to Egypt, and spent 10 years building a chain of nightclubs before forming Solutions Leisure Group. The company's portfolio includes the internationally acclaimed STK JBR and STK Downtown venues, Q43 Dubai, Karma Kafe, Asia Asia, Lock Stock & Barrel Barsha, Lock, Stock & Barrel, District as well as Wavehouse, the joint venture with leading hotel operator Atlantis The Palm. This year, his award-winning hospitality company has opened three venues in Kazan, Russia: Asia Asia, Lock, Stock & Barrel and a new brand, The Central.

Originally from Scotland, UK, **Carolyn Coe** started her career as a management performance coach back in 2009. With a keen understanding of how emotions influence decisions in and away from the workplace, she has worked with some of Dubai's leading entrepreneurs, including Paul Evans himself.

As Paul's mindset coach through his series of impactful life events during his formidable years in Dubai, Carolyn later became the in-house management performance coach for the Solutions Leisure Group. It is during this time, having an up-close and professional relationship with him, she wrote Paul's story. Carolyn lives in Dubai with her husband, and is planning to write her second book.